I0824994

Thomas Sully's Philadelphians

Thomas Sully's Philadelphians

Painting the Athens of America

Peter Conn

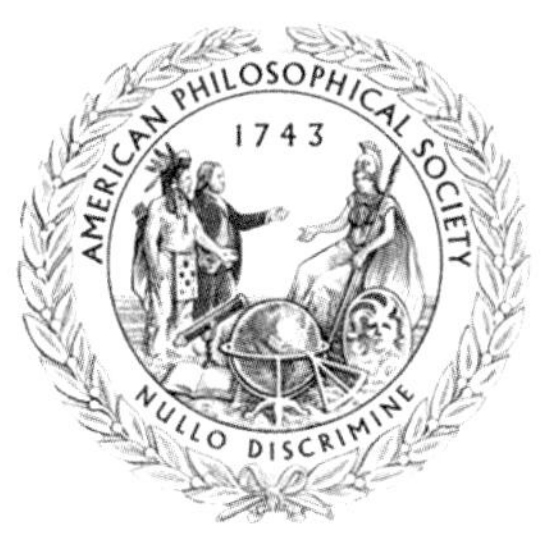

American Philosophical Society Press
Philadelphia

Published by
The American Philosophical Society Press
Philadelphia, Pennsylvania 19106-3387
www.amphilsoc.org

Printed in the United States of America on acid-free paper
10 9 8 7 6 5 4 3 2 1

Library of Congress Cataloging-in-Publication Data
Names: Conn, Peter J., author.
Title: Thomas Sully's Philadelphians : painting the Athens of America / Peter Conn.
Description: Philadelphia : American Philosophical Society Press, 2025. | Summary: "In the course of a career that reached across more than six decades, Sully painted over two thousand portraits and was one of America's most prominent painters. This book describes and discusses several of Sully's portraits as history painting that documents the history of Philadelphia in the first half of the nineteenth century"— Provided by publisher.
Identifiers: LCCN 2024028386 (print) | LCCN 2024028387 (ebook) | ISBN 9781606180495 (hardback) | ISBN 9781606180501 (epub)
Subjects: LCSH: Sully, Thomas, 1783-1872—Criticism and interpretation. | Portrait painting, American—19th century. | Philadelphia (Pa.) —Biography—Portraits. | Philadelphia (Pa.) —History—19th century.
Classification: LCC ND1329.S84 C66 2025 (print) | LCC ND1329.S84 (ebook) | DDC 759.13—dc23/eng/20240919
LC record available at https://lccn.loc.gov/2024028386
LC ebook record available at https://lccn.loc.gov/2024028387

Hardback: 9781606180495
E-book: 9781606180501

Cover design by Eugenia B. González.

In memory of my mother and father,

Alice St. Onge Conn and Ira Francis Conn

Contents

Illustrations

Acknowledgments

I am indebted to those who encouraged, assisted, suggested, queried, or otherwise made this book better than it would have been: Kayla Anthony, Linda Kimiko August, Tristan Bella, Maxim Bouchard, David Brigham, Zachary Brintlinger-Conn, Mary Ellen Budney, Susannah Carroll, Steven Conn, Terry Conn, Lynn Dolby, Peter Dougherty, J. M. Duffin, Lynn Farrington, Barbara Foley, Kathleen Foster, Briana Giasullo, Eduardo Glandt, Susan Glassman, Judith Guston, Robert Hauser, Jessica Hilburn-Holmes, Judy Ivy, Randy Ivy, Sherri Jackson, Brian Kirk, Pamela Lankas, Michael Lewis, Victor Mair, Anna Marley, Margaret Maxey, Lexy Niles, Tara O'Brien, James O'Donnell, Lauris Olson, Stacey Peeples, John Pollock, George Ritchie, Carton Rogers, Matt Rowe, Casey Schweiger, Steve Smith, Carol Soltis, Wendy Steiner, Stacey Swigart, Maria Thompson, Michael Thompson, Hoang Tran, John Vick, Mackenzie Warren, Julie Zeftel, and Jobi Zink.

1

Introduction

In his long career, Thomas Sully (1783–1872) produced a few history paintings, most notably *Washington's Passage of the Delaware* (1819), once celebrated but long overshadowed by Emmanuel Leutze's later version (1851).[1] Sully also painted a handful of landscapes, including studies of Niagara Falls, scenes from the life of Christ, and copies of work by Reynolds, Hogarth, Titian, Raphael, and others. His lifelong commitment, however, was to portraiture. Over the course of a career that reached across more than six decades, Sully painted over two thousand portraits.[2]

In the opinion of Milton Brown, Sully was "undoubtedly the best portrait painter of his generation."[3] According to Allen Fern, "In Sully's lifetime he enjoyed a reputation as one of America's most prominent painters; after the death of Gilbert Stuart, he was probably the principal portrait painter in the land."[4] Jules

[1] Although it is no masterpiece, Sully's painting of the legendary scene is both aesthetically and historically superior to Leutze's sentimental fabrication.

[2] In addition to the portraits, Sully painted several hundred miniatures, and genre and theme paintings—what he called his "fancy pictures."

[3] Milton W. Brown, *American Art to 1900* (New York: Harry N. Abrams, 1977), 229.

[4] Alan Fern, "Foreword," in Monroe H. Fabian, *Mr. Sully, Portrait Painter: The Works of Thomas Sully (1783–1872)* [exhibition cat.] (Washington, DC: Smithsonian Institution Press, 1983), 6. These high opinions of Sully's painting were widely shared during his lifetime. William Dunlap, in 1834, wrote that Sully "has long stood at the head of his profession as a portrait painter." William Dunlap, *A History of the Rise and Progress of the Arts of Design in the United States*, vol. 2 (New York: George P. Scott and Company, 1834; repr.,Toronto: Dover Publications, 1969), 101.

Prown described Sully as "the leading American portrait painter of the first half of the nineteenth century."[5] Michael Lewis has called Sully "the most successful" portrait painter "of the Romantic era."[6] Sully "also had that most elusive of artistic gifts," according to Lewis, "a keen grasp of expression, not the rigid petrified face of his late colonial rivals, but a face alert and lively, capable of swift change, and flickering with humor and intelligence."[7]

The qualities of Sully's best work—and he was often at his best, especially in the years between about 1810 and 1840—have been summed up by Carol Soltis: "luminous color, a dramatic or nuanced quality of light, a rich but refined handling of paint and description of form, tightly integrated compositions that underline a narrative or dramatic moment, flowing lines handled with refinement and well-integrated into the overall composition."[8]

In this book, I describe and discuss several of Sully's portraits as a different kind of history painting: as documents in the history of Philadelphia in the first half of the nineteenth century.[9] Gathered under headings that include individuals, institutions, professions, and contemporary events, these portraits offer points of entry into much that was going on in early nineteenth-century Philadelphia. The pages that follow explore education, politics, theater, medicine, journalism, commerce, philanthropy, religion, and the fierce debate over slavery.

From its founding in the seventeenth century, Philadelphia's economy was based on commerce. By the middle of the eighteenth century, the city's merchants were doing business with all

---

[5] Jules David Prown, "Two Manuscript Notebooks of Thomas Sully," *The Yale University Library Gazette* 39, no. 2 (October 1964): 73.

[6] Michael J. Lewis, *American Art and Architecture* (London: Thames & Hudson, 2006), 76.

[7] Michael J. Lewis, "Thomas Sully's Philadelphia." Lecture at the Wagner Free Institute of Science in Philadelphia, October 4, 2003.

[8] Carol Eaton Soltis, "Sully's Women: Real and Imagined," in William Keyse Rudolph and Carol Eaton Soltis, *Thomas Sully: Painted Performance* (New Haven, CT: Yale University Press, 2013), 47.

[9] Without suggesting an equivalence between the two artists, I was interested to note a similar proposal about Vermeer, who "made his own form of history painting from domestic interludes." Claudia Swan, "Looking Behind the Curtain," *Times Literary Supplement* (May 5, 2023): 15. I am also reminded of Walter Benjamin's often-quoted pronouncement, "To write history means giving dates their physiognomy" (*Arcades Project*) 476.

the important Atlantic and Gulf ports, exporting a wide variety of manufactured goods, along with meat, grain, and flour, and importing cotton, sugar, molasses, rice, fish, and textiles.[10] In 1800, forty Philadelphia ships were involved in the China trade. Beginning in about that same year, the city also began to develop a significant manufacturing capacity.

After the national capital moved to the District of Columbia and New York began to emerge as the nation's financial center, Philadelphia could still claim eminence in law, medicine, science, music, and publishing.[11] The city also remained a center of painting. In1825, "one of the places where Americans were most likely to see portraits was the public art gallery. In this year, Philadelphia, boasting the most advanced art market in America, housed four of those galleries."[12]

In short, well into the Early National period, the years in which Sully settled and worked in Philadelphia, the city remained the nation's most cosmopolitan, the place that "set the standards of early nineteenth-century American culture, expressed in natural history, art and architecture, theater, political oratory, and science."[13]

The people whose portraits are included in this book were among those who set those standards. And given the relatively small size of the city's early nineteenth-century economic and social elite, many of its members knew each other. Through the early decades of the nineteenth century, the same names tend to appear in the leadership and on the boards of Philadelphia's major cultural institutions: the Library Company, the American Philosophical Society, the Pennsylvania Academy of the Fine

---

[10] Bernard S. Levin and F. R. Kirkland, "Society News and Accessions," *The Pennsylvania Magazine of History and Biography* 64, no. 3 (July 1940): 430–48.

[11] Gary B. Nash, *First City: Philadelphia and the Forging of American Memory* (Philadelphia: University of Pennsylvania Press, 2002), 108. Along with dozens of newspapers, Philadelphia's book publishers had produced several hundred thousand volumes by 1810.

[12] Valentijn Byvanck, "Public Portraits and Portrait Publics," *Pennsylvania History: A Journal of Mid-Atlantic Studies* 65 (1998): 200.

[13] Nash, *First City*, 149. Nash is right to include architecture in the summary of Philadelphia's cultural centrality. William Strickland, Benjamin Latrobe, John Notman, and John Haviland were all active in the city in the Early National period and designed important buildings, many of which survive. Sully apparently completed two portraits of William Strickland, both of which have disappeared.

Arts, the Athenaeum of Philadelphia, the Board of Trustees of the University of Pennsylvania, along with Pennsylvania Hospital, and a few other organizations.[14] There was some justice in the widely circulated phrase, usually attributed to Gilbert Stuart, that Philadelphia could claim to have become "the Athens of America."[15] Today, after two centuries and more, all of these institutions—more than half of which count Benjamin Franklin (Figure 1.1) as father or godfather—continue to play a singular role in Philadelphia's cultural and communal life.

To be sure, Thomas Sully's Philadelphia was not all of Philadelphia. His sitters were typically merchants, physicians, senior clergy, lawyers, and bankers, along with their wives and children. Some of these men had earned their prosperity; others were heirs of affluence or even wealth. In short, these were, by and large, people who could afford to have their portraits painted. The child of theatrical parents, Sully also painted numerous actors and actresses, some of whom he chose to paint, others whose portraits were commissioned.

Although Sully's portraits do not explicitly represent Philadelphia's working people, or its poor, or its large concentration of Black men and women, the stories attached to a few of these paintings encompass a number of those subjects.

Samuel Coates was a long-time manager of the Pennsylvania Hospital, founded in 1751 specifically to serve the city's "sick poor and lunatics." Coates compiled a notebook describing the lives and behaviors—and most significant—the conversations, of some of the institution's mental patients. In those pages, still unpub-

---

[14] Lee L. Schreiber, "Bluebloods and Local Societies: A Philadelphia Microcosm," *Pennsylvania History: A Journal of Mid-Atlantic Studies* 48, no. 3 (July 1981): 251–66. For a breezy but encyclopedic survey of these "Old Philadelphians," see Nathaniel Burt, *The Perennial Philadelphians: The Anatomy of an American Aristocracy* (Boston: Little, Brown, 1963). That local aristocracy lingered for generations. Shortly after the turn of the twentieth century, journalist Christopher Morley described Philadelphia as "a surprisingly large town at the confluence of the Biddle and Drexel families."

[15] In fact, the phrase was in use as early as 1733, in a petition that Franklin drafted soliciting Thomas Penn's approval of the plan for the proposed Library Company: "May your Philadelphia be the future Athens of America!" "Directors of Library Company to Thomas Penn and Reply, 16 May 1733," *Founders Online*, National Archives, https://founders.archives.gov/documents/Franklin/01-01-02-0095.

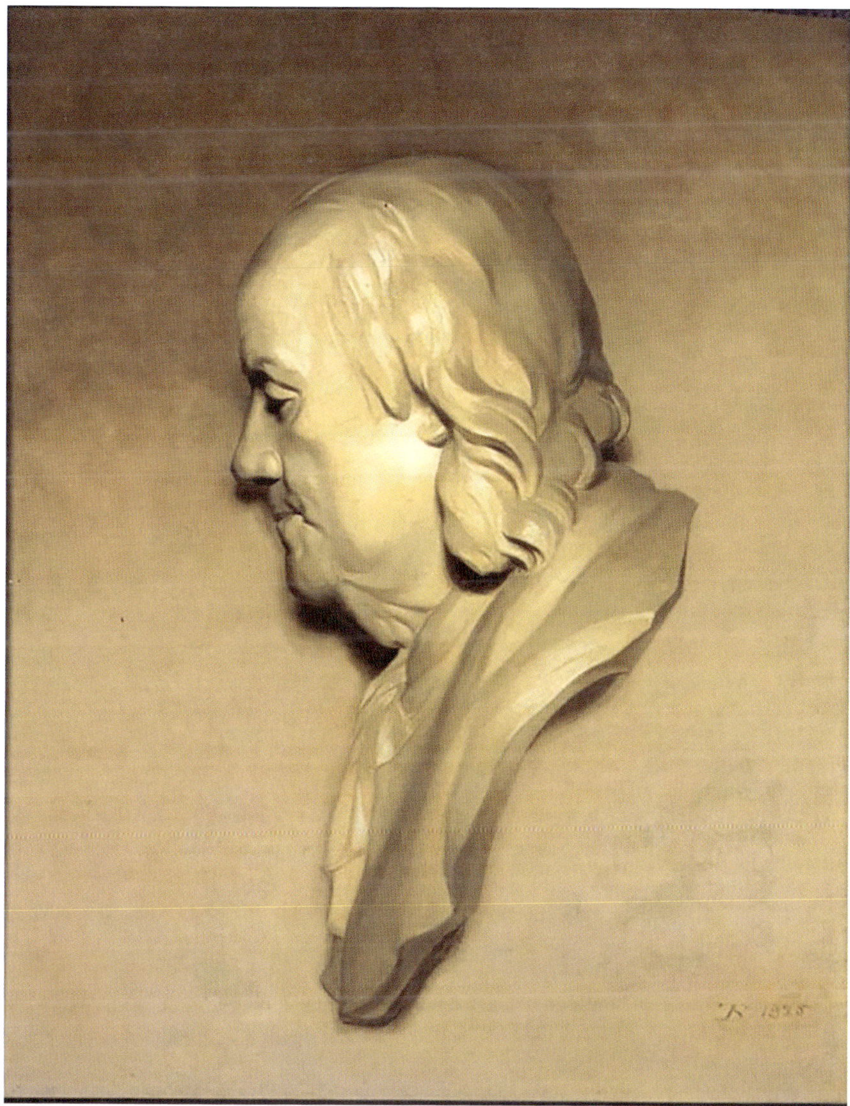

Figure 1.1 Sully presented his portrait of Benjamin Franklin as bas-relief (1825) to the Franklin Institute.

Courtesy of the Franklin Institute.

lished, Coates provides a valuable account of these afflicted men and women.[16]

A Unitarian minister, William Henry Furness, bravely distinguished himself with his outspoken—and unpopular—sermons denouncing slavery.[17] Addressing slavery from a different direction, Benjamin Coates and others, including Sully himself, stood high in the leadership of the Pennsylvania Colonization Society. The work of these men, along with those of their female allies and adversaries, and the debates among them, can only be understood in the context of the racial violence that erupted repeatedly in Philadelphia through much of the first half of the nineteenth century.[18]

Philadelphia's small Jewish community seldom suffered overt discrimination. Nonetheless, its members were separated by their religion from the overwhelming Christian majority, and they were always aware of "the delicate balance of tolerance."[19] Sully's many portraits of the members of the Gratz family—Rebecca's is the most famous, but also those of Michael, Benjamin, Rachel Gratz Etting, and Rachel Gratz Moses—help to illuminate the story of Philadelphia's Jews.[20]

In his influential book, *Portraiture,* Richard Brilliant writes, "so many viewers feel compelled to ascertain the names given to the images of men, women, and children in portraits—once the art works are known to be portraits—when the same viewers feel no similar compulsion to do so in their encounter with art works in other genres."[21]

Brilliant's assertion may in fact not be true of everyone who looks at a portrait. But it does capture my own response: Who

---

[16] Several excerpts from Coates's notebook are printed in Thomas G. Morton, *The History of the Pennsylvania Hospital, 1751–1895* (New York: Arno Press, 1973 [1895]), 139ff. I include additional quotes from the unpublished notebook in Chapter 3.

[17] Elizabeth M. Geffen, "William Henry Furness: Philadelphia Antislavery Preacher," *The Pennsylvania Magazine of History and Biography* 82, no. 3 (July 1958): 259–92.

[18] Contributing to the racial violence was the fact that in the Early National years Philadelphia was almost certainly home both to the largest population of free Black people in the country and to the largest assemblage of abolitionist societies.

[19] Edwin Wolf 2nd and Maxwell Whiteman, *The History of the Jews of Philadelphia from Colonial Times to the Age of Jackson* (Philadelphia: The Jewish Publication Society, 5717/1957), 44.

[20] Including the several Gratz portraits, Hannah London concluded that Sully had painted more than two dozen pictures of Jews. Hannah R. London, *Portraits of Jews by Gilbert Stuart and Other Early American Artists* (New York: William Edwin Rudge, 1927).

[21] Richard Brilliant, *Portraiture* (Cambridge, MA: Harvard University Press, 1991), 8.

were these people and what did they contribute, two centuries ago, to life in Philadelphia? As a person who has lived in the city for over fifty years and is happily burdened by an unquenchable curiosity about Philadelphia's past, I have felt this response especially when standing in front of portraits by Thomas Sully. Sully was born elsewhere, but over decades of residence, he became the city's foremost portraitist. His scores of paintings of antebellum Philadelphians comprise an invitation to know more about them and, through them, more about the city's history. No other American city offers the same opportunity: to study what is in effect an important city's group portrait, painted over several decades, by the same artist.[22]

[22] My comments on Sully's portraits avoid the interpretive error of claiming to deduce anything about the character or inner life of his subjects from the evidence of his paintings. That commonplace but misguided response, as Harry Berger observed, is "motivated by ... a belief that the painter can and should make the sitter's face an index of his or her mind." Harry Berger, Jr., "Fictions of the Pose: Facing the Gaze of Early Modern Portraiture," *Representations* 46 (Spring 1994): 89. All such assertions are of course mere speculation, telling us more about the critic than about the portraits.

2

A Brief Biography

THE SEVERAL BIOGRAPHICAL SOURCES REHEARSE THE same information.[1] Thomas Sully was born in Horncastle, England, in 1783. His actor parents, Matthew and Sarah, emigrated to the United States with their nine children in 1792. They first set up house in Richmond, Virginia, where one of their relatives managed a theater. From there they moved to Charleston, South Carolina. Thomas was apprenticed to an insurance broker, who, noticing that the young man did more sketching than calculating, encouraged him to find a teacher. Several quite modestly talented men, including his older brother Lawrence, provided a few of the rudiments.

When Lawrence died in 1804, Thomas assumed the support of his widowed sister-in-law and her three children. The couple married in 1806, eventually having nine children of their own.

[1] There is no full-length biography of Thomas Sully. Along with his *Journal*, *Register*, and notebooks, sources include Edward Biddle and Mantle Fielding, "Memoirs of Thomas Sully," in Biddle and Fielding, *The Life and Works of Thomas Sully* (Philadelphia: Wickersham Press, 1921); Monroe H. Fabian, "Introduction," *Mr. Sully, Portrait Painter: The Works of Thomas Sully (1783–1872)*, 10–24; Steven Eric Bronson, *Thomas Sully: Style and Development in Masterworks of Portraiture, 1783–1839* (PhD diss., University of Delaware, 1986); "Thomas Sully (1783–1872)," Worcester Art Gallery, https://www.worcesterart.org/collection/Early_American/Artists/sully/biography/index.html; and Robert L. Gale, "Thomas Sully," in *American National Biography*, vol. 21 (New York: 1999), 129–31.

After moving around for eighteen months, from North Carolina to New York to Hartford, the Sullys settled in Philadelphia, where the painter (Figure 2.1)[2] would live for most of the next six decades.

Searching for guidance, Sully traveled to Boston in 1807, to visit Gilbert Stuart. His three weeks in Stuart's studio comprised the only more or less formal training in oil painting Sully ever received.

He traveled to England twice. In 1809, early in his career, he crossed the Atlantic with financial support from a number of subscribers and carrying a letter of introduction from Charles Willson Peale. He was able to visit and get advice from Benjamin West, study anatomy with Henry Fuseli, and copy pictures by Raphael, Correggio, Reynolds, and others. Sully was ambivalent about the work of Thomas Lawrence, though the influence of the stylish and successful English portraitist would become a commonplace of art-historical opinion.

Sully's second visit to England took place during 1837–38. Now at the height of his career, and after quite a bit of back-and-forth, he secured an invitation to paint a full-length portrait of the new monarch, teenaged Queen Victoria. The picture was met with wide approval on both sides of the Atlantic and earned further prestige for the painter.[3]

There is some evidence that Sully initially intended to pursue history painting. Eighteenth-century aesthetic theory conferred a higher status on history than portraiture. And, in Europe at least, history paintings sold for the highest prices. Sully's version of Washington's crossing of the Delaware River, mentioned earlier, is a large and impressive accomplishment.[4] But Sully, with a large family to support, had a keen appreciation of American taste in the Early National period. In 1805, Aaron Burr wrote to John

---

[2] "Of the artist's twenty or so self-portraits, this one, painted in his prime, is without doubt the finest." Monroe H. Fabian, *Mr. Sully, Portrait Painter: The Works of Thomas Sully (1783–1872)* [exhibition cat.] (Washington, DC: National Portrait Gallery, 1983), 76.

[3] The entries in Sully's *Journal*, from March 22 through May 14, 1838, contain extended and generally admiring comments on the young queen.

[4] For several years after settling in Philadelphia, and as late as 1829, Sully identified himself as an "Historical and Portrait Painter" in catalogues for the annual exhibitions at the Pennsylvania Academy. Edward Biddle and Mantle Fielding, *The Life and Works of Thomas Sully, 1783–1872* (Philadelphia: Wickersham Press, 1921), 28.

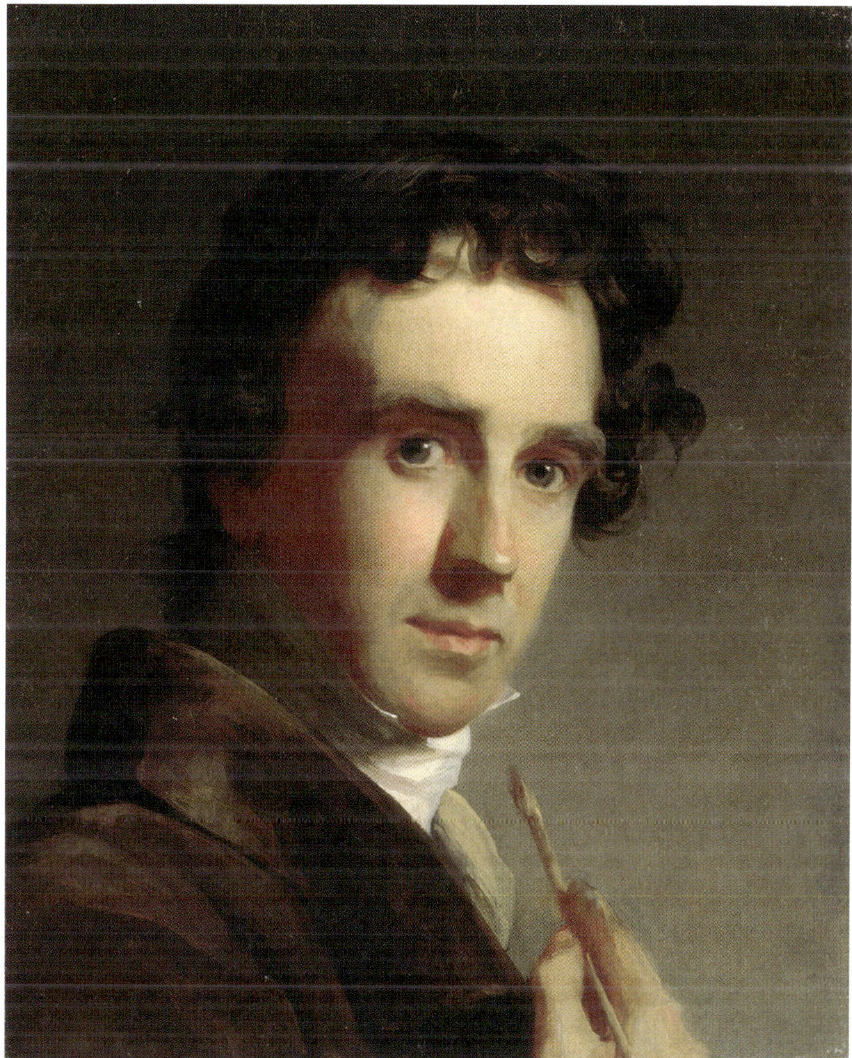

Figure 2.1 Thomas Sully, *Portrait of the Artist* (1821).

Courtesy of the Metropolitan Museum of Art. Gift of Mrs. Rosa C. Stanfield, in memory of her father, Henry Robinson, 1894.

Vanderlyn, then in Paris, advising Vanderlyn to come home from Paris because "if you are to send in some portrait painting, this is the best country for here is the rage for portraits."[5]

Two years later, the first *Salmagundi* paper reported, "everyone is anxious to see his phiz on canvas, however stupid and ugly it may be." John Neal wrote that portraits "abounded in our country. You can hardly open the door of the best room anywhere without surprising, or being surprised by, a picture of somebody plastered to the wall and staring at you with both eyes and a bunch of flowers."[6] During the first four decades of his career, Sully earned a substantial income from his portraits. (He included his estimate of each painting's asking price in his *Register.*)[7]

Throughout his long residence in Philadelphia, Sully also made frequent trips to other cities, always in search of new business. His travels took him to The Hermitage in Tennessee (to paint Andrew Jackson), Charleston, Washington (to paint John Quincy Adams), West Point, Monticello (to paint Jefferson), Baltimore, Boston, Oak Hill in Virginia (to paint James Monroe), and New York. As his reputation grew, he was honored with gestures of esteem, among them membership in the Pennsylvania Academy of the Fine Arts (PAFA), the Franklin Institute, the National Academy of Design, and Edinburgh's Royal Scottish Academy. In 1842, he was elected president of PAFA's board of directors but declined the appointment.

Sully also corresponded with some of the nation's most prominent figures. In December 1811, he wrote to inform Thomas Jefferson that he had been elected an associate member of the recently founded Society of American artists. In early January, Jefferson replied at courteous length, among other comments confessing: "I fear that I can be but a very useless associate. Time, which withers the fancy, as the other faculties of the mind and

[5] Cited in Ellen Miles, ed., *Portrait Painting in America: The Nineteenth Century* (New York: Main Street/Universe Books, 1977), 56.

[6] Cited in James Thomas Flexner, *The Light of Distant Skies: American Painting, 1760–1835* (New York: Harcourt, Brace and Co, 1969 [1954]), 200.

[7] In 1830, Sully published a price list for his portraits: "Head — $80; Bust — $100; Kit-Kat — $200; Half Length — $300; Bishop's Half Length — $350; Whole Length — $600."

body, presses on me with a heavy hand, and distance intercepts all personal intercourse."[8]

Late in his life (Figure 2.2), Sully became active in the Pennsylvania Colonization Society, one of many similar organizations advocating the emigration of Black Americans to Africa. He thus became involved in the most contentious debate of Philadelphia's antebellum years.

We know a great deal about Sully's professional and public life, his Philadelphia homes, his travels. Newspapers carried occasional stories about the meetings he attended and the organizations he belonged to. We know the names of his wife and their children, and something about a few of them. We know who many of his friends and colleagues were, and his *Register* tells us the names of almost everyone who sat for him. We know about the advice he gave, both as teacher and writer, to younger painters.[9]

One of Sully's students was Robert Douglass, Jr., a Black painter whose *Portrait of a Gentleman* was included in the 1834 exhibition of the Pennsylvania Academy of Fine Arts. Douglass was denied entry into the exhibition because of his race. In 1840, carrying a letter of introduction from Sully, Douglass was able to gain entry to the National Gallery in London.[10] Those two dates may support the speculation that Sully's refusal to accept the presidency of PAFA in 1842 was connected to the institution's treatment of Douglass.

We know that Sully was devoted to music: He was an accomplished amateur flutist and was for many years an officer of the Musical Fund Society. Sully's *Journal* records dozens of occasions when he joined with other friends for evenings of chamber music,

---

[8] Both sides of the correspondence were published in *The Enquirer* (Richmond, Virginia), February 25, 1812.

[9] Sully's *Hints to Young Painters* was drafted in 1851, revised in 1871, and printed posthumously in 1873. Aside from offering pages of detailed practical and technical advice, Sully occasionally includes an interesting aside. He tells us that Gilbert Stuart "considered the nose the most important feature" in a portrait, whereas Sully himself believed "the mouth to be the most important feature." The 1965 Reinhold Publishing Corporation reprint, 32.

[10] See Rebecca Bayeck, "Robert Douglass Jr., 19th Century African American Artist," New York Public Library, https://www.nypl.org/blog/2020/05/22/robert-douglass-jr-african-american-artist.

though his *Journal* tells us that he did not dance. Evidently, he had favorite poems: He included lengthy excerpts from Oliver Goldsmith's "The Deserted Village" and Thomas Gray's "Elegy Written in a Country Churchyard" in the opening pages of one of his notebooks.[11] He enjoyed exercise: His *Journal* records his vigorous swimming, his eight- and eleven-mile walks, and his pride, at the age of fifty, in being the first of his party to reach the summit of Mount Holyoke.[12]

Along with many nineteenth-century artists, Sully employed skilled engravers, among them John Sartain, to reproduce his portraits in multiple copies. Cheaper and more accessible than his originals, the engravings and mezzotints were intended to raise the visibility of his work and increase demand for commissions. He partnered with influential magazine publishers, most importantly Sarah Josepha Hale, who included a number of Sully's pictures in *Godey's Lady's Book*, the most popular magazine in antebellum America. Edward Lea Carey's seasonal *The Gift* also featured some of Sully's portraits.

We read many testimonials to Sully's generosity and kindness, though we also know that he could offer sharp appraisals of some of his contemporaries: "Trumbull does not paint as well as he did ten years ago ... R. Peale and Copely [*sic*] are too painstaking and hard ... Ingham's pictures are too much wrought and consequently hard ... Morse too fond of process in his coloring until the work looks soiled."[13] He was also and often critical of his own efforts. "My leading error," he writes in his *Journal* on May 16, 1838, "is the want of force."

Sully was moderately active in Whig politics. One of the last entries in his *Journal* reveals that he voted for Henry Clay in the election of 1844. We also know that Sully was a regular churchgoer. He attended the Unitarian Church and was friends for many years with the minister, William Henry Furness. The friendship eventually foundered over the question of abolition.

---

[11] MSS 196, Beinecke Library, Yale University.

[12] We even know what the wallpaper in Sully's Fifth Street house looked like: The Athenaeum of Philadelphia has preserved a sample in its important collection of decorative arts.

[13] Sully's *Journal*, July 21, 1825. New York Public Library, Roll #18. By far, the majority of entries in the *Journal* deal with his portrait commissions, his earnings, travels, and his technical opinions.

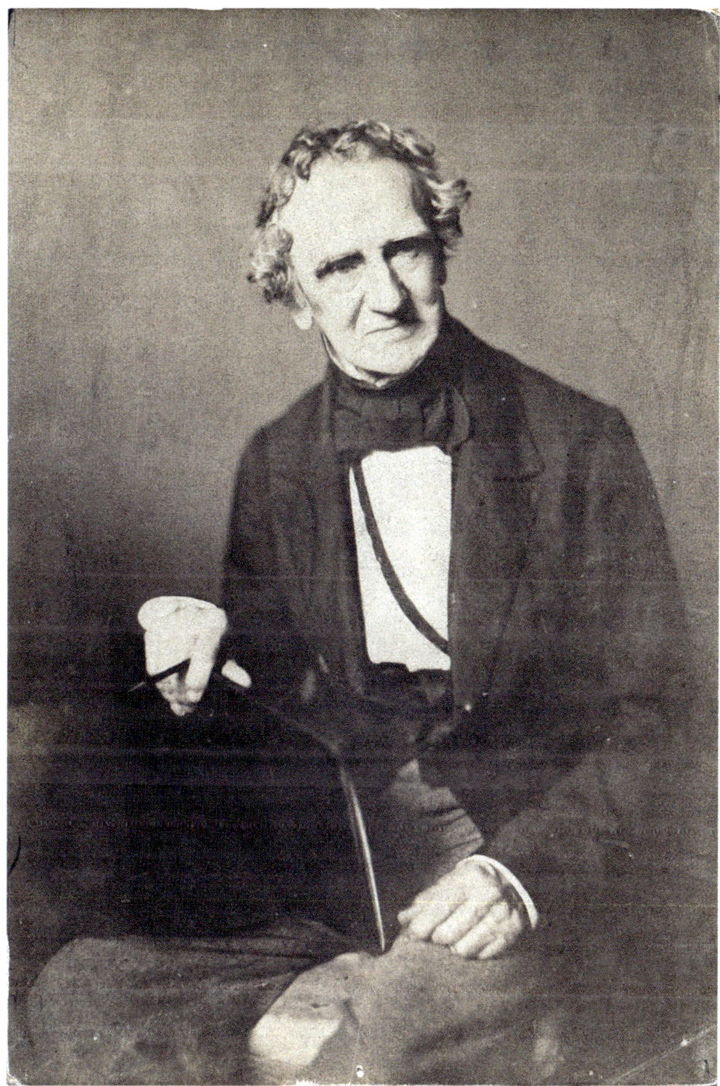

Figure 2.2 Thomas Sully in 1869.

Beyond that we do not know much about his opinions and convictions. We have only a few letters, no personal diary, no transcriptions of table talk. We can catch a glimpse of what might be called his belief in a kind of artistic democracy in a letter he co-signed in 1819 on learning of Joseph Delaplaine's plans to open a Gallery of Portraits in Washington, DC.

> It appears to the undersigned that Mister Delaplaine's gallery of portraits has two principal objects in view, one to promote the arts of the country by encouraging rising genius, the other to hand down to posterity the likenesses of distinguished Americans. The first of these objects we are of opinion cannot be affected to the extent that could be felt or that would come within the scope of the plan unless a liberal regard is shown to the number and variety of subjects. We cannot conceive that the portrait of any distinguished man could be lessened in the interest which it might impart by placing alongside of it that of another person less known.[14]

In short, find room on the gallery walls for the average American, not just the good and the great. A modestly Emersonian generosity.

In the later decades of his career, Sully's practice faced two decisive challenges. American taste had begun to turn away from portraiture toward a preference for landscape. What had begun in the 1820s, with the work of the Hudson River artists, flourished through the rest of the century as a quasi-patriotic preference for renderings of America's natural wonders. In addition, the rapid emergence of photography, beginning in the 1840s, offered Americans who wanted their portraits made access to a medium that promised a quicker, cheaper, and in many cases more accurate transcript.

Though his income and reputation declined in the final decades of his life, Sully remained well known and respected in the city that had long been his home. In the closing years of his life, he was the beneficiary of an unusual gesture of respect. An ordinance was passed to widen Ranstead Street between Fourth and Fifth Streets. The act was repealed "when it was found that such an undertaking would necessitate the demolishing of the

---

[14] The letter was published in several newspapers, including the *National Register*, Washington, DC (September 1, 1819).

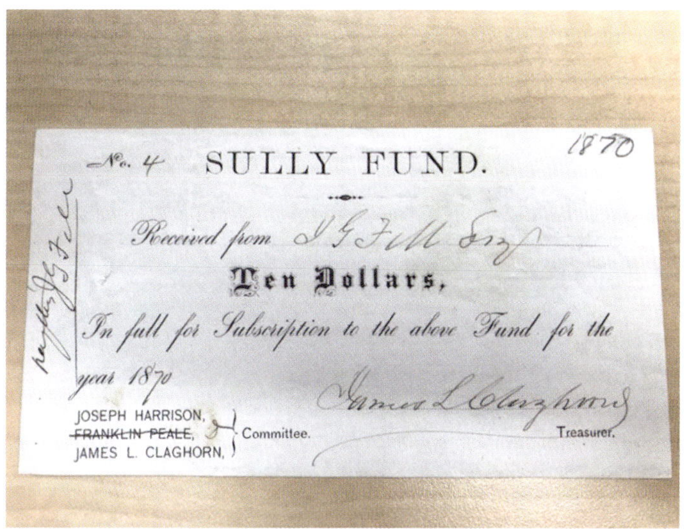
1870

No. 4 SULLY FUND.

Received from

Ten Dollars,

In full for Subscription to the above Fund for the year 1870

James L Claghorn Treasurer.

JOSEPH HARRISON,
~~FRANKLIN PEALE~~,
JAMES L. CLAGHORN, Committee.

Figure 2.3 Receipt for payment to the Sully Fund.

old artist's home."[15] In 1867, the board of the Pennsylvania Academy of the Fine Arts voted to create the "Sully Fund" (Figure 2.3) to which PAFA members contributed $10.00 or more, the proceeds to be given to Sully. A check was sent each year; in 1869, the amount was $1,000.[16]

Sully died in 1872, a few months before his ninetieth birthday. The citizens of Philadelphia mourned, and his death was reported in newspapers across the country.

---

[15] "Introduction," in *Catalog of the Memorial Exhibition of Portraits of Thomas Sully* (Philadelphia: Pennsylvania Academy of Fine Arts, 1922), 7.

[16] PAFA Archives, MS.053, Box 13, Folder 1.

3

Pennsylvania Hospital

THE HISTORY OF MEDICAL SCIENCE IN America begins in Philadelphia. Pennsylvania Hospital, the nation's first, received its charter in 1751. Formal education in medicine began in 1765, when John Morgan, recently returned from Edinburgh, partnered with William Shippen to found the country's first medical school.[1] Both institutions enabled Philadelphia to secure a leading position in clinical care and medical research, and to sustain that status for decades. In the words of historian Whitfield Bell: "Philadelphia at the beginning of the nineteenth century was pre-eminently the place in America to study medicine."[2]

In 1751, the year Pennsylvania Hospital received its charter, the thriving port of Philadelphia had a population of fifteen thousand, making it the largest city in the colonies, and the second largest—behind London—in the British Empire. Growing prosperity, however, was inevitably attended by growing poverty

[1] One scholar estimates that "there were about 3500 medical practitioners in America at the time of the Revolution. However, less than 10% were doctors of medicine." In the absence of hospitals and medical schools, most would-be physicians learned their trade by serving as apprentices; periods of apprenticeship varied widely, from a few months to a year or more. Ira M. Rutkow, *Surgery: An Illustrated History* (St. Louis: Mosby-Yearbook, 1993), 308.

[2] Whitfield J. Bell, *The Art of Philadelphia Medicine* (Philadelphia: Philadelphia Museum of Art, 1965), 39.

and disease. The well-to-do had access to medical care, receiving their treatments at home; surgery was performed on kitchen tables. The poor could only turn to the Philadelphia Almshouse, which opened in 1732, and offered almost nothing in the way of medical care. The place more resembled a disciplinary homeless shelter than a medical facility. In the words of one historian, "[many] indigents avoided the institution because it functioned less as a refuge and more as a prison where officials tried to control the poor and to shape their morals. Locked gates and a brick wall confined inmates to the grounds."[3] The mortality rate was exceptionally high.[4] In short, the poor went to the Almshouse to die.

Just a year before the Almshouse opened, Benjamin Franklin had published an appeal to his readers in *The Pennsylvania Gazette*, urging them to show "a tender regard for the afflicted."[5] Twenty years later, Dr. Thomas Bond returned from a tour of hospitals in London, Edinburgh, and Paris with the fixed purpose of establishing a similar institution in Philadelphia: a hospital to serve the needs of the sick poor.[6] After failing to secure adequate donations for the project, he enlisted his friend Benjamin Frank-

[3] Billy G. Smith, ed., *Life in Early Philadelphia: Documents from the Revolutionary and Early National Periods* (University Park: The Pennsylvania State University Press, 1995), 36.

[4] Maria Katkins, "Almshouses (Poorhouses)," *The Encyclopedia of Greater Philadelphia*, https://philadelphiaencyclopedia.org/essays/almshouses-poorhouses.

[5] Benjamin Franklin, "Compassion and Regard for the Sick," *The Pennsylvania Gazette* (March 18, 1731). For the most comprehensive account of Franklin's role in the establishment of Pennsylvania Hospital, see J. A. Leo Lemay, *The Life of Benjamin Franklin, Volume 3: Soldier, Scientist and Politician, 1748–1757* (Philadelphia: University of Pennsylvania Press, 2009), 265–86.

[6] Dr. Bond's concern for the poor suggests that he was a large-minded man. A further indication of his character can be found in his views of America's indigenous people. In a lecture delivered in November 1766, defending the importance of practical experience over theory in medical care, Bond noted that the native Americans, without recourse to the learning of physicians, "have been found possessed of Skill in the Cure of Diseases [and] from their discoveries the present practice of Physic has been enrich'd with some of the most valuable Medicines now in use." Cited in Francis Randolph Packard, *The History of Medicine in the United States* (Philadelphia: J. B. Lippincott, 1901), 178.

lin, who secured a matching grant from the Colonial government.[7]

The hospital was founded to serve "the sick poor and lunatics." The physicians and surgeons included several of the nation's most distinguished practitioners: John Morgan, William Shippen, Philip Syng Physick, and Benjamin Rush, to name only a handful. Most of the earliest patients were servants, enslaved women and men, paupers, and the insane relatives of upper-class families. Men and women suffering from a wide range of maladies—skin diseases, asthma, knife and gunshot wounds, leprosy, bone fractures, putrid fever, ulcers, and rheumatism—sought relief at the hospital.

In the years following its founding, the hospital's managers and physicians collaborated on a long list of innovations, many of which would influence American medicine for generations: the first outpatient clinic (1752), first hospital pharmacy (1755), first medical library (1762), first medical resident (1773), and first surgical amphitheater (1804).[8]

Franklin opened his 1751 petition to the Pennsylvania Assembly for the creation of a hospital by addressing the problem of mental illness:

> That with the numbers of people, the numbers of Lunaticks, or Persons distempered in mind, and deprived of their rational faculties, hath greatly increased in this province. That some of them going at large are a Terror to their Neighbours, who are daily apprehensive of the Violences they may commit; and others are continually wasting their substance, to the great injury of themselves and families, ill-disposed persons wickedly taking

[7] When rural legislators proved reluctant to provide funds for a city hospital, Franklin devised a scheme. The politicians accepted his proposal that he would only make a formal request after he had raised two thousand pounds from private citizens. The plan worked, since the legislators believed the task would prove impossible. However, as he predicted, the promise of a matching grant enabled Franklin to raise the money—every donated pound would be doubled, he assured his contributors—which, when the requisite funds had been raised, compelled the legislature to provide a like amount. Looking back on what he called his "cunning" triumph, Franklin wrote, "I do not remember any of my political manoeuvres, the success of which gave me at the time more pleasure." Peter Conn, ed., *The Autobiography of Benjamin Franklin* (Philadelphia: University of Pennsylvania Press, 2006), 97.

[8] The glass-domed amphitheater restricted surgery to sunlight hours. Replaced as a working surgical facility in 1868, it survives as an artifact of medical history.

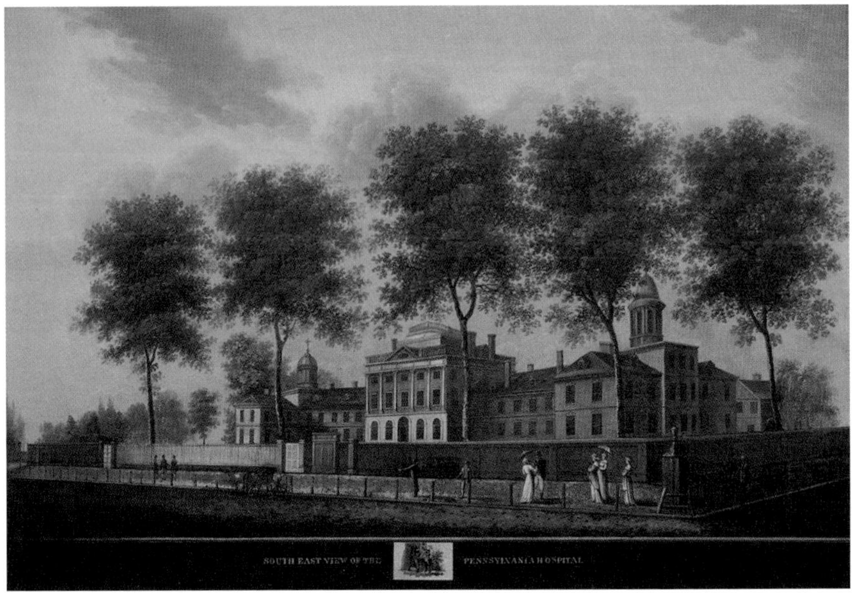

Figure 3.1 Pennsylvania Hospital. The building was constructed in three stages and completed in 1804.

> advantage of their unhappy condition, and drawing them into unreasonable bargains.[9]

Four of the first six patients admitted to the hospital were persons suffering from some sort of mental illness, and through its first several decades these made up at least half of all the persons admitted.

The first published record of Pennsylvania Hospital's (Figure 3.1) founding was Benjamin Franklin's *Some Account of the Pennsylvania Hospital* (1754). Although its roots lay in the examples of voluntary hospitals in London, Edinburgh, and Paris, Pennsylvania Hospital was from the beginning distinctive in its governance. All decisions about staffing, budgets, construction, and the hospi-

---

[9] The forty-page 1751 petition is printed in full in I. Bernard Cohen's facsimile edition of Franklin's *Some Account of the Pennsylvania Hospital* (Baltimore, MD: The Johns Hopkins Press, 1954).

tal rules resided with a board of managers. The twelve managers, answerable to no authority inside or outside the hospital, selected replacements for the board when vacancies occurred.[10] Through the first several decades of the hospital's operation, most of the managers were Quakers, usually a mix of lawyers, merchants, and bankers. Physicians were never appointed to the board, though the managers did frequently consult with hospital's medical staff.

SAMUEL COATES

Samuel Coates was born in Philadelphia in 1748, the son of Samuel Coates and his wife, Mary Langdale. Following the death of his parents, Coates was taken in by his uncle and mentor, John Reynell, who helped establish Coates as a merchant when he joined Reynell's firm in 1771. Ten years later, Coates took ownership of the company, and prospered, importing and exporting products of all sorts throughout the colonies and back and forth across the Atlantic.

Cathy Matson has summoned up the workplace that Coates and Reynell shared in the 1760s:

> The young clerk Samuel Coates spent hours every day in the small counting rooms he shared with merchant John Reynell during the 1760s. Stuffed with evidence of the British Empire's expansion, these two windowless spaces were at the rear of the first floor of a three-story building at Front and Walnut Streets in Philadelphia, a dwelling and business space that was about eighteen feet wide at the front of the building and ran twenty-one feet deep. Each of the two counting chambers measured a little less than six by nine feet. They were filled with the material objects and accounts of an Atlantic world trader whose connections stretched not only to the farthest corners of the British Empire but also into the shops and homes of nearly two hundred Philadelphians.[11]

---

[10] Technically, the Managers were elected by the Contributors (donors of £10 or more) at the Annual Meeting each May, but the slate of candidates proposed by the Managers themselves was routinely approved.

[11] Cathy Matson, "Putting the *Lydia* to Sea: The Material Economy of Shipping in Colonial Philadelphia," *The William and Mary Quarterly* 74, no. 2 (April 2017): 303.

Coates's success in business was accompanied by an impressive commitment to public service. He served as an overseer of Philadelphia's public schools, as a director of the First Bank of the United States, and as treasurer of the Library Company of Philadelphia.

Of most interest to us in this account, Coates also served for four decades as manager and for thirteen years as president of the Pennsylvania Hospital. In 1793, Coates was among the small handful of managers who stayed in Philadelphia during the yellow fever epidemic. He worked with the banker Stephen Girard, who headed up a relief committee, its members doing what they could to relieve the sick and bury the dead. The Pennsylvania Hospital's records include some of Coates's eye-witness testimony. "I think our disorder doth not much abate," he wrote on October 9, 1793. He then named some of the sick and dead of his acquaintance: David Rittenhouse "very ill," Josiah Hewes and Richard Wells "better," Jonathan Dickinson Sergeant "dead," and "my poor brother's family terribly afflicted with sickness."[12]

In 1798, in the midst of a recurrence of yellow fever, Coates wrote to a friend that more than 3,000 people had died "in a city which has been scourged a third time since the year 1792 with a pestilential fever."[13] As he had in the previous visitations of plague, Coates remained at the hospital, doing what he could to comfort the sick and dying. Throughout his long volunteer career at the hospital, Samuel Coates showed a particular interest in the mentally afflicted. When the original facilities for housing the mentally disturbed became overcrowded, Coates led a fundraising effort that led to the construction in 1796 of the west wing of the hospital: One hundred beds reserved exclusively for these patients. According to one nineteenth-century writer, "when additional funds were needed, Coates was among the first called on for aid, either directly, or indirectly by the influence of his character on other and wealthier citizens. Foremost among these was his warm friend, Stephen Girard, to whom an appeal was rarely

---

[12] Cited in Walter Hayes, *The Captain from Nantucket and the Mutiny on the "Bounty"* (Ann Arbor, MI: The William L. Clements Library, 1996). The brother was Benjamin Coates.

[13] Samuel Coates collection, Clements Library, University of Michigan.

made by Samuel Coates in vain."[14] Coates was also generous in his everyday transactions with patients. The hospital's Steward Receipt book records that on November 13, 1819, Coates paid "eleven dollars & forty Cents in full for 285 sweet oranges bought for distribution among all the patients of the Pennsylvania Hospital @ 4 Cents."[15]

George Morton, a nineteenth-century Pennsylvania Hospital physician and historian of the institution, remarked on another dimension of Coates's interest. According to Morton, Coates "always carried with him a rather large, leather-bound memorandum book, in which he noted, in ink, his reflections upon madness and his deductions drawn from his observations, with notes of the histories of especially interesting cases and incidents, which came under his notice."[16] Coates called the notebook "Cases of Several Lunatics, and the Causes Thereof in Many Cases." The historian of medicine Nancy Tomes concluded that "the character of madness in late eighteenth and early nineteenth century Philadelphia is nowhere better captured" than in Coates's pages.[17]

Coates may have been moved to examine the lives and misfortunes of these men and women by his religious convictions. In the eighteenth and nineteenth centuries, Quakers distinguished themselves for their energetic acts of philanthropy, founding or taking part in many of the progressive movements that marked those years. Though some held and sold enslaved persons, Quakers were among the most vocal opponents of slavery.

Measured by later standards of care, the conditions in which the mentally ill were confined in Pennsylvania Hospital were undeniably harsh and sometimes inhumane. Shackles were used to confine disruptive individuals, and the rooms in which they

---

[14] James J. Levick, "Benjamin Hornor Coates, M.D., One of the Founders of the Historical Society of Pennsylvania, and for Many Years Its Senior Vice-President" *The Pennsylvania Magazine of History and Biography* 6, no. 1 (1882): 23. By 1841, increased demand for housing the mentally ill led to the construction of an entirely separate facility in West Philadelphia.

[15] Steward Receipt books, 1819–1831 (6 vols.) box 151, Pennsylvania Hospital archives.

[16] Thomas G. Morton, *The History of the Pennsylvania Hospital, 1751–1895* (New York: Arno Press, 1973 [1895]), 139.

[17] Nancy Tomes, "The Domesticated Madman: Changing Concepts of Insanity at the Pennsylvania Hospital, 1780–1830," *The Pennsylvania Magazine of History and Biography* 106, no. 2 (April 1982): 271.

were housed were routinely referred to as *cells.*[18] At the same time, much evidence survives of kindness and sympathy. The hospital itself was referred to as *the house,* and the patients were often called part of *a family.*

> The hospital staff believed that the lunatics should be disciplined "with leniency, as a parent would correct a child. … Indeed, for a serious crime, James F., the "outrageous madman," received a very childish form of reprimand: an old-fashioned spanking. As Coates' cases also make clear, the staff countenanced parental indulgence along with the discipline. Hannah L. had her chair at the "family" table, Daniel T. presided over a religious service called specially for him, and Charles P. got a fine coffin and grave for his beloved dog Romeo. For all its occasional callousness, the hospital "family" evinced a remarkable tolerance, even appreciation of the lunatic patients as individual characters.[19]

A few examples of the people and incidents Coates describes confirm his attention as an observer and his responses—sometimes merely curious, but often sympathetic—to the suffering he encountered on an almost daily basis.[20]

Hannah Lewis (formerly Hannah Garrett), suffered from a "lunacy that became apparent soon after the death of her husband." Among other symptoms of her condition, she announced that she was the eldest daughter of King George III and would inherit his crown. For some years, Coates enjoyed a friendship with Hannah; the friendship ended when he—merely as a small joke—claimed a part ownership in her Palace.

Coates had become friendly with a patient named George Searle. On one of his visits, he asked what Searle is writing: "A power for you to settle my estate. I mean to practice Physick, which I have followed above 40 years, and understand better than all of your Kuhns, Rushes, Shippens or any other Quack Doctor in the World."

---

[18] Explaining if not justifying the occasional use of shackles, recall that a substantial portion of the men and women confined in the hospital had exhibited violent behavior.

[19] Tomes, "The Domesticated Madman," 278–79.

[20] These excerpts are transcribed from a microfilm copy of Coates's unpublished notebook at the American Philosophical Society. The entries in the notebook are not dated.

Elisabeth Matthewson was "a very lively, interesting woman, I think must have been 30 years in the Hospital and Alms [House], insane by reason of a brutal Sea Captain's behavior to her."

Coates attempted to make conversation with a patient named William Knox, who repeatedly demanded that Coates take off his hat. Coates politely but repeatedly refused, explaining, "I am a Quaker; it is a going from our principles to pull the hat off to any man." When Knox once again makes the same demand, Coates at last replies, "if it would be the means of relieving my friend, I would freely bend to his wishes." He then adds, "Really I did not intend to; but for this once I will gratify my friend Knox—so off goes my hat!"

Sully completed this portrait (Figure 3.2) of Samuel Coates in 1813.

Monroe Fabian provides a brief description: "Coates is shown standing at his desk in an office on the first floor of the hospital. The painting is almost a grisaille, with only the flesh tints and the pink of the sky as a relief from the white, brown, and gray green of the rest. The architectural details and the desk are carefully delineated and are more colored drawing than painting."[21]

It is a large painting, nearly life-size, shrewdly composed. Sully's management of light draws our attention to Coates, dressed in his plain gray Quaker suit, standing at his desk. Every surface—wood, brass, fabric, quill feather, glass—is handled with virtuoso panache. Every page of the stack of papers on which he is writing seems magically visible. Coates stands on a raked floor, covered in a splendidly rendered carpet, which suggests a stage set. His pose creates a dramatic interaction with the viewer. He is working, his right hand holding the quill with which he is writing up his notes. He has turned his calm, confident face to see—not quite yet to greet—a visitor. Each of us who returns his gaze is that visitor.

[21] Monroe H. Fabian, *Mr. Sully, Portrait Painter: The Works of Thomas Sully (1783–1872)* [exhibition cat.] (Washington, DC: Smithsonian Institution Press, 1983), 60. Sully made a gift of the portrait to Pennsylvania Hospital. Fabian offers the interesting speculation that self-promotion may have played a part in the benefaction. The hospital was "one of the most visited public buildings in Philadelphia," and the Coates portrait would be seen by a stream of staff, patients, and visitors.

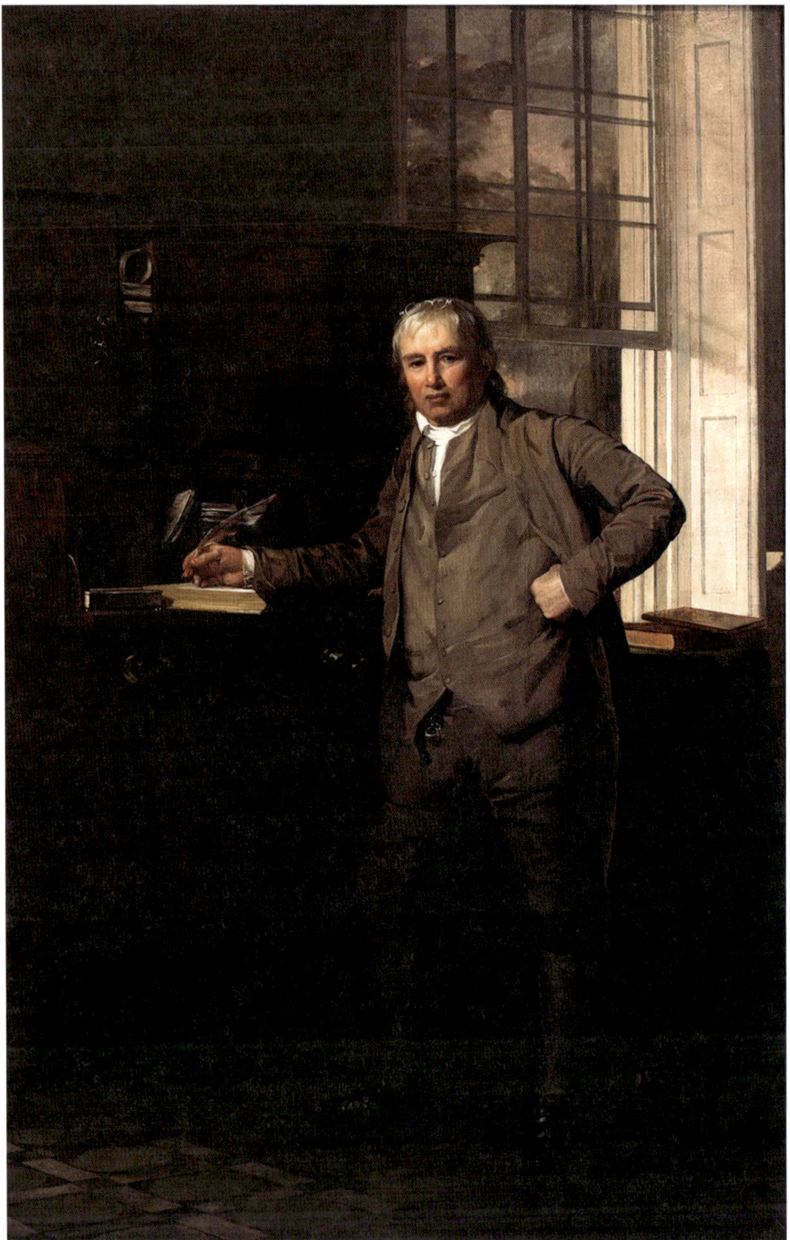

Figure 3.2 *Samuel Coates.*

Courtesy of the Pennsylvania Hospital Historic Collections, Philadelphia. Photographed by Robert Neroni.

On a shelf to Coates's right rests his Quaker hat: I like to believe it is the hat that he generously took off for William Knox.

BENJAMIN RUSH

The subject of at least seven full-length biographies, along with scores of articles and book chapters, Benjamin Rush was the most celebrated—and controversial—physician in nineteenth-century America. In the words of historian Whitfield Bell, "The quarter century after 1790 might properly be called the age of Rush. He was not the only medical figure in the city, or even perhaps the ablest, but he was tireless, devoted, informed, and self-confident, an effective speaker and writer, and an appealing teacher. He was the most famous physician in America, and also the most influential."[22]

In 1867, a half-century after Rush's death and over a century after the founding of Pennsylvania Hospital, Dr. Charles Meigs, one of the hospital's resident surgeons, published a brief history of the institution in the first volume of *Pennsylvania Hospital Reports.* "We esteem the greatest name of the men who, in that now somewhat distant day, served in the Pennsylvania Hospital, was the name of Dr. Benjamin Rush."[23]

When Rush died in 1813, Thomas Jefferson wrote to John Adams that "Another of our friends of 76. is gone, my dear Sir, another of the Co-signers of the independence of our country. And a better man, than Rush, could not have left us, more benevolent, more learned, of finer genius, or more honest."[24] Adams replied that he knew "of no Character living or dead, who has done more real good in America."[25]

---

[22] Bell, *The Art of Philadelphia Medicine,* 34.

[23] Morton, *The History of the Pennsylvania Hospital,* 450. Rush trained more than twenty-five hundred medical students. One writer has claimed that "every outstanding American physician down to the Civil War was either a pupil of Rush or of a Rush pupil." Alyn Brodsky, *Benjamin Rush: Patriot and Physician* (New York: St. Martin's Press, 2004), 5.

[24] "To John Adams from Thomas Jefferson, 27 May 1813," *Founders Online,* National Archives, https://founders.archives.gov/documents/Adams/99-02-02-6041.

[25] "John Adams to Thomas Jefferson, 11 June 1813," *Founders Online,* National Archives, https://founders.archives.gov/documents/Jefferson/03-06-02-0171.

Not everyone agreed, either in Rush's lifetime or in the two centuries since. "A polarizing figure in historical analysis as he sometimes was in life, Rush is usually cast as hero or villain."[26] His achievements and failures often coincided. He was an advocate for women's education, but in large part to shape women fit to raise patriots.[27] His call for prison reform was sincere, though it led him to endorse the creation of Eastern State Penitentiary, the Benthamite panopticon that Charles Dickens and eventually many others found repugnant to common sense.[28]

He was an eloquent opponent of slavery, who chided clergymen for their failure to support the abolitionist cause: "In vain," he wrote, "will you command your flocks to offer up the incense of faith and charity, while they continue to mingle the sweat and blood of negro slaves with their sacrifices."[29] At the same time, and like many white opponents of slavery, he harbored views on race that were offensive. In a paper he delivered at the American Philosophical Society in 1799, Rush argued that Africans' black skin was the consequence of leprosy, brought on by the intense heat of the African continent.[30]

Born in 1745, in a town outside Philadelphia, Rush graduated from the College of New Jersey at the age of seventeen, was apprenticed to the physician John Redman, and earned his medical degree at Edinburgh in 1768. He then spent a year visiting

---

[26] Sari Altschuler and Christopher J. Bilodeau, "The Republics of Benjamin Rush," *Early American Studies* 15, no. 2 (Spring 2017): 234.

[27] Rush was among those who supported the creation of the Young Ladies' Academy, the first legally chartered school for women. He delivered the school's first commencement address, "Thoughts Upon Female Education," arguing that education was compatible with "the domestic character of women."

[28] Charles Dickens, *American Notes for General Circulation* (London: Chapman & Hall, 1842), Chapter VII, "Philadelphia, and its Solitary Prison." Earlier in the chapter, Dickens commented favorably on several Philadelphia institutions. "Among them a most excellent Hospital—a quaker establishment, but not sectarian in the great benefits it confers; a quiet, quaint old Library, named after Franklin; a handsome Exchange and Post Office; and so forth. In connection with the quaker Hospital, there is a picture by West, which is exhibited for the benefit of the funds of the institution. The subject is, our Saviour healing the sick, and it is, perhaps, as favourable a specimen of the master as can be seen anywhere. Whether this be high or low praise, depends upon the reader's taste. In the same room, there is a very characteristic and life-like portrait by Mr. Sully, a distinguished American artist."

[29] Cited in N. G. Goodman, *Benjamin Rush, Physician and Citizen* (Philadelphia: University of Pennsylvania Press, 1934), 273.

[30] Bernard Bailyn, ed., *The Great Republic* (Boston: Little, Brown, 1977), 411.

hospitals in London and Paris. Benjamin Franklin liked him, and introduced him to such eminent figures as Samuel Johnson, Oliver Goldsmith, and Sir Joshua Reynolds. In evidence already is the combination of intelligence, charm, excellent talk, and good looks that would serve Rush well throughout his life. He also displayed the complete self-confidence, often rising to arrogance, that would embroil him in nearly continuous controversy: "always outspoken, often dogmatic and seldom conciliatory."[31]

Rush set up his practice in Philadelphia in 1769. In the same year, he was appointed professor of chemistry in the College of Philadelphia, the first such position in America. Over the next several years, he was named physician to the Pennsylvania Hospital in 1783 and professor of the Institutes of Medicine in the University of Pennsylvania in 1791.

An enthusiastic supporter of America's break with Great Britain, Rush signed the Declaration of Independence, then served as a senior medical officer during the Revolution. A bitter dispute with Dr. William Shippen eventually led to Rush's forced resignation, but he acquitted himself honorably and usefully during his year of service. He also made a major contribution to the welfare of active-duty soldiers. According to one of his biographers, Rush's essay, "Directions for Preserving the Health of Soldiers," was a founding document in the development of preventive military medicine. Based on his frontline experience, Rush opened the essay with the crucial insight—not widely understood at the time—that "a greater proportion of men have perished with sickness in our armies than have fallen by the sword." Published as a pamphlet in 1778, it was reissued throughout the nineteenth century, the final edition appearing in 1908.[32]

Rush remained on the staff of Pennsylvania Hospital for thirty years, until his death in 1813. Early in his tenure, in 1789, he published the first volume of his *Medical Inquiries and Observations*, which included "An account of the bilious remitting fever." During the eighteenth century, no one knew what caused or how to cure any of the dozen or more diseases that besieged the citizens

---

[31] Carl Binger, MD, *Revolutionary Doctor: Benjamin Rush, 1746–1813* (New York: W. W. Norton, 1966), 156.

[32] Ibid., 124.

of Philadelphia and other cities: typhoid, yellow fever, dysentery, malaria, cholera, typhus. But Rush's talent for observation often enabled him to differentiate the symptoms, and thus the probable prognoses, for some of these plagues.

Rush's medical interventions during the yellow fever epidemic of 1793, controversial at the time, have left an indelible stain on his memory. Like most other cities around the world, Philadelphia suffered from periodic outbreaks of contagious disease throughout its early history. However, the eruption of yellow fever in the summer of 1793 proved to be the most devastating. Rush was among the first to realize how serious this outbreak was going to become.

Most physicians blamed the spread of the disease on "noxious miasma," produced by rotting vegetation—of which there was an abundance on the hot August wharves—or perhaps by bags of putrefying coffee beans that had recently arrived on a ship from San Domingo. Neither fires nor gunfire had any effect. Nor did smoking cigars, or chewing garlic cloves, or aggressively scrubbing every household surface.

As many as five thousand men, women, and children died in a city of about forty-five thousand: By proportion, this was one of the deadliest epidemics in American history. As many as ten thousand, not only the affluent and wealthy, escaped to the surrounding countryside. All three branches of the federal government, still located in Philadelphia, moved out of the city. By late August, Rush wrote, even many doctors were "flying from the city."[33] Historian James Flexner described the terror and chaos of that summer: "husbands abandoned sick wives, mothers their children. ... Many persons died alone in empty houses, their screams going on and on through the silent night while hundreds of anguished listeners stopped their ears. Sometimes a sufferer would use his last strength to stagger out into the deserted street, and pound unavailingly at the bolted doors of his neighbors. The next morning his corpse would be found lying face down in the gutter."[34]

---

[33] Cited in Stephen Fried, *Rush: Revolution, Madness, and Benjamin Rush, the Visionary Doctor Who Became a Founding Father* (New York: Crown Publishers, 2018), 339.

[34] James Thomas Flexner, *Doctors on Horseback: Pioneers of American Medicine* (New York: Viking Press, 1937), 95.

Rush behaved with exceptional courage throughout the plague. He worked to the point of exhaustion for months, often sleeping no more than two or three hours a night. He charged no fees for his services and went deeply into debt. (Samuel Coates offered to lend him £50, equivalent to more than $8,000 today.)[35] However, the "heroic" remedies he administered, a combination of aggressive purging and repeated bleeding, were vigorously and often vehemently opposed by many of his fellow physicians. "It was said of him that his purges were meant for a horse, and that he had waded through the epidemic in a bath of his patients' blood."[36] He was sometimes defamed as the "prince of bleeders" or "Doctor Vampire."

Rush's critics were right to claim that his practices were probably doing more harm than good, although no one in the 1790s had any real understanding of the causes—infection by Aedes mosquito—or any effective therapy. In any event, in the opinion of several scholars, Rush's "popularity as a writer teacher spread the blight of heroic practice across the United States for half a century, 1800–1850."[37]

From the beginning of his tenure at Pennsylvania Hospital in 1783, Rush had charge of the mentally ill patients. He first turned his attention to the conditions in which the "lunatics" were housed, doing what he could to improve sanitation, food, and clothing. He encouraged his colleagues and students to reconceive of madness as a medical problem, not as evidence of moral failure. He also insisted that physicians should listen to what the patients had to say (as the layman Samuel Coates had long been doing).

In 1812, just a year before his death, he published, *Medical Inquiries and Observations Upon the Diseases of the Mind,* the first comprehensive American text on mental illness. In a letter to Thomas Jefferson, he wrote that the book was "the result of the reading, experience and reflections of fifty years upon all the

---

[35] Fried, *Rush,* 355.

[36] Binger, *Revolutionary Doctor,* 217.

[37] Richard Harrison Shryock, *Medicine in America: Historical Essays* (Baltimore, MD: The Johns Hopkins Press, 1966), 9.

forms of madness, and upon all the other diseases of the mind."[38] In nineteen chapters, Rush reviewed the symptoms, the putative causes, and the possible cures of a broad spectrum of mental derangements.

Some of Rush's speculations may sound daft to a modern reader. In Chapter V, "Of General Intellectual Derangement," for example, Rush summarizes the evidence for and against the influence of the moon in inducing madness. "There is," he concludes" an equal portion of truth on the side of both these opinions."[39] Far more important, however, is the book-long commitment—reflecting Rush's lifelong commitment—to a new and more humane conception of madness. Madness was an illness, a disease of the entire body. It had its sources in a myriad of physical and psychological reversals. It was neither a demonic possession nor punishment for sin. Rush provided examples of madness apparently provoked by head injuries, rage, grief, sun stroke, apoplexy, terror, "excessive intake of alcoholic beverages," and obsessive intellectual overwork.

Although they influenced medical theory and practice through much of the nineteenth century, few of the hypotheses Rush recorded in *Medical Inquiries* have proven durable. However, by reorienting attitudes toward the mentally ill, he made a monumental contribution to the history of medicine. In 1965, canonizing a term that had often circulated informally, the American Psychiatric Association recognized Rush as the "father of American psychiatry."

Based on sketches made over several years, Sully's portrait of Benjamin Rush (Figure 3.3) was painted in 1814, a year after the doctor's death, at the request of his colleagues and students.[40] Although Rush was the subject of dozens of paintings and drawings in his lifetime, Sully's portrait is the iconic representation,

---

[38] "Letter of Benjamin Rush to Thomas Jefferson, April 26, 1812," in *Letters of Benjamin Rush, Volume II, 1793–1813*, ed. Lyman Henry Butterfield (Princeton, NJ: Princeton University Press, 2019 [1951]), 1131.

[39] Benjamin Rush, *Medical Inquiries and Observations Upon The Diseases of the Mind*, facsimile edition (New York: Hafner Publishing Company, 1962), 171.

[40] Along with countless portraits, Rush has been memorialized in at least two life-size statues. The first, unveiled in the early twentieth century, stands outside the Navy's Bureau of Medicine and Surgery in Washington, DC. A replica was installed in 2004 at Dickinson College, of which Rush was a principal founder.

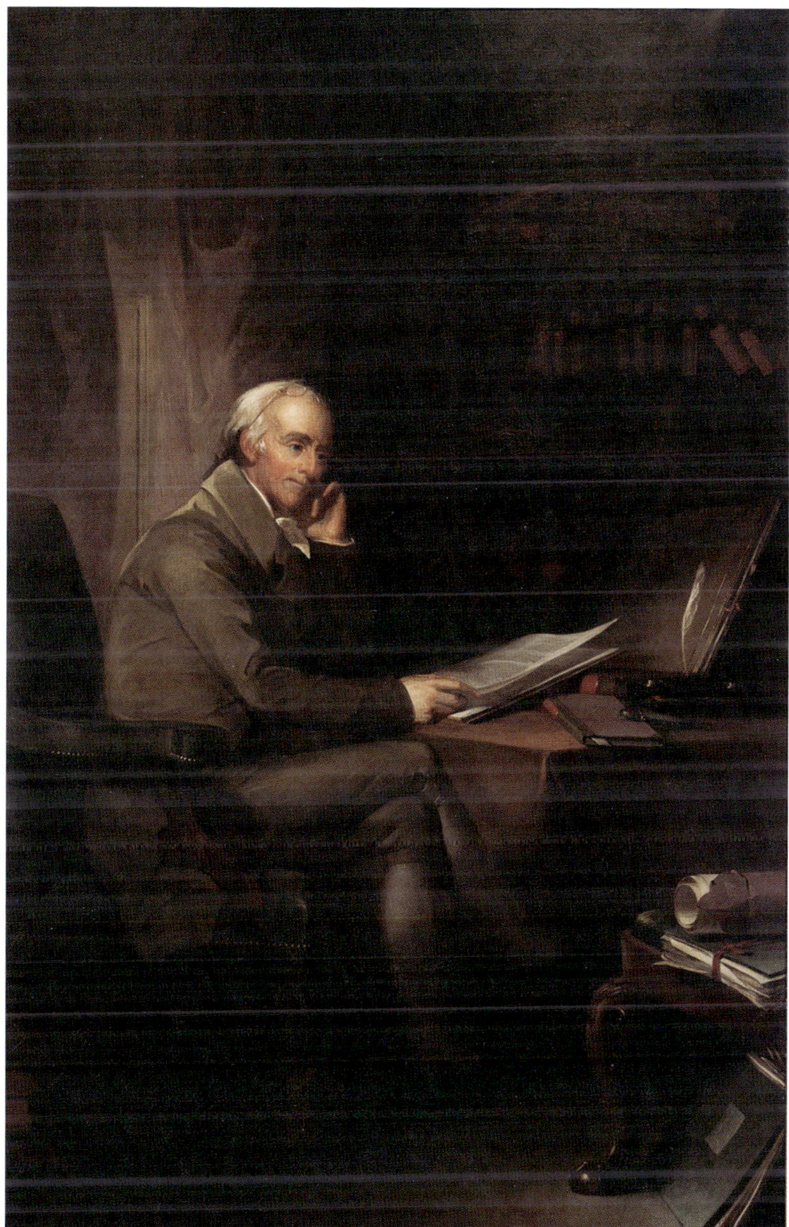

Figure 3.3 *Benjamin Rush/Attending Physician.*

Courtesy of the Pennsylvania Hospital Historic Collections, Philadelphia. Photographed by Robert Neroni.

reproduced scores of times in articles and books and on book jackets.[41]

Comparing the painting with a detailed description of Rush written by one of his students, Carl Binger concluded that the portrait closely resembles Rush's appearance near the end of his life: a slender build, a thin face and aquiline nose.[42] Finely dressed, as he almost always was, Rush is presented in a rather casual pose, his face showing the age and fatigue that marked his last years. Sully provides an elegant account of Rush's right hand, holding his place in the text he is reading. Rush's glance is slightly averted from the document. He has paused, spectacles perched on the top of his head, reflecting either on the subject of his reading or any one of the dozens of topics that engaged him.

He sits on a handsome mahogany chair, upholstered in leather. A companion footstool occupies the lower right corner of the painting, given over to manuscripts. Rush is surrounded by books, a realistic detail but at the same time an emblem of his long immersion in reading and writing. The palette is subdued, in keeping with the meditative tone. Strong light entering from the left illuminates Rush and his famously broad and high forehead. Dr. David Hosack had urged Rush to sit for a portrait, writing that Sully "is sufficiently acquainted with your *mind* as well as your *face,* to blend them on the canvas." Hosack was right. Sully has produced an arresting image of a man thinking.[43]

---

[41] Sully had painted two portraits of Rush in 1809 and 1812. His posthumous portrait was based in part on those earlier pictures.

[42] Binger, *Revolutionary Doctor,* 294.

[43] Cited in William Dunlap, *A History of the Rise and Progress of the Arts of Design in the United States,* vol. II (New York: George P. Scott, 1834, facsimile reprint Dover, 1969), 269. Hosack, who had a distinguished career, is mainly known to history as the physician who attended Alexander Hamilton following Hamilton's fatal duel with Aaron Burr.

4

The Second Bank of the United States

NICHOLAS BIDDLE

Andrew Jackson's protracted campaign against the Second Bank of the United States (BUS) "was one of the most controverted episodes of American history."[1] Jackson's principal opponent was Nicholas Biddle, president of the bank from 1822 to 1836. These were the years following the devastating Panic of 1819, a critical period in the nation's economic history. Biddle's decisions and his eventual defeat by Jackson have remained the subject of intense and sometimes vehement dispute for nearly two centuries. What is not in dispute is Biddle's centrality to those years, both in Philadelphia's history and the nation's: Nicholas Wainwright called his essay on the period "The Age of Nicholas Biddle."[2]

Born in 1786, Biddle was the talented, precocious, and ambitious child of a prominent Philadelphia family. One of his uncles

[1] Bray Hammond, *Banks and Politics in America from the Revolution to the Civil War* (Princeton, NJ: Princeton University Press, 1957), 286.

[2] Nicholas B. Wainwright, "The Age of Nicholas Biddle, 1825–1841," in *Philadelphia: A 300-Year History,* ed. Russell F. Weigley (New York: W. W. Norton 1982), 258–307.

had served with distinction and lost his life in the Revolutionary Navy; his father was a successful merchant and a confidant of Benjamin Franklin. According to William Shade, young Nicholas "hardly had a boyhood at all, entering the University of Pennsylvania at ten," then transferring to the College of New Jersey at Princeton, from which he graduated in 1801, at fifteen, as valedictorian.[3] After studying law for three years, he accepted an invitation from retired General John Armstrong, US minister to France, to join him as his unpaid personal secretary.

Apparently, young Biddle did not devote much time to his secretarial duties. He spent most of his three years in Europe traveling through eastern France, Switzerland, Austria, Italy, Sicily, and Malta. His encounter with Greece—he was reputedly the second American to visit the country as a tourist—provoked a lifelong fascination with Greek history and especially ancient Greek architecture.[4] Biddle's visit to Greece coincided with the removal of the Parthenon Marbles and their shipment to England. Outraged by what he saw, Biddle called Lord Elgin a "Scotch vandal" who "robbed for gold."[5] The twenty-one-year-old Biddle completed his European tour in London, where he took up the position of temporary secretary to James Monroe, then serving as American ambassador. From London, he traveled to Cambridge, where he reportedly "delighted the dons with his facility in Greek."[6]

Exceptionally well traveled and well connected, the twenty-three-year-old Biddle had already come to the admiring attention of Thomas Jefferson. "Biddle we know," the President wrote to a

---

[3] William G. Shade, "Nicholas Biddle," *American National Biography*, vol. 2 (New York: Oxford University Press, 1999), 734.

[4] R. A. McNeal, ed., *Nicholas Biddle in Greece: The Journals and Letters of 1806* (University Park: Pennsylvania State University Press, 1993), 199.

[5] John Clubbe, *Byron, Sully and the Power of Portraiture* (Aldershot, UK: Ashgate, 2005), 142. Thomas Sully did not share Biddle's outrage. After visiting the Parthenon statuary on May 1, 1838, he confided his response in his *Journal*: "These wonderful remains of ancient art deserve all the extravagant praise that has been written about them." He also declared that he was "much pleased with a colossal bust of the Duke of Wellington, cut by Postrucci from a block of marble taken from the Parthenon."

[6] E. Digby Baltzell, *Philadelphia Gentlemen: The Making of a National Upper Class* (Glencoe, IL: The Free Press, 1958), 90.

HISTORY

OF

THE EXPEDITION

UNDER THE COMMAND OF

CAPTAINS LEWIS AND CLARK,

TO

THE SOURCES OF THE MISSOURI,

THENCE

ACROSS THE ROCKY MOUNTAINS

AND DOWN THE

RIVER COLUMBIA TO THE PACIFIC OCEAN.

PERFORMED DURING THE YEARS 1804—5—6.

By order of the

GOVERNMENT OF THE UNITED STATES.

PREPARED FOR THE PRESS

BY PAUL ALLEN, ESQUIRE.

VOL. II.

PHILADELPHIA:

PUBLISHED BY BRADFORD AND INSKEEP; AND

ABM: H. INSKEEP, NEWYORK.

J. Maxwell, Printer.

1814.

Figure 4.1 Title page of Volume Two of the *Journals of Lewis and Clark.* Biddle requested that his name be left off the title page. Paul Allen had made the final edits and supervised publication.

friend in September 1808, "and have formed an excellent opinion of him."[7]

The young man returned to Philadelphia and was admitted to the Pennsylvania bar in December 1809. The law did not suit him. Having no need to work to support himself and the family he had begun with Jane Craig, he turned to literature, serving briefly as editor of *The Port Folio,* probably the most important literary journal of its day. In 1812 he began work on the *History of the Expedition of Captains Lewis and Clark.* Biddle's edition of the journals (Figure 4.1), published in 1814, has long been super-

[7] Cited in Hammond, *Banks and Politics in America,* 290.

seded by more accurate versions. It nonetheless remains a substantial achievement, the first draft, as it were, of what novelist Larry McMurtry has called "our only real American Epic."[8]

Biddle was elected to the lower house of the Pennsylvania legislature in 1810. The BUS, headquartered in an imitation Roman temple on Third Street in Philadelphia, was a major subject of debate, both in the state and in the US Congress. Opponents, then as later, warned of the potentially abusive economic power that a national bank could wield. Supporters, including Biddle, defended the bank as guarantor of stability and an engine of American enterprise. His long and well-argued speech in defense of the bank, "the most important in his entire public career," established his credentials as an authority "on banking, currency, and governmental finance."[9]

Some years later, at President Monroe's request, Biddle compiled *Commercial Regulations* (1819), a digest of the laws and regulations of foreign countries on commerce, money, and weights and measures. More consequential, Monroe then appointed Biddle as one of the five government directors of the bank. The appointment coincided almost exactly with the crash of 1819, a collapse that quickly undermined local economies across the country. New York's almshouse was overrun with the impoverished and homeless. Three-fourths of Philadelphia's workforce "was reported idle in 1820, and hundreds were imprisoned for nonpayment of debts."[10] The suffering devastated rural areas as well as urban centers.

The causes of the crash included a dramatic shift in international commerce. Following the final defeat of Napoleon in 1815, Britain flooded the American market with manufactured goods that had been warehoused during the long European wars. That, together with high-risk speculation in land and cotton, and a shortage in gold and silver, hollowed out the American economy. The BUS's president, Langdon Cleves, chose deflationary policies,

---

[8] Larry McMurtry, *Sacagawea's Nickname: Essays on the American West* (New York: New York Review Books, 2001), 139.

[9] Thomas Payne Govan, *Nicholas Biddle: Nationalist and Public Banker, 1786–1844* (Chicago: The University of Chicago Press, 1959), 27.

[10] Sean Wilentz, *The Rise of American Democracy: Jefferson to Lincoln* (New York: W. W. Norton & Company, 2005), 207.

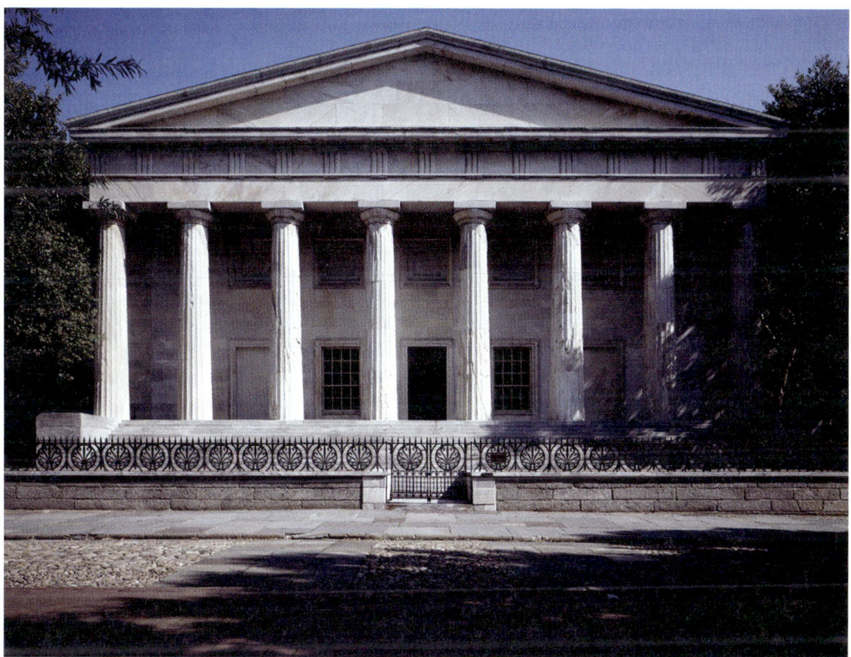

Figure 4.2 The Second Bank of the United States.

which contributed to the chaos. Biddle initially cooperated with Cleves, but his failure of leadership "left Biddle frustrated and disenchanted"; he left the governing board in December 1821.[11]

Prior to his resignation, Biddle persuaded the directors to commission a competition for the bank's new quarters. The design specifications published in May 1818 called for "a chaste imitation of Grecian architecture, in its simplest and least expensive form."[12] The young Philadelphia architect William Strickland won the competition. The building, a splendid example of the Greek Revival, stands as a testament to Biddle's influence (Figure 4.2).

---

[11] "Biddle, Nicholas," Papers of Abraham Lincoln Digital Library, https://papersofabrahamlincoln.org/persons/BI47179.

[12] Bray Hammond, *The Second Bank of the United States.* Transactions of the American Philosophical Society, n.s. 43, pt. 1 (Philadelphia: American Philosophical Society, 1953), 80.

Cleves resigned as president of the bank in 1822. President Monroe and Treasury Secretary William Crawford urged Biddle to take the position; he reluctantly agreed. On November 25, 1822, the stockholders elected thirty-seven-year-old Biddle as president; he would hold the position for the next fourteen years. During the first decade of his presidency, Biddle rehabilitated the bank's reputation and became America's foremost financier. He had preserved the species reserves of the nation's banks from loss to the East India trade, and to the import trade generally; he retired public debt without upsetting the money market; he stabilized both domestic and foreign exchange rates.[13] Leading what was by far the largest bank in the country, indeed, the largest corporation in the country and the only financial institution armed with a national mandate, Biddle was able to compel state banks to maintain adequate reserves as surety for their paper money.[14]

Despite Biddle's success in managing its operations, the bank remained controversial. The debate turned into a crisis with the election of Andrew Jackson as president in 1828. Jackson's antipathy to the BUS was a long-standing commitment. In an 1833 letter to James K. Polk, Jackson wrote, "Every one that knows me does know, that I have always been opposed to the U. States Bank, nay all banks."[15] The Second Bank, in Jackson's frequently quoted opinion, was "a Monster Institution." In a meeting with several advisors, Jackson summarized his objections to the bank, calling it "unconstitutional" and "dangerous to liberty."[16] In this opinion, Jackson contradicted the US Supreme Court, which, in *McCulloch v. Maryland* (1819), had affirmed that BUS was a constitutional entity.

The bank's charter was set to expire in 1836. Biddle, in what proved to be a ruinous miscalculation, agitated for the charter's

---

[13] Shade, "Nicholas Biddle," *American National Biography*, 735.

[14] Daniel Walker Howe, *What Hath God Wrought: The Transformation of America, 1815–1848* (New York: Oxford University Press, 2007), 374.

[15] Cited in Wilentz. *The Rise of American Democracy*, 361.

[16] Cited in Marquis James, *The Life of Andrew Jackson* (Indianapolis: The Bobbs-Merrill Company, 1938), 559.

renewal in 1832, ostensibly to remove it as an issue in the presidential contest. Jackson interpreted the move as an arrogant attempt to influence the election.

The Bank War had begun. According to historian Roy Nichols, "Biddle saw Jackson as a ruthless megalomaniac trying to destroy the nation's economy to satisfy his lust for power. Jackson saw Biddle as a greedy capitalist trying to control politics for his own enrichment. Truth did not enter into the contest."[17] Although this is an obvious overstatement, both of the antagonists in the struggle understood that the stakes were exceptionally high: nothing less than the finances of a rapidly growing and volatile national economy.

Congress did pass legislation to re-charter the bank in the summer of 1832. However, on July 10, 1832, Jackson "issued the most important presidential veto in American history."[18] Jackson took the position that the "executive and legislative branches were not bound by the judiciary and could judge constitutional questions for themselves," defending his decision in a message that Bray Hammond called "legalistic, demagogic, and full of sham."[19] Biddle thought the veto message "has all the fury of a chained panther biting the bars of his cage. It is really a manifesto of anarchy—such as Marat or Robespierre might have issued to the mob of the Faubourg St. Antoine."[20] The election of 1832 "constituted a referendum on Jackson himself. Was he a tyrant ('King Andrew the First,' as a famous National Republican cartoon called him) or a popular tribune?"[21] If that was the question, the voters provided an unequivocal answer. Jackson ran on the veto and won by a wide margin: 700,000 votes to Henry Clay's 480,000.

By 1834, the war over the BUS was concluded. After firing two Treasury Secretaries who refused the order, Jackson appointed Roger Taney to the post for the sole purpose of removing

---

[17] Roy Nichols, review of Thomas Payne Govan, *Nicholas Biddle*, in *The Journal of Southern History* 26, no. 2 (May 1960): 243–44.

[18] Hammond, *Banks and Politics in America*, 379.

[19] Hammond, *Banks and Politics in America*, 405.

[20] Biddle to Henry Clay, August 1, 1832. Cited in Govan, *Nicholas Biddle*, 202–3.

[21] Howe, *What Hath God Wrought*, 383.

federal deposits from the bank and distributing the funds to state banks of his choosing.[22] This was almost certainly illegal. By a vote of 26–20, the Senate passed a resolution of censure—the only one in American history—which Jackson ignored.[23] Biddle shared his outraged response in a letter to District Court Judge John Hopkinson: "This worthy President thinks that because he has scalped Indians and imprisoned Judges he is to have his way with the Bank. He is mistaken—and he may as well send at once and engage lodgings in Arabia."

In fact, of course, Jackson was not mistaken. He had his way with the bank, destroying it and destroying Biddle's reputation into the bargain. His single-minded vendetta was not only unconstitutional, it was also economically catastrophic. In 1837, the nation collapsed in a depression that would continue for fifteen years.

Biddle is represented in "a long list of likenesses, including miniatures, paintings, and sculptured busts. ... The inventory includes two portraits by Jacob Eichholtz, one by Rembrandt Peale, miniatures by Benjamin Trott, Henry Inman, and George Freeman, one attributed either to W. Brown or John Robinson, and one attributed to Anna Claypoole Peale, along with two engravings by John Sartain, and marble busts by E. Luigi Persico, Robert Ball Hughes, and Hugh Cannon."[24]

Perhaps the motive for so many likenesses was vanity. Diarist Sidney George Fisher described Biddle as "a curly-headed darling in youth, inordinately handsome in maturity, Biddle possessed features both regular and chiseled."[25] Of the many paintings, miniatures, engravings, and marble busts that Biddle commissioned, Sully's portrait (Figure 4.3) is the most provocative and memorable. Completed in 1828, when Biddle was at the height of his career, the painting confounds any expectations that viewers

[22] To reward Taney for his collaboration in shuttering the bank, in 1835 Jackson appointed him Chief Justice of the United States. In that capacity, of course, Taney wrote the 7–2 majority opinion in one of the Court's most notorious decisions, *Dred Scott v. Sandford.*

[23] Howe, *What Hath God Wrought*, 389.

[24] Nicholas B. Wainwright, "Nicholas Biddle in Portraiture," in *Portrait Painting in America: The Nineteenth Century*, ed. Ellen Miles (New York: Universe Books, 1977), 149.

[25] Nicholas B. Wainwright, ed. *A Philadelphia Perspective: The Diary of Sidney George Fisher Covering the Years 1834–1871* (Philadelphia: The Historical Society of Pennsylvania, 1967), 154.

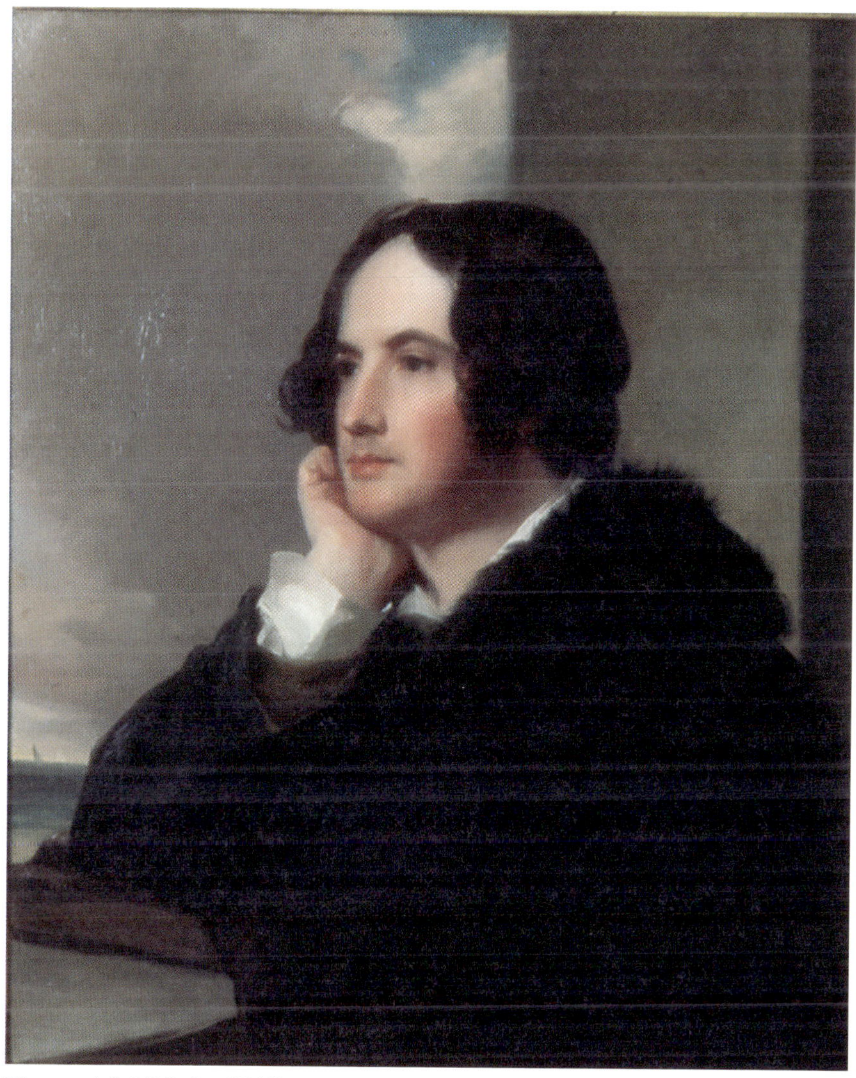

Figure 4.3 *Nicholas Biddle.*

Courtesy of Andalusia Historic House, Gardens & Arboretum.

might bring—then or now—to the likeness of a powerful financier. (Think of Edward Steichen's famous photograph of J. P. Morgan.)

Instead, this is Biddle the Romantic polymath, resting his still abundant curly-haired head on his hand, indifferent to our presence, gazing in meditative mood, alone with his thoughts. Those thoughts are presumably aesthetic and literary, not political or financial. His arm rests on the wide stone sill of the opening in a thick wall, a book supporting his elbow. In the distance, a glimpse of a single ship sailing under a brooding, cloudy sky, broken only by an emblematic patch of light directly over Biddle's head. The dark fur of his cloak, combined with his long dark hair and the generally muted palette of most of the picture, casts Biddle's face into dramatic relief. This is a man of learning and letters, a writer and thinker, the lover of all things Greek. The painting's composition resembles another of Sully's portraits, that of Lord Byron, also a fervent admirer of ancient and modern Greece. The two men were near contemporaries, and the two paintings were completed at about the same time.

In his book *Byron, Sully and the Power of Portraiture,* John Clubbe explores the connections at eccentric, entertaining, and often convincing length. The sixth chapter of his book, "Byronic Biddle," discusses the two men's shared passion for Greece, the Greek revival in architecture, and Byron's enthusiastic response to Biddle's edition of the Lewis and Clark journals.[26]

[26] Clubbe, *Byron, Sully and the Power of Portraiture,* 137–60.

5

The Theater

MANY YEARS AGO, GEORGE CHURCHILL, a professor of English at Amherst College, wrote that "It is in Philadelphia in 1749 that America's theatrical history begins. There a company of actors, apparently partly amateur and partly professional, gave for two months some plays of which Addison's *Cato* is the only one for certain known. They were soon prohibited by the magistrates."[1]

A century of scholarship suggests that Churchill's pronouncement was more confident than accurate. In fact, we simply do not know when or where the first play was performed in the American colonies. What we can state with assurance is that, in the Early National period, Philadelphia had emerged as one of the two or three most important theatrical centers in the country.

As late as the opening of the American Revolution, opposition to theaters, led primarily by Quakers, had kept the theater restricted to the fringes of the city.[2] In 1759, the House of Representatives of the Colony of Pennsylvania passed a law "forbidding

[1] George B. Churchill, "Shakespeare in America," *Jahrbüch der Deutschen Shakespeare-Gesellschaft* 42 (1906). Reprinted in Peter Rawlings, ed., *Americans on Shakespeare, 1776–1914* (Aldershot, UK: Ashgate, 1999), 419.

[2] Gary B. Nash, *First City: Philadelphia and the Forging of American Memory* (Philadelphia: University of Pennsylvania Press, 2002), 198.

the showing and acting of plays, with a penalty of 500 pounds."[3] The first Continental Congress, meeting in Philadelphia in 1774, passed a resolution denouncing "every species of extravagance and dissipation, especially all horse-racing, and all kinds of gaming, cock-fighting, exhibition of shews, plays, and other expensive diversions and entertainments."[4] Young Jacob Ehrenzeller was accepted as Pennsylvania Hospital's first apprentice in 1773. Along with prohibitions against dice playing and fornication, his bond commanded that he was not to "haunt Ale-houses, Taverns, or Playhouses."[5]

Following the Revolution, the situation changed. George Washington, resident of Philadelphia throughout his presidency, was "a famously avid theater-goer." His enthusiasm for plays helped to legitimize theatrical performances.[6] Needless to say, opposition to theaters did not simply disappear. Perhaps that explains the rhetorical gestures that some productions deployed through the 1790s. Theater managers often advertised plays as "moral lectures." *Richard III* instructed us in "The Fate of Tyranny," and *Hamlet* taught a lesson in "Filial Piety."[7] In any event, by 1800, entertainment had overwhelmed piety and theater had become "one of the chief forms of entertainment for all but the bottom quarter or third of society."[8]

The most notable of the several Philadelphia theaters built in response to the growing appetite for drama was the Chestnut Street Theatre. Work began in 1791, was suspended during the yellow fever epidemic of 1793, and the theater opened in 1794. Palladian in style, and loosely copied from the Royal Theatre at Bath, it could accommodate some two thousand people, nine

---

[3] Don B. Wilmeth and Christopher Bigsby, *The Cambridge History of American Theatre, Volume One: Beginnings to 1870* (New York: Cambridge University Press, 1988), 5.

[4] "*Journals of the Continental Congress—The Articles of Association*; October 20, 1774," Lillian Goldman Law Library, Yale Law School, https://avalon.law.yale.edu/18thcentury/contcong10-20-74.asp. Similar resistance to plays and players was led by residual Boston Calvinists and dour Dutchmen in New York.

[5] Pennsylvania Hospital Archives.

[6] "Washington the Theater-Goer," George Washington's Mount Vernon, https://www.mountvernon.org/george-washington/colonial-life-today/entertaining-george-washington.

[7] Russell Blaine Nye, *The Cultural Life of the New Nation, 1776–1830* (New York: Harper & Row, 1963), 264.

[8] Nash, *First City*, 198.

hundred in the more expensive boxes. Sculptures by William Rush adorned the exterior. With some renovations added by Benjamin Latrobe in 1805, the theater was hailed as the finest in America.

Over the next two decades, the Chestnut Street Theatre maintained its reputation as the country's best equipped and most lavishly decorated playhouse, sometimes referred to as one of the *Seven Wonders of America*"[9] The theater burned down in 1820 and was rebuilt in 1822 using a design by Latrobe's former student William Strickland (Figure 5.1). This structure, which could also hold two thousand spectators, survived until 1855.[10]

What did Philadelphians come to see on the several stages in the city? David Grimsted surveyed the categories of plays on offer between 1800 and 1850 and concluded that the great majority of tragedies and comedies were English.[11] American dramatists struggled to attract attention, which may in turn either explain or be explained by the mediocrity of their work.

Shakespeare was by far Philadelphia's favorite playwright. As early as the 1770s, Shakespeare's plays "served as a mainstay in the repertory for the touring companies that performed in all the major southern and some of the northern cities, with the most popular being *Richard III* and *Romeo and Juliet*."[12]

In the years that followed, Shakespeare's domination of the American stage continued to grow. Arthur Hobson Quinn's history of early American theater is worth quoting at length:

> Fortunately, we have in Wood's Diary such a carefully recorded list of plays.[13] In the Philadelphia season of 1810–11, extending from November 26th to April 30th, were offered eighty-eight

---

[9] Felicia Hardison Londré and Daniel J. Watermeier, *The History of North American Theater: From Pre-Columbian Times to the Present* (New York: Continuum, 1998), 82.

[10] A third Chestnut Street Theatre, a few blocks west of the original buildings, opened in 1862. It was demolished in 1913.

[11] David Grimsted, *Melodrama Unveiled: American Theater and Culture, 1800–1850* (Chicago: The University of Chicago Press, 1968).

[12] Frances Teague, *Shakespeare and the American Popular Stage* (New York: Cambridge University Press, 2006), 19.

[13] Reese David James, ed., *Old Drury of Philadelphia: A History of the Philadelphia Stage, 1800–1835, Including the Diary or Daily Account Book of William Burke Wood, Co-manager with William Warren of the Chestnut Street Theatre, Familiarly Known as Old Drury* (Philadelphia: University of Pennsylvania Press, 1932).

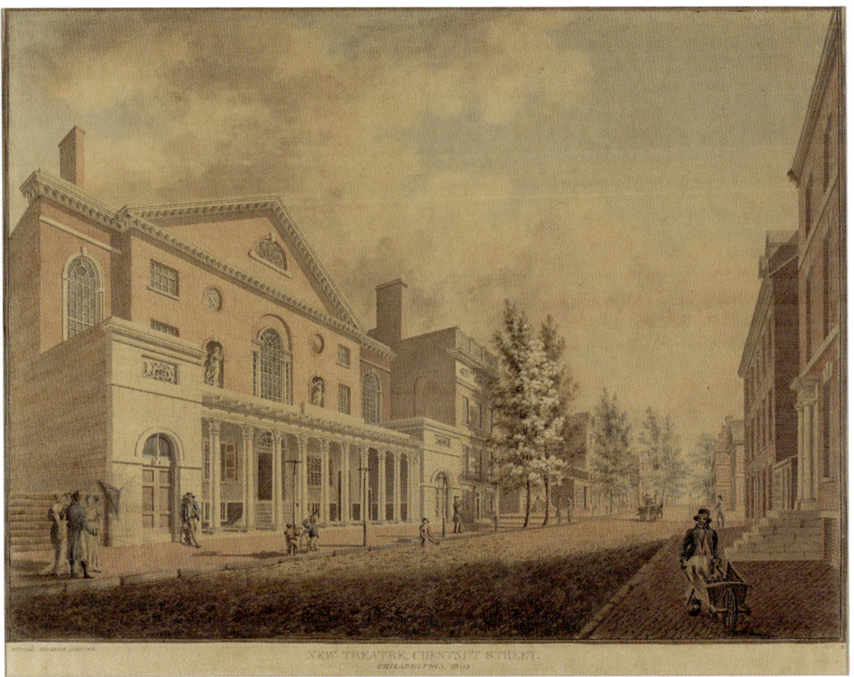

Figure 5.1 William Strickland, *New Theatre, Chestnut Street*, 1808.

Courtesy of the Pennsylvania Academy of the Fine Arts. Gift or Mr. and Mrs. William Jeanes, 1975.19.

> performances. Of these, twenty-two were devoted to Shakespeare, the plays being *Macbeth, Richard III, King Lear, Hamlet, Othello, Romeo and Juliet, Merchant of Venice, Coriolanus,* and *Katherine and Petruchio.* These performances were the most profitable, for Shakespeare ... was the main support of the season. During the season of 1811–12, performances were given on 108 nights, and again exactly one-quarter of them, twenty-seven, were devoted to Shakespeare. In addition to the plays offered the previous season, *Much Ado About Nothing, The Merry Wives of Windsor,* and *King John* were put on, and *Coriolanus* was dropped.[14]

Adopting a tradition that reached back to the 1590s, a number of these Shakespearean productions concluded with

[14] Arthur Hobson Quinn, *A History of American Drama: From the Beginning to the Civil War*, 2nd ed. (New York: Harper & Bros, 1943 [1923]), 162.

lighthearted entertainment. In 1810, to give just one example, the actor Thomas Abthorpe Cooper played the title role in *Macbeth* at the New-Theatre in New York. The promotional handbill promised the audience that Shakespeare's tragedy would be followed by a two-act farce, *Old Maid.*[15]

GEORGE FREDERICK COOKE

Born in London in 1756, George Frederick Cooke spent years acting in provincial theaters, gaining experience along with a growing reputation. In 1801, he appeared at the Theatre Royal, Covent Garden in *Richard III.* The role would become his most celebrated. Cooke, "the great dramatic delineator of dark passions and base minds,"[16] as one critic called him, has been judged the "most electric star" of the early 1800s.[17]

He was also given to frequent, alcohol-fueled, angry outbursts, which increasingly tested the patience of London's theater managers. Angry at what he regarded as managerial impertinence, and perhaps drunk, Cooke agreed to come to the United States in 1810. His prospective American audience was "at first incredulous, for Cooke was a luminary of the English stage. ... Why should an actor of Cooke's stature risk the long sea voyage to act in a wilderness?"[18]

Cooke's arrival in Philadelphia "caused unusual excitement, a crowd remaining in the street all night to be present betimes at the opening of the box office."[19] Despite intermittent alcoholic absences, euphemistically described as episodes of "indisposition," Cooke's American tour was a triumph. Fellow actor Charles Durang attended one of Cooke's performances and recalled that

[15] *Early American Imprints*, Series II: Supplement 3 from the American Antiquarian Society, 1801–1819, no. 56270 (AAS supplement).

[16] G. C. Verplank, "Garrick: His Portrait in New York, Its Artist and History," *The Crayon* IV (March 1857): 71.

[17] Bruce McConachie, "American Theatre in Context, from the Beginnings to 1870," in *The Cambridge History of American Theatre, Volume One: Beginnings to 1870*, eds. Don B. Wilmeth and Christopher Bigsby (New York: Cambridge University Press, 1988), 141.

[18] Barnard Hewitt, *Theatre U.S.A., 1665 to 1957* (New York: McGraw-Hill, 1959), 82.

[19] Ellis Oberholzer, *The Literary History of Philadelphia* (Philadelphia: George W. Jacobs & Co., 1906), 222. For an extended and frequently hilarious account of the excitement that Cooke's arrival in Philadelphia provoked, see the article, "Mr. Cooke," in *The Mirror of Taste and Dramatic Censor* 3, no. 3 (March 1, 1811): 43–56.

"his Richard was received with shouts. His death scene was truly appalling. As he lifted up his left arm over his forehead and gave the last withering look at Richmond, the expression of his eyes—as they for a moment vividly rolled, then became fixedly glazed, and all vision seemed gone—was peculiar and thrilled the audience."[20] In the opinion of theater historians, Cooke's critical and financial success initiated the "star system in America."[21]

A group of Cooke's Philadelphia fans offered Sully three hundred dollars for a portrait of the actor. The subscribers wanted Cooke to pose as Richard III. Cooke (Figure 5.2), reputed to be the master of soliloquies, is pictured in costume. The portrait depicts the point at which Cooke is delivering four lines from Shakespeare's *Henry VI, Part III*, which he shrewdly inserted for the dramatic effect they produced:

> Why I can smile, and murther whiles I smile,
> And cry 'Content' to that which grieves my heart,
> And wet my cheeks with tears,
> And frame my face to all occasions.
> (Act 3, scene 2, ll. 182–85)

In the eighteenth and nineteenth centuries, theatrical portraits proved to be immensely popular in both Britain and the United States. John Boydell opened the Shakespeare Gallery in Pall Mall, London, in 1786. Richard Altick has counted at least fifty paintings of actors playing Richard III in the eighteenth and nineteenth centuries.[22] Sully's portrait of Cooke reveals both his knowledge of and indebtedness to his English predecessors, and above all to Thomas Lawrence.[23]

---

[20] Charles Durang, *The Philadelphia Stage from the Year 1749 to the Year 1855* (Philadelphia: Thomas Westcott, 1860). Cooke was undoubtedly performing in Colley Cibber's version of the play.

[21] Simon Williams, "The Actors: European Actors and the Star System in the American Theatre, 1752–1780," in *The Cambridge History of American Theatre, Volume One: Beginnings to 1870*, eds. Don B. Wilmeth and Christopher Bigsby (New York: Cambridge University Press, 1988), 314. Cooke's earnings in America, reported to be $20,000, would be worth over half-a-million dollars today.

[22] Richard Altick, *Paintings from Books: Art and Literature in Britain, 1760–1900* (Columbus: The Ohio State University Press, 1985), 281–83.

[23] Many scholars have discussed Sully's artistic descent from British predecessors. See, for an extended example, Christopher M. S. Johns, "Theater and Theory: Thomas Sully's 'George Frederick Cooke as Richard III,'" *Winterthur Portfolio* 18, no. 1 (Spring 1983): 27–38. Johns also documents Sully's absorption in the aesthetic theories of Joshua Reynolds and Henry Fuseli.

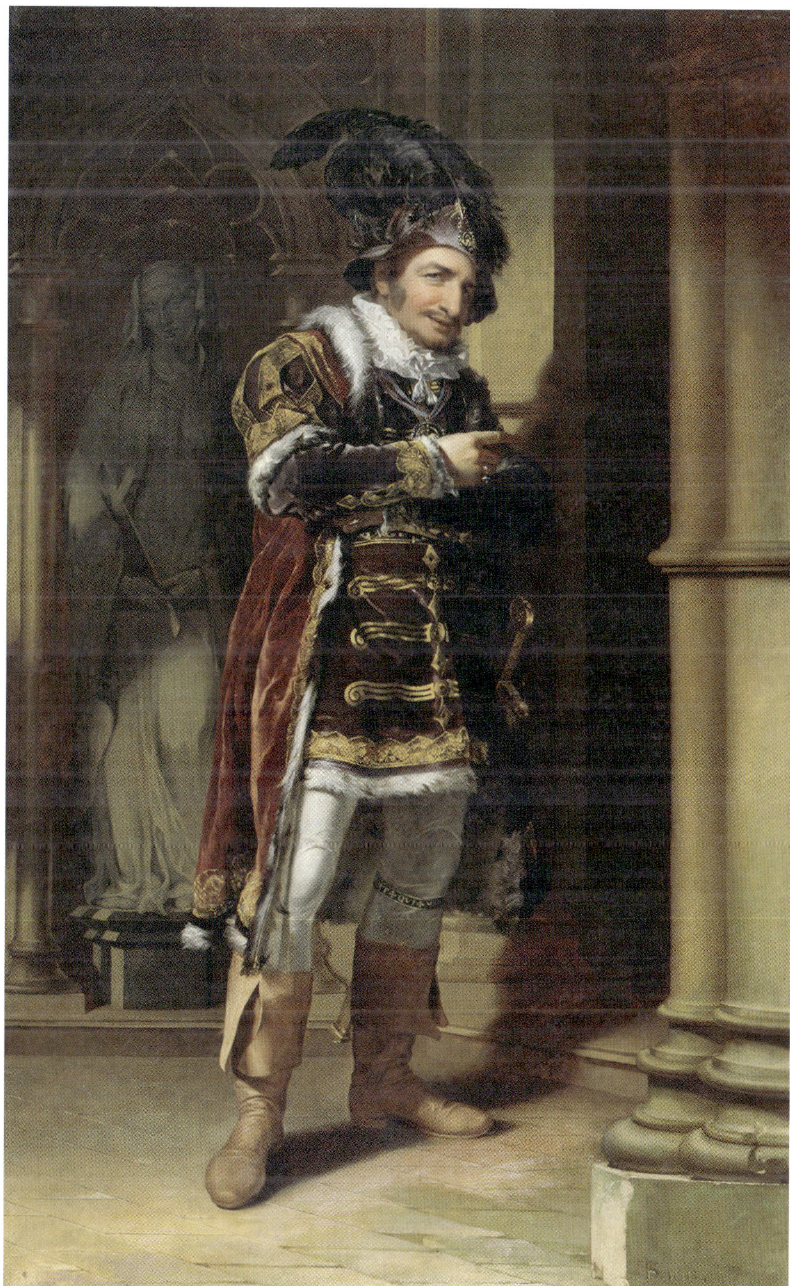

Figure 5.2 *George Frederick Cooke.*

Courtesy of the Pennsylvania Academy of the Fine Arts 1812.1.

Whatever its antecedents, Sully's portrait of Cooke as Richard III, completed in June 1811, is intensely dramatic, psychologically revealing, filled with meaningful detail. This is a villain fully embracing and indeed enjoying his villainy. He looks directly at us as he speaks his fatal lines, his mouth curved in a small smirk of self-satisfaction. His pose confirms Cooke's decision never to wear the customary artificial hump most actors employed.

Both the costume and the setting are rendered with bravura technique, capturing the opulence, even the deliberate extravagance, of Richard's self-presentation. The surfaces and fabrics—fur, velvet, stone, gilding—dazzle. The elaborate purple plume of his hat points ironically toward the statue of the female saint behind him: Evil displaying its contempt for sanctity. Indeed, the magnitude of Richard's perfidy is enhanced by the setting: a Gothic church.

Sully was just twenty-eight-years old when he produced this remarkable painting; it secured his reputation.[24]

A few weeks after the painting was completed, Cooke suffered what one scholar has called a "sudden, but hardly surprising death."[25] The apparent cause was cirrhosis. Cooke died in New York early on the morning of September 26, 1812, and was buried there in the cemetery of St. Paul's Church. On Friday evening, October 5, his colleagues at the Chestnut Street Theatre in Philadelphia presented "a respectable remembrance of their deceased favorite." Sully's portrait of Cooke in the role of Richard III was the centerpiece.[26]

FANNY KEMBLE

In 1872, in Rome, twenty-nine-year-old Henry James was introduced to sixty-three-year-old Fanny Kemble. More or less immedi-

---

[24] In December 1816, Sully complained to his *Journal* that "The subscribers to the whole length of Cooke, as Richard IIId, have not made good the amount of the picture—$70 is still due."

[25] Judithe Douglas Speidel, *The Theatre and Early Romanticism in America* (PhD diss., Boston University, 1983), 66.

[26] Monroe H. Fabian, *Mr. Sully, Portrait Painter: The Works of Thomas Sully (1783–1872)* [exhibition cat.] (Washington, DC: Smithsonian Institution Press, 1983), 57.

ately, they embarked on a friendship that lasted until Kemble's death in 1893.[27] In his memorial essay, James wrote that "her conversation swarmed with people and with criticism of people, with the ghosts of a dead society. She had, in two hemispheres, seen every one and known every one, had assisted at the social comedy of her age."[28]

The compliment is barely an exaggeration. Fanny Kemble's friends, acquaintances, admirers, and antagonists included Emerson; Washington Irving; Leigh Hunt; Catherine Sedgwick; the Shakespearean editor Horace Furness; John Quincy Adams; Alfred, Lord Tennyson; Daniel Webster; Nathaniel Hawthorne; Margaret Fuller; William Thackeray; Oliver Wendell Holmes; Edmund Kean; Andrew Jackson; Charlotte Cushman; Walt Whitman; Sir Frederick Leighton; John Marshall; and Sir Walter Scott. And Thomas Sully, as we will see.

Kemble spent only five years on the stage, and reluctantly, but secured a place among the finest actors of the nineteenth century. Daughter of Charles Kemble, and thus a member of a distinguished family of English actors, Frances Anne Kemble had little interest in following in the family trade. Her father, facing bankruptcy, convinced her to play Juliet at his Covent Garden theater. After three weeks of rehearsal, she made her first appearance on October 5, 1829. The audience and critics loved her. One of her biographers describes the curtain call: "the applause was tumultuous and rapturous. The large audience hailed this girl of nineteen as the worthy successor to her incomparable aunt [Sarah Siddons]."[29]

Noting the financial opportunities now on offer in the United States, father and daughter sailed for New York in September 1832. In her first appearance, on September 18th, she played Bianca in Henry Hart Milman's *Fazio* at the Park Theatre. The *United States Gazette* reprinted reviews, among them this: "The *New York Enquirer* of yesterday says—Miss Fanny Kemble made her first

[27] For a thoughtful commentary on this affectionate two-decade relationship, see Tamara Follini, "The Friendship of Fanny Kemble and Henry James," *The Cambridge Quarterly* 19, no. 3 (1990): 230–42.

[28] Henry James, "Frances Anne Kemble," in *Essays in London and Elsewhere* (New York: Harper & Brothers, 1893), 120.

[29] Leota S. Driver, *Fanny Kemble* (New York: Negro Universities Press, 1969), 36.

appearance last evening. ... As an actress she stands unrivalled before the American public, and never have we seen one who can compare with her."[30]

Diarist Philip Hone saw *Fazio* in New York and reached for superlatives: "I have never witnessed an audience so moved, astonished, and delighted. Her display of the strong feelings which belong to the part was great beyond description ... we have never seen her equal on the American stage."[31]

The reception Kemble received in Philadelphia, from audiences and critics, was uniformly ecstatic. A young man of the town named Henry Wikoff recorded the audience's response to Kemble's performance in *Fazio*.

> The theatre was crowded to suffocation to witness the débu of Fanny as Bianca in Milman's Tragedy of Fazio. Her first appearance impressed and delighted the house: above medium height, a symmetrical figure, an expressive countenance, flashing dark eyes, with luxurious hair to match. When she spoke, her rich resonant voice captivated every ear. Her bearing and attitude were so natural and withal *distingué* that the audience was half won before she had essayed to act. ... But when she rose with the action of the play and began to display her power—when she gave to the fierce passions of the role the agonized threats of the half-maddened wife—the spectators were transported with enthusiasm and wept and applauded wildly by turns.[32]

Throughout Kemble's American tour, the wealthy planter and slaveholder Pierce Butler had followed—one might say stalked—her, showing up at her dressing room with flowers and sometimes playing a flute. After several refusals, and with some of the same reluctance she felt for the stage, she married Butler in 1834, gave up the theater with no particular regrets, and followed him to his Georgia plantation.

Kemble's first-hand experience of the brutality of slavery ultimately compelled her to return to Philadelphia, and eventually

[30] Quoted in *Portraits of the American Stage, 1771-1971: An Exhibition in Celebration of the Inaugural Season of The John F. Kennedy Center for the Performing Arts* (Washington, DC: Smithsonian Institution Press, 1971), 42.

[31] *The Diary of Philip Hone* (New York: Dodd, Mead, 1927), 77–78.

[32] Cited in Dorothie Bobbé, *Fanny Kemble* (New York: Minton, Balch & Company, 1931), 75–76.

to divorce Butler. She wrote a strongly anti-slavery account of what she had seen in *Journal of a Residence on a Georgian Plantation in 1838–1839.* The cover (Figure 5.3) includes a quotation from the infamous "Cornerstone Speech" that the Confederacy's Vice President Alexander Stephenson delivered on March 21, 1861, just six weeks after the attack on Fort Sumter.

The unpublished book circulated among abolitionists for decades.[33] Kemble decided to publish it in 1863, in response to Lincoln's Emancipation Proclamation and also to reports of British hostility to the Union cause. Historians have suggested that her vivid descriptions of slavery's cruelty helped erode British support for the Confederacy.[34]

In 1849, after her divorce from Butler was finalized, Kemble returned to the stage, this time as a solo performer. For the next two decades, she enjoyed success in a series of one-woman recitations from the plays of Shakespeare. She made it clear that she would never tour in the South.

Sully's first portrait sketch of Kemble, in the role of Juliet, was completed after viewing her on stage.[35] A long and close friendship between painter and actor, indeed between the Sully and Kemble families, began during those first weeks in Philadelphia. Over the next thirty years, Sully completed more than a dozen likenesses of Kemble, both in costume and in her daily clothing.

Among those many images, critics and scholars have generally judged as the finest Kemble in the role of Beatrice in Shakespeare's *Much Ado About Nothing* (Figure 5.4). The painting was completed in 1833, in the middle of the Kembles' American tour.

Kemble seems to rise out of billows of pink and gray. Her face is brought into sharp focus by the dark and then darker

---

[33] As early as 1835, Kemble had written an anti-slavery article. Writing from Philadelphia to her friend Harriet St. Leger, she said she had not dared to publish it, "lest our fellow-citizens should tear our house down, and make a bonfire of our furniture—a favorite mode of remonstrance in these parts with those who advocate the rights of the unhappy blacks." Cited in Elizabeth M. Geffen, "William Henry Furness: Philadelphia Antislavery Preacher," *The Pennsylvania Magazine of History and Biography* 82, no. 3 (July 1958): 271.

[34] The most extensive study of Kemble's anti-slavery writing can be found in Catherine Clinton, *Fanny Kemble's Civil Wars* (New York: Simon & Schuster, 2000).

[35] Fabian, *Mr. Sully, Portrait Painter*, 88.

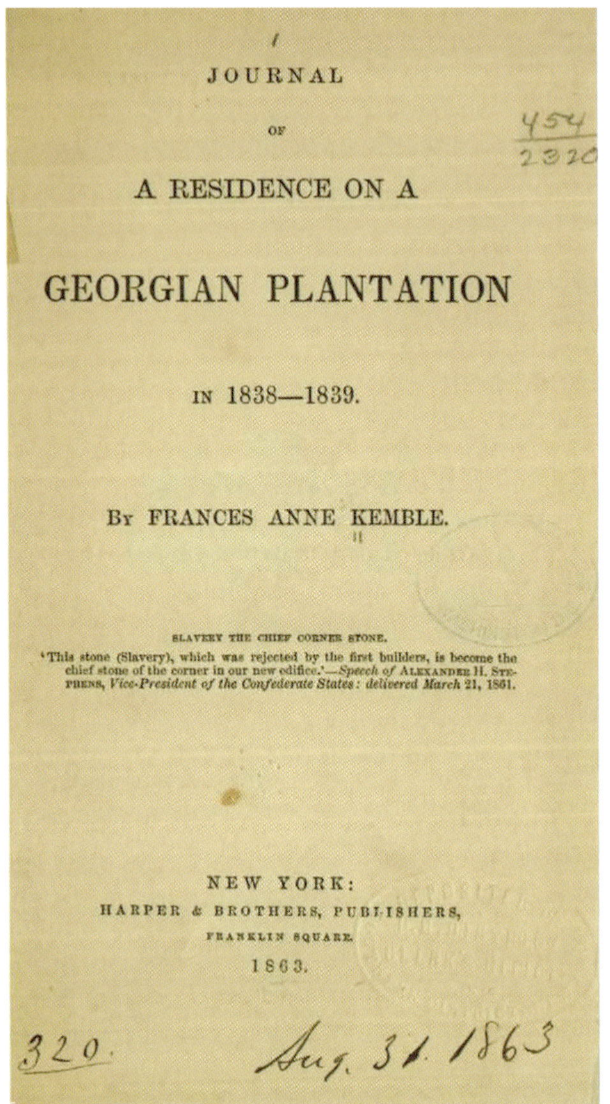

JOURNAL

OF

A RESIDENCE ON A

GEORGIAN PLANTATION

IN 1838—1839.

BY FRANCES ANNE KEMBLE.

SLAVERY THE CHIEF CORNER STONE.

'This stone (Slavery), which was rejected by the first builders, is become the chief stone of the corner in our new edifice.'—*Speech of* ALEXANDER H. STEPHENS, *Vice-President of the Confederate States: delivered March* 21, 1861.

NEW YORK:
HARPER & BROTHERS, PUBLISHERS,
FRANKLIN SQUARE.
1863.

Figure 5.3 Title page of *Journal of a Residence on a Georgian Plantation in 1838–1839.*

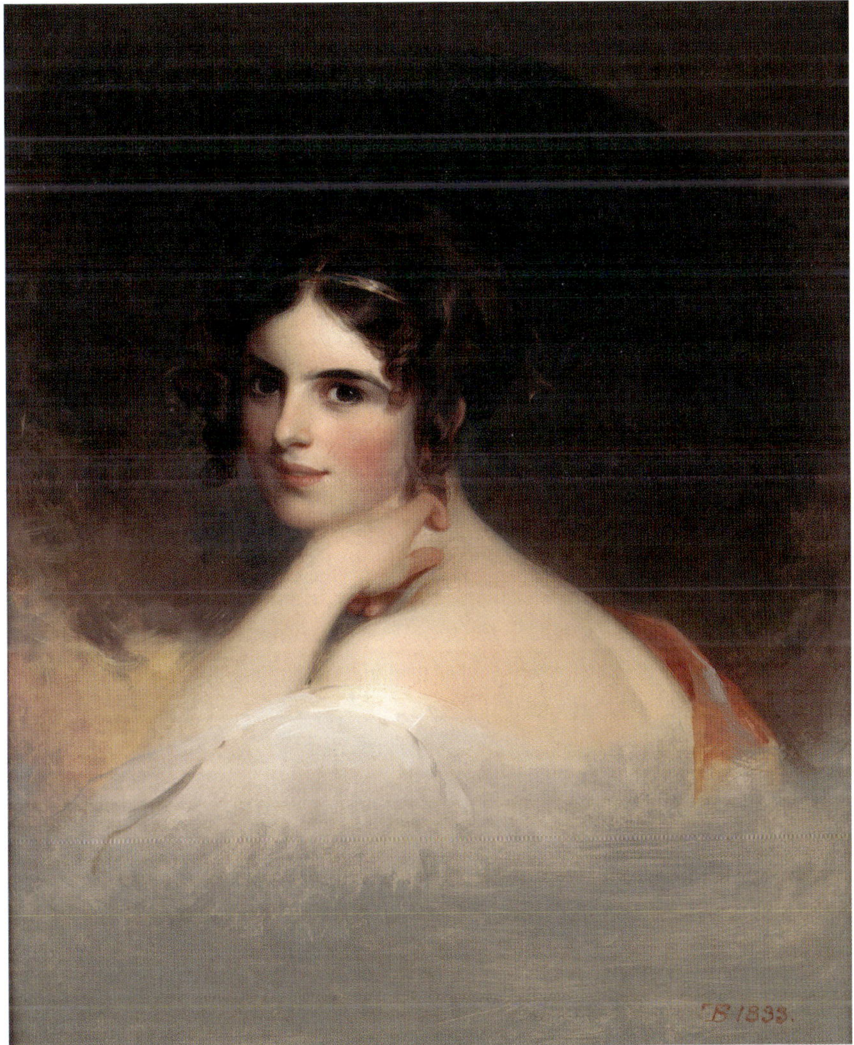

Figure 5.4 *Frances Anne Kemble as Beatrice.*

Courtesy of the Pennsylvania Academy of the Fine Arts 1879.8.24. Bequest of Henry C. Carey (The Carey Collection).

background behind her. She turns to face the viewer, her face framed by ringlets, her hair parted in the middle and held in place by a thin gold clasp. Her gaze is steady, appraising, a declaration of her confidence. Sully himself valued the painting highly. He brought it with him to London in 1837, proof of his skill, which he deployed to persuade Queen Victoria to pose for him. She did.[36]

CHARLOTTE CUSHMAN

A century ago, the theater historian George Churchill, whom we met at the beginning of this chapter, wrote that many American actors "were good, a few eminent; and there are two whom the judgment of the world has pronounced great—Edwin Booth and Charlotte Cushman."[37] Half-a-century later, Barnard Hewitt offered a similar opinion: "Charlotte Cushman was ... America's first great actress."[38]

Cushman had initially hoped to pursue an operatic career. Gifted with a rich contralto voice, the eighteen-year-old sang the role of Countess Almaviva in *The Marriage of Figaro* in a well-received 1834 Boston concert. Her success led to an invitation to join a company at the St. Charles Theatre in New Orleans. In her first appearance, straining to reach the back of the large hall, her top notes failed. The critic for the *New Orleans Bee* wrote that he would rather "hear a peacock attempting the carols of a nightingale" than listen to Cushman's "squalling caricature of singing."[39]

Resilient in the face of failure and humiliation, she quickly turned to acting. In 1836, she played Lady Macbeth in New Orleans, receiving enormous applause for the intensity and, in some

---

[36] Carrie Rebora Barratt, *Queen Victoria and Thomas Sully* (Princeton, NJ: Princeton University Press, 2000).

[37] Churchill, "Shakespeare in America," 421. In the fourth act of *Long Days Journey Into Night,* James Tyrone, echoing Eugene O'Neill's opinion, calls Edwin Booth "the greatest actor of his day."

[38] Hewitt, *Theatre U.S.A.*, 126.

[39] Cited in Joseph Leach, "Charlotte Cushman," *American National Biography*, vol. 5 (New York: Oxford University Press, 1999), 921.

accounts, the sheer terror she could summon. Acclaim in New York followed, and within a couple of years she had become a star attraction on both sides of the Atlantic. In 1844 she made her London debut at the Princess Theatre "and took critics and audiences by storm."[40]

One of Cushman's younger contemporaries, the actor James Murdoch, recalled the unnerving power of her voice: "There was always in Miss Cushman's vocal effects a quality of aspiration and a woody or veiled tone more becoming the expression of wilful passion suppressed and restrained than that emotion which seeks a sympathetic recognition of outspoken vocality, pure, ringing, and elastic—the former being Nature's mode of utterance for the evil passions, while the latter speaks to the noble, pure, and bright."[41]

Although this is mostly melodramatic tosh, there seems to be a kernel of truth here. At her most histrionic, Cushman had the power to frighten not only her audiences but even some of her fellow actors. She made a total commitment to each role. In 1837, when she played Nancy, the impoverished prostitute in Charles Dickens's *Oliver Twist*, she prepared by living for several days in the slums of New York's Lower East Side. She even bought ragged clothing from the women she met to make her costume more authentic.[42] Whether authentic or not, her performance was electrifying. One awestruck critic wrote that Cushman's "portrait of female depravity … was fearfully natural, dreadfully intense, horribly real."[43]

Cushman frequently played Meg Merrilies, the old and ugly gypsy in the melodrama *Guy Mannering*, adapted from the second of Walter Scott's Waverley Novels. Her explosive first entrance stunned the audience. John Braham, who played Bertram,

---

[40] Hewitt, *Theatre U.S.A.*, 127.

[41] James E. Murdoch, *The Stage or Recollections of Actors and Acting from and Experience of Fifty Years* (Philadelphia: J. M. Stoddart & Co., 1880), 237.

[42] "Cushman; Charlotte (1816–1876)," GLBTQ: an encyclopedia of gay, lesbian, bisexual, transgender and queer culture, https://web.archive.org/web/20070418152943/http://www.glbtq.com/arts/cushman_c.html.

[43] Cited in Faye Dudden, *Women in the American Theatre: Actresses and Audiences* (New Haven, CT: Yale University Press, 1994), 89.

"started in sudden fright at the wizened face, the demented eyes glaring through shredded grey wisps of hair, the wrinkled chin and twisted bones held rigid."[44]

Along with her memorable performances in female parts, Cushman also earned much applause—and some insults—for the many male characters she played. "Breeches roles" were not uncommon in the nineteenth century, though there is no consensus among critics or scholars about the reasons for this. Cushman appeared as Hamlet, Cardinal Wolsey, and especially Romeo, which became her signature role, and which she sometimes played opposite her sister Susan as Juliet.[45]

When Cushman first came to Philadelphia, she was introduced to Thomas Sully and his family. If Fanny Kemble—who probably made the introduction—was a good friend of the Sullys, Cushman became virtually part of the family. She called Thomas "Dad," and grew especially close to Sully's daughter Rosalie, herself a painter of talent.[46] They sometimes slept together, and Cushman's diary entry for July 6th, 1844, reads: "R. Saturday, July 6th 'married'."[47]

The painting (Figure 5.5) was completed and delivered to Cushman on April 27, 1843, along with $10.10 Sully said was a refund for her overpayment. The next day she sent this remarkable letter. "Dear Mr. Sully—had I *over*-paid you twenty times it

---

[44] Cited in Lisa Merrill, *When Romeo Was a Woman: Charlotte Cushman and Her Circle of Female Spectators* (Ann Arbor: The University of Michigan Press, 1999), 100. The merchant Joseph Sill, an avid theatergoer, swooned over Cushman's portrayal of Meg Merrilies. In a diary entry for November 10, 1849, he comments that the "strength and vigor" of her performance "gave a life-like character to the Gypsy Hag. Some of her attitudes and speeches assumed the highest tragic force." A tireless memoirist, Sill's diary covers the years 1832 to 1854, and runs to more than 4,300 unpublished pages. Historical Society of Pennsylvania, Am.1525, Volume 9.

[45] In the view of one British critic, "The best Romeo ever seen on the English stage, or that I have ever seen on the London stage, is Miss Cushman, the American." W. J. Fox, "The Common Interests of Great Britain and America," *The People's Journal* 1 (1846): 177.

[46] Rosalie's painting, *The Student* is in the Metropolitan Museum of Art. According to Lisa Merrill, Thomas Sully "recognized his daughter Rosalie's talent and ambition as an artist by choosing to depict her as an art student with her portfolio in hand." Merrill, *When Romeo Was a Woman,* 73. Based on years of research, Merrill's book is the most exhaustive account of Cushman's relationships with the Sully family.

[47] Ibid., 6.

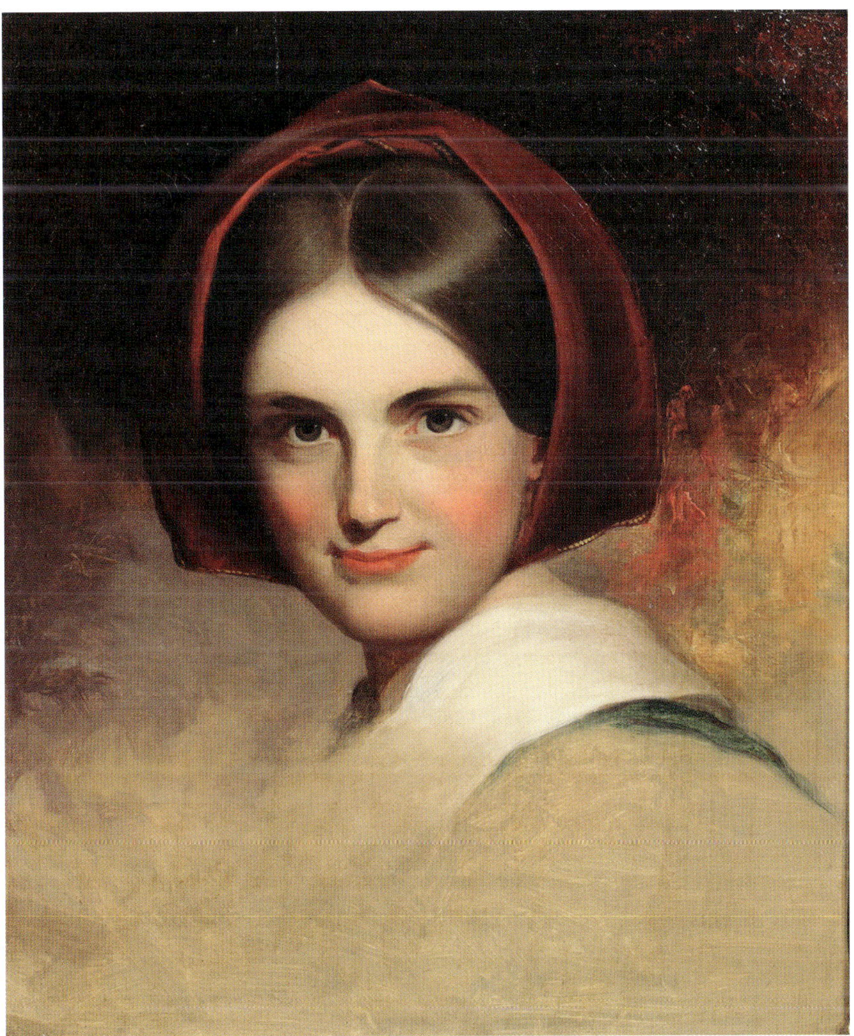

Figure 5.5 *Charlotte Saunders Cushman "of the Walnut Street Theater."*
Courtesy of the Library Company of Philadelphia.

could not half *re*pay the obligations I should be under to you for the most excellent terms you have put me upon with my unfortunate *Mug!* for I have established it in my mind that I *am beautiful.* Can you wonder that I should have made a blunder—under such a monomania?"[48]

Charlotte Cushman was an immensely gifted actor, in both female and male roles. But she was in no sense conventionally beautiful. Her face and indeed her body had heavy, masculine features. Photographs taken not long after Sully did the "portrait" demonstrate that the picture is, deliberately, nothing approaching a likeness. Instead, it represents a generous and admiring token of affection, almost purely imaginative, and a tribute to the transformative power that this remarkable actor displayed every time she stepped on stage.

[48] Fabian, *Mr. Sully, Portrait Painter,* 104.

6

The Library Company of Philadelphia

ZACHARIAH POULSON

During the course of his long life (1761–1844), Zachariah Poulson more or less simultaneously pursued two quite different but successful careers: journalist and librarian.

Poulson had learned the printer's trade during the tumultuous and indeed dangerous years preceding and during the Revolution. In a letter to William Rawle in 1791, Poulson recalled some of the repeated threats he and his father faced.

> James Humphreys was to have taught me printing. Before I was bound [as an apprentice] he was necessitated to fly on account of the troubles which then agitated our country. After his materials were packed up and secreted, I went with my Father to Hall and Seller's office, where we remained until the first rumor of the approach of the British army. We then worked with Joseph Cruikshank until they [the British] took possession of the city, when we returned to James Humphreys and remained with him until it was evacuated. After its evacuation, we went again to Joseph Cruikshank. While here we experienced all the hardships

> which malicious neighbors and unfeeling fine collectors could occasion.[1]

Following the war, Poulson established himself as an important independent publisher. His books included *Poulson's Town and Country Almanac,* 1788–1801; Robert Proud's *History of Pennsylvania* in two volumes, 1797–98; and the *Journals of the General Conventions of Delegates from the Abolition Societies of the United States,* 1794 to 1801.

Among his most important publications were the tabulations of Philadelphia's births and deaths, which appeared in fourteen issues of his *Town and Country Almanacs* in the late eighteenth and early nineteenth centuries. After studying these reports, Susan E. Clepp concluded that the "demographic data about Philadelphia contained in the first fourteen issues of Poulson's almanacs are superior to any sources known for eighteenth-century urban America."[2]

In the years before the turn of the century, Poulson considered founding his own newspaper, but concluded that the competition made a new publication too risky. During the Early National period, American cities large and small were awash in newspapers. A list of those that were being published in Philadelphia during some or all of the two decades from 1800 to 1820 would include *The American Centinel, The Aurora, Claypoole's American Daily Advertiser, The Democratic Press, The Freeman's Journal, The Independent Gazetteer, The Pennsylvania Evening Post, The Pennsylvania Gazette, The Pennsylvania Journal, The Pennsylvania Mercury, The Pennsylvania Packet*—the first daily newspaper in the United States, *The Spirit of the Press, The True American,* and *The United States Gazette,* among others.[3]

Rather than gambling on another new journal, Poulson purchased *Claypoole's American Daily Advertiser,* successor to the *Pennsylvania Packet,* in 1800. He renamed it *Poulson's American*

---

[1] Zachariah Poulson Jr., Edward Burd, and Richard Peters, "Some Biographical Letters," *The Pennsylvania Magazine of History and Biography* 23, no. 2 (1899): 196.

[2] Susan E. Clepp, "The Demographic Characteristics of Philadelphia, 1788–1801: Zachariah Poulson's Bills of Mortality, 1788–1801," *Pennsylvania History: A Journal of Mid-Atlantic Studies* 53, no. 3 (July 1986): 202.

[3] Edward Connery Lathem, ed., *Chronological Tables of American Newspapers, 1690-1820* (Barre, MA: The American Antiquarian Society, 1972).

Daily Advertiser and served as editor and publisher for the next thirty-nine years. As the paper's name, *Advertiser*, accurately implied, columns of advertisements outnumbered columns of news by about three to one. The *Advertiser*'s longevity indicates that this suited the preferences of a large audience. Subscribers included merchants, lawyers, bankers, and at least one president; see this note from Thomas Jefferson:

> Account with Zachariah Poulson, Jr., 12 March 1802
>
> His Excellency the President [Jefferson pays for his subscription] of the United States, Philadelphia, March 12th. 1802. To Zachariah Poulson, junr. Dr. For the American Daily Advertiser, from the first day of October, 1800, to the last day of December 1801, } $11.25

The enclosed check appears to settle an overdue account.[4]

A lifelong member of the Moravian Church, Poulson led or participated in several charitable organizations. He was a founder of the Philadelphia Society for Alleviating the Miseries of Public Prisons, and he served as one of the managers of the Pennsylvania Hospital. He also served, for thirty-five years, as a director of the Philadelphia Contributionship for the Insurance of Homes from Loss by Fire, founded in 1752 by Benjamin Franklin as the first fire-insurance company in America.

Through the years of editorship of the *Advertiser*, a period of bitter partisan wrangling, Poulson secured and maintained a reputation for probity: "during the most exciting periods, he never made an enemy or lost a friend."[5]

Along with his newspaper, Poulson's main association was with the Library Company of Philadelphia. His connection with the library, which was to continue for nearly fifty-nine years, began in 1785.[6]

---

[4] "Account with Zachariah Poulson, Jr., 12 March 1802," *Founders Online,* National Archives, https://founders.archives.gov/documents/Jefferson/01-37-02-0041.

[5] Edwin Wolfe 2nd and Marie Elena Korey, eds., *Quarter of a Millennium: The Library Company of Philadelphia, 1731–1981* (Philadelphia: The Library Company of Philadelphia, 1981), 160.

[6] Despite his long and influential career at the oldest and one of the most important American public libraries, Poulson was not included among the hundreds of individuals whose careers were surveyed in the *Dictionary of American Library Biography* (Littleton, CO: Libraries Unlimited, Inc., 1978).

The Library Company had its source in the Junto, a group of middling folk that Benjamin Franklin organized in 1727: "a printer, several clerks, a glazier, two surveyors, a shoemaker, a cabinetmaker." The two entwined purposes of the weekly conversations were "self-improvement and doing good for society."[7]

Concluding that Philadelphia needed a publicly accessible subscription library—or, more accurately, concurring in Franklin's proposal about such a need—the Junto drew up a charter in 1731. The document included such details as initiation fees and annual dues. Within four months, and mainly through Franklin's exertions, fifty subscribers had joined.[8]

The next step was to identify the books that should be purchased; Franklin consulted widely, but above all with James Logan, "the most learned man in Pennsylvania."[9] Almost all the books were imported. The first lists included: "Pufendorf on jurisprudence, Hayes on fluxions, Keill on astronomy, Sidney on government, L'Hospital on conic sections, Gravesande on natural philosophy; Palladio, Evelyn, Addison, Xenophon's *Memorabilia,* Defoe's *Compleat English Tradesman, Gulliver's Travels,* the *Spectator, Tatler, Guardian,* Homer's *Iliad* and *Odyssey,* Dryden's *Virgil,* Bayle's *Critical Dictionary.*"[10]

Peter Collinson, Franklin's agent in London, donated a copy of Newton's *Principia* and a dictionary of gardening. In 1738, John Penn donated an air pump, "with some other things to shew the nature and power of the air."[11]

---

[7] Gordon Wood, *The Americanization of Benjamin Franklin* (New York: The Penguin Press, 2004), 42.

[8] Austin K. Gray, *Benjamin Franklin's Library, 1731–1931* (New York: Macmillan, 1937), 8–9. (Originally printed privately in 1936 as *The First American Library.*)

[9] H. W. Brands, *The First American: The Life and Times of Benjamin Franklin* (New York: Doubleday, 2000), 112.

[10] Carl Van Doren, *Benjamin Franklin* (New York: Viking Press, 1938), 105. For a complete list of the volumes in the first rounds of collecting, see Albert J. Edmunds, Thomas Godfrey, William Parsons, Philip Syng Jr., Benjamin Franklin, Anthony Nicholas, and Robert Grace, "The First Books Imported by America's First Great Library: 1732," *The Pennsylvania Magazine of History and Biography,* 30, no. 3 (1906): 300–8.

[11] This and the following excerpts from the minutes are taken from George Maurice Abbot, *A Short History of the Library Company of Philadelphia* (Philadelphia: The Library Company, 1913), 7ff.

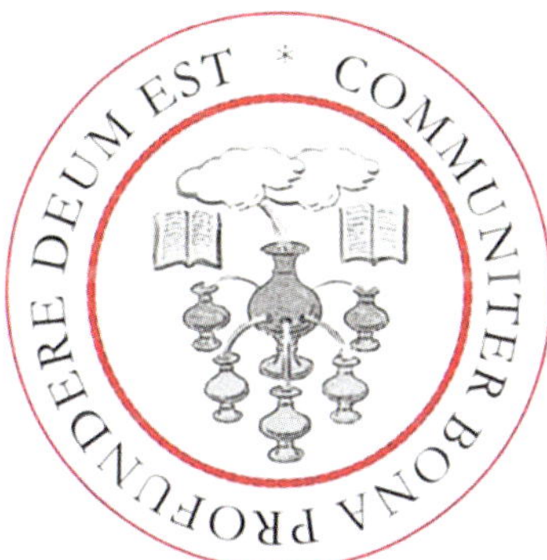

Figure 6.1 The Library's seal, devised by the founders and still in use.

Franklin himself reportedly devised the seal for the Library Company (Figure 6.1).[12] After reviewing the early history of the library in his *Autobiography*, Franklin indulged in a certain amount of well-earned pride in the result: "The books were imported; the library was opened one day in the week for lending to subscribers. ... The institution soon manifested its utility, was imitated by other towns, and in other provinces."[13] On the eve of the Revolution, Franklin went further, claiming for the several subscription libraries a political utility: "These Libraries have improved the general Conversation of Americans, made the common Tradesmen and Farmers as intelligent as most Gentlemen from other Countries, and perhaps have contributed in some

[12] The central image includes a bizarre allegorical emblem presumably representing the distribution of knowledge (perhaps heavenly, given the angelic wings) from the larger vessel—the library—into the smaller ones—the readers. The image is surrounded by a motto in what a classics professor friend of mine calls "simply bad Latin, in two ways: (1) erroneous (*deum* is just wrong) ... (2) *communiter bona profundere* is the sort of thing you get by using an English–Latin dictionary without having any ear for how to say things." In what might generously be called a free translation, the intention of the quote seems to be something like "to share benefits for the common good is divine."

[13] Peter Conn, ed., *The Autobiography of Benjamin Franklin* (Philadelphia: University of Pennsylvania Press, 2006), 63.

Degree to the Stand so generally made throughout the Colonies in Defence of their Privileges."[14]

Although it was a subscription library, by 1774 the membership included far more tradesmen than persons "of distinction and fortune." All were welcome, as long as they conformed with the regulations governing attendance, among them the command that readers who "had to be awakened twice," or showed "any evidence of 'pulex irritans [fleas]'" would be expelled.[15]

According to one historian, the Library Company was "not dismayed by the surrounding turmoil" of the Revolution. During the British occupation of Philadelphia, the library "had books to lend and it lent them with generous impartiality to congressmen and British officers alike, as long as they obeyed the rules."[16]

From the Revolutionary War to 1800, when the nation's capital moved to Washington, the Library Company also served as the Library of Congress. Until the 1850s it was the largest public library in America.[17]

The minutes of the early meetings include quite a few noteworthy items.

> December 11th, 1732, At this meeting, 'B. Franklin was asked what his charge was for printing a catalogue ... for each subscriber; and his answer was that he designed them for presents, and should make no charge for them.'

> November 12th, 1762, 'Mr. Byrnes complained that he had provided a supper for the last meeting and nobody came but the Sec'y, it was agreed that for the future every absentee should pay a fine of one shilling for his absence, which should go to the house as a recompense.'

---

[14] Cited in Donald G. Davis Jr., review of *Quarter of a Millennium: The Library Company of Philadelphia, 1731–1981: A Symposium, an Exhibition, a Man, The Journal of Library History* 17, no. 3 (Summer 1982): 328.

[15] Gary B. Nash, *First City: Philadelphia and the Forging of Historical Memory* (Philadelphia: University of Pennsylvania Press, 2002), 17.

[16] Harry M. Tinkum, "The Revolutionary City, 1765–1783," in *Philadelphia: A 300-Year History*, ed. Russell F. Weigley (New York: W. W. Norton, 1982), 149.

[17] *"At the Instance of Benjamin Franklin": A Brief History of the Library Company of Philadelphia*, revised and enlarged ed. (Printed for the Library Company of Philadelphia by York Graphic Services, 1995), 20.

December 14th, 1767 ... 'The Secretary reported that Mr. Benjamin West, formerly of this city but now of London, historical painter, had presented to the Company with his respectful compl't a woman's hand taken from an Egyptian mummy, in good preservation.'

In 1784 the Librarian was removed for his inattention to the duties of his office.

August 5th, 1824, 'Resolved that the use of the Library be offered to General LaFayette.'

January 6th, 1831, while a meeting of the Directors was being held in a room next to the Library building, there was an alarm of fire. One of the Directors put his head out of the window and called to a passer-by, 'Friend, can thee tell me where the fire is?' 'It's your darned old building that's a'burning' was the reply, and so it was.[18]

Zachariah Poulson's association with the library extended across nearly sixty years, from the 1780s until his death in 1844. For twenty-one years he was its librarian, for six years its treasurer, and for thirty-two years a director.

Appointed librarian in 1785, Poulson worked to rationalize lending procedures and reorganize cataloguing: tedious and apparently pedestrian tasks that elevated the library's usefulness. "He compiled and printed an indexed catalogue in 1789, kept admirable accounts of books borrowed, and set up 'A Chronological Register' of shares that retrospectively listed the original and successive owners of each share from 1731 on. The register has been kept up and is still in use."[19]

---

[18] A portrait of James Logan was destroyed in the 1831 fire. Thomas Sully repainted the portrait from memory. In recognition of his work, Sully was named the sixth honorary member of the Library Company—joining George Washington, John Adams, Lafayette, John Bartram, and Logan himself. Austin K. Gray, *Benjamin Franklin's Library* (New York: The Macmillan Company, 1937), p. 38.

[19] *"At the Instance of Benjamin Franklin,"* p. 37. Some years ago, the Library Company re-incorporated itself as a research library rather than a subscription library. Franklin's original model did indeed inspire copies across much of the United States in the eighteenth and nineteenth centuries. Most of those institutions—nearly a hundred at their nineteenth-century peak—have closed. Today, only about a dozen subscription libraries are still in business, including the Athenaeum of Philadelphia, founded in 1814.

In addition to his work as writer, publisher, editor, and librarian, Poulson also made drawings of many Philadelphia buildings. Housed today in the Library Company, these sketches include the President's House on Market Street and the residence of Washington and Adams before the nation's capital was moved to the District of Columbia.[20]

According to Monroe Fabian, this portrait of the eighty-two-year-old Zachariah Poulson (Figure 6.2) is "considered by many critics to be one of Sully's finest portraits of a male sitter." It was completed in just ten days in June 1843.[21]

The painting's lights and shadows bring its subject vividly to life. Poulson's illuminated face, framed between his high white cravat and his gleaming tall top hat, emerges confidently from the artist's muted palette. Poulson's gaze is contemplative but confident. The wisps of his white hair, along with the hint of a smile, bring us close to this benevolent old man.

---

[20] Joseph Jackson, "Iconography of Philadelphia," *The Pennsylvania Magazine of History and Biography* 59, no. 1 (1935): 57–73.

[21] Monroe H. Fabian, *Mr. Sully, Portrait Painter: The Works of Thomas Sully (1783–1872)* [exhibition cat.] (Washington, DC: Smithsonian Institution Press, 1983), 105.

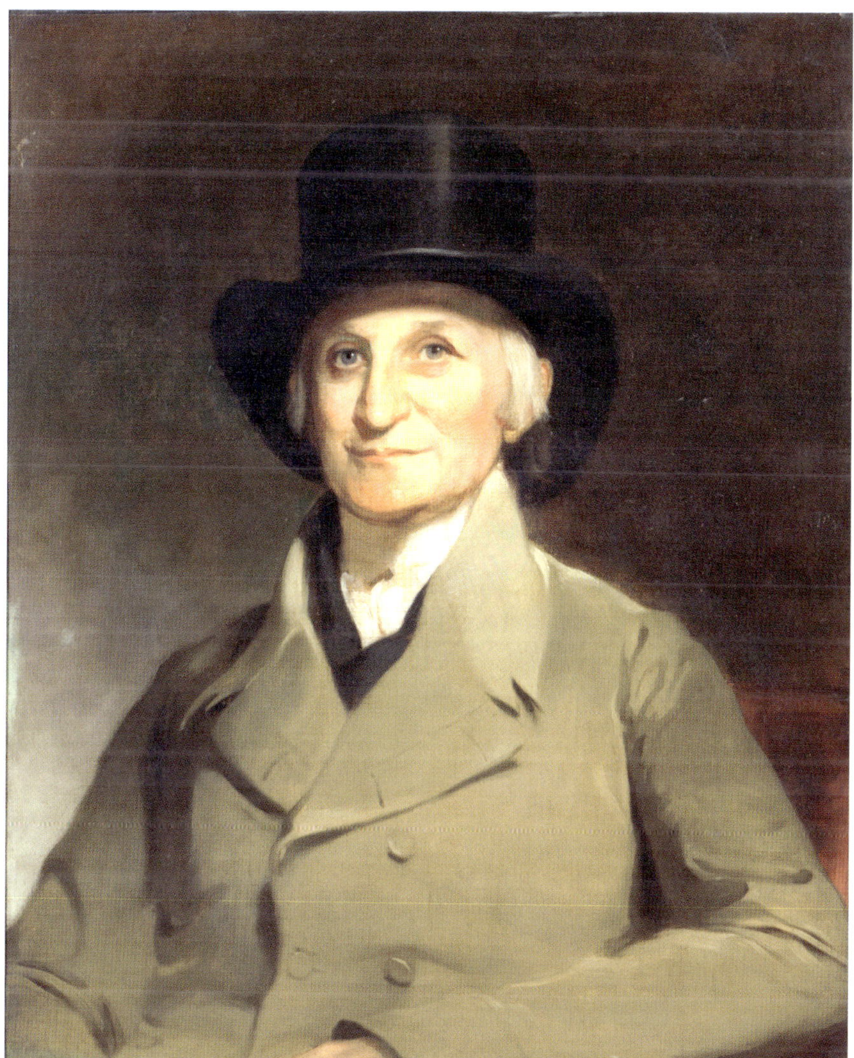

Figure 6.2 *Zachariah Poulson.*

Courtesy of the Library Company of Philadelphia.

7

The Jews of Philadelphia

REBECCA GRATZ

In 1831, Alexis de Tocqueville spent nine months touring the United States, ostensibly to study prisons and penitentiaries. Four years after his return to France, he published *Democracy in America*, one of the nineteenth century's most important works of political analysis. Among other subjects, he commented extensively on the influence of religion in American life and politics.

> Upon my arrival in the United States, the religious aspect of the country was the first thing that struck my attention; and the longer I stayed there the more did I perceive the great political consequences resulting from this state of things. ... In France I had almost always seen the spirit of religion and the spirit of freedom pursuing courses diametrically opposed to each other; but in America I found that they were intimately united, and that they reigned in common over the same country. ... For the Americans the ideas of Christianity and liberty are so completely mingled that it is almost impossible to get them to conceive of the one without the other.[1]

[1] Alexis de Tocqueville, "Chapter XVII: Principal Causes Maintaining The Democratic Republic—Part I," in *Democracy in America* (London: Saunders and Otley, 1835; repr. New York: Library of America, 2004).

From its Colonial beginnings, America was understood to be a Christian polity. Naomi Cohen surveyed the charters for the original thirteen colonies and found that many of them "employed a Christian vocabulary and often included the promotion of Christianity as a primary aim." In the decades following the founding documents, Cohen notes: "statutory law reinforced the Christian character of society. Civil law prohibited blasphemy and public worship on the part of minorities. It also mandated church attendance, Sunday observance, and financial support of the colonies' established church and its schools. Political rights—citizenship, voting, office holding, service as jurors and witnesses—were usually limited, if not to church members, then at least to those who took oaths of allegiance formulated in christological terms."[2]

The laws undoubtedly reflected popular sentiment: Most Americans believed they were inhabitants of a Christian, specifically Protestant, nation. "Christian assertions about the nature of God and the role of Jesus in securing eternal life appeared in many new state constitutions. Attempting to control corrupt politicians, most states included statements about an afterlife of rewards and punishments in their oaths of office."[3]

The eruption of evangelical Christianity, beginning in the early nineteenth century, affirmed and intensified the conflation of Protestant religion and politics. The Second Great Awakening proved to be "one of the most decisive developments of the early nineteenth century. ... This was the period in which the United States began its career as the most religious of Western nations."[4]

Because Christianity has been cankered with antisemitism virtually from its beginnings, the upsurge of evangelicalism pre-

---

[2] Naomi W. Cohen, *Jews in Christian America: The Pursuit of Religious Equality* (New York: Oxford University Press, 1992), 15.

[3] Dianne Ashton, *Rebecca Gratz: Women and Judaism in Antebellum America* (Detroit: Wayne State University Press, 1997), 39. South Carolina's constitution of 1669, written by John Locke, in a remarkable exception, granted "Jews, Heathens, and other Dissenters" the freedom to worship. By the end of the eighteenth century, in part because of this guarantee, Charleston was home to five hundred Jews, the largest Jewish community in the country. (Other sections of the constitution are decidedly less enlightened. After affirming hereditary nobility, Locke declared that "every freeman of Carolina shall have absolute power and authority over his negro slaves, of what opinion or religion soever.")

[4] Jean V. Matthews, *Toward a New Society: American Thought and Culture, 1800–1830* (Boston: Twayne Publishers, 1991), 26. The most comprehensive account of the evangelical revival can be found in Jon Butler, *Awash in a Sea of Faith: Christianizing the American People* (Cambridge, MA: Harvard University Press, 1992).

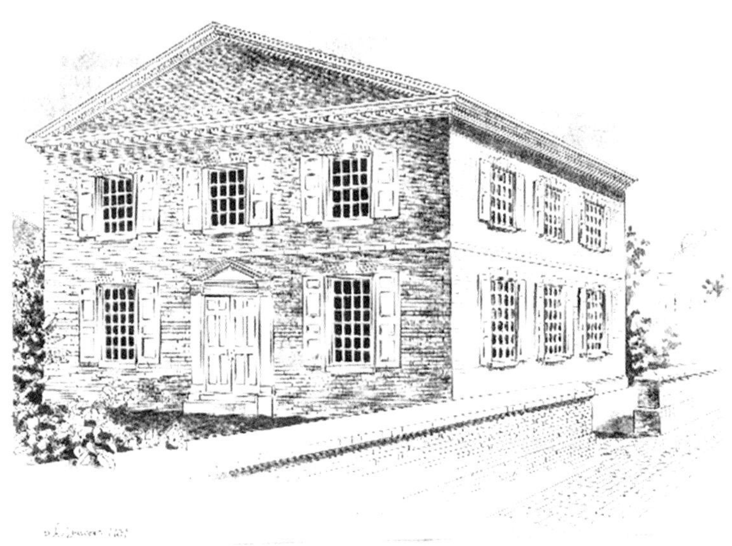

Figure 7.1 Philadelphia's oldest synagogue, Mikveh Israel, was built in 1782 at the corner of Third and Cherry Streets.

sented a potential and sometimes a real threat to the tiny Jewish population of Philadelphia. The threat was not physical—in the early nineteenth century the city's white rioters directed their violence against Black people, not Jews. Rather, Jews faced intrusive and often aggressive missionary efforts at conversion. Despite their relentless efforts, Christian evangelists failed to convert more than a handful of Philadelphia's Jews. An 1816 issue of the *Niles Weekly Register* joked about missionary groups that were spending "$500,000 over five years for the conversion real or supposed of five Jews."[5] Nonetheless, the evangelical crusade, which received continuous and often noisy support from journalists and politicians, served as a continuing reminder of the marginal status of the Jewish community.

Jews had lived in Philadelphia since the early eighteenth century, but their numbers were minuscule (Figure 7.1). In 1775,

[5] Cited in Hasia Diner, *A Time for Gathering: The Second Migration, 1820–1880* (Baltimore, MD: The Johns Hopkins University Press, 1992), 177.

among a population of 25,000, an estimated three hundred were Jews.[6] They suffered intermittent insult and harassment. For example, in 1784, during a debate over the establishment of a national bank, the Quaker Miers Fisher attacked "Jew Brokers."[7] By and large, however, Philadelphia's Jews found a larger degree of acceptance than those in New York and especially those in Boston: "Puritan Boston ... sent its first known Jew back to England."[8]

The main source of Jewish anger and anxiety lay in discriminatory Pennsylvania laws regarding voting and officeholding. The first draft of a proposed state constitution, published in September 1776, provided that any adult male who was a resident and freeman could vote by taking this oath: "I do believe in one God, the Creator and Governor of the universe." This formulation met with concerted resistance from several journalists, who opposed giving the franchise to "Jews or Turks." The oath was amended to include belief in both the Old and New Testaments, effectively barring Jews. Over Benjamin Franklin's objection, the revised phrasing was accepted. Only in 1790, following the ratification of the Constitution and its Bill of Rights, was the exclusion abolished.

Despite the occasional affronts and their struggle for equal rights, a number of Philadelphia's Jews earned financial success and social acceptance. Among them were men such as merchants Isaac Moses and Isaac Franks; entrepreneurs Moses Cohen and Samuel Judah; and broker Haym Salomon, who served as assistant to Robert Morris in financing the Revolution.[9]

From the mid-eighteenth century, several of the city's more affluent Jews reached beyond the circle of their co-religionists to participate in Philadelphia's cultural and civic life. In 1761, Mathias Bush donated £10 to the Pennsylvania Hospital. Perhaps

---

[6] Fritz Hirschfeld, *George Washington and the Jews* (Newark: University of Delaware Press, 2005), 50. As late as 1830, according to Richard Brilliant, Jews numbered "perhaps no more than four thousand persons" in the entire country. *Facing the New World: Jewish Portraits in Colonial and Federal America* (New York: Jewish Museum, 1997), 1.

[7] Edwin Wolf 2nd and Maxwell Whiteman, *The History of the Jews of Philadelphia from Colonial Times to the Age of Jackson* (Philadelphia: The Jewish Publication Society, 5717/1957), 111.

[8] Murray Friedman, ed., *Jewish Life in Philadelphia, 1830–1940* (Philadelphia: Institute for the Study of Human Issues, 1983), 3.

[9] Extensive information about all these men can be found in Jacob R. Marcus, *United States Jewry, 1776–1985*, vol. I (Detroit: Wayne State University Press, 1989).

inspired by Benjamin Franklin's ecumenical convictions, the Academy that would become the University of Pennsylvania enrolled Jewish men as early as 1760. "Four Jews—Samuel Hays, Mark Prager, Jr., Isaac Franks, and Michael Prager—were among the earliest subscribers to the new Chestnut Street Theatre in 1792."[10] Jews were represented among the subscribers and sat on the boards of the Athenaeum and the Library Company.

The members of the Gratz family emerged as the most prominent Jewish Philadelphians.[11] Their Philadelphia story begins with Barnard and Michael Gratz, immigrants born in Silesia. In the years before the Revolution, they developed a successful trading business, importing Caribbean sugar and rum, exporting leather goods, tobacco, and iron bars to England. Like other merchants, they were also active in the coastal trade, selling lumber, hardware, and jewelry to cities from Boston and New York to Charleston.[12] Both brothers energetically supported the Revolution, as did most of Philadelphia's Jews.

The Gratz brothers' business was continued by Michael's sons: Simon, Hyman, Joseph, Jacob, and Benjamin. Michael's daughters included Rebecca, now the most well-known member of the family, and the most celebrated Jewish woman of the nineteenth century.

Born in 1781, Rebecca Gratz grew up deeply committed to her Jewish faith from childhood to the end of her long life. As a young woman she was also an eager participant in Philadelphia's social life. She attended dances and teas, and spent time with local dignitaries, including the French exiles Joseph Bonaparte and Lucien Murat.[13] Her conversation was reputed to be lively and perceptive.

She was an avid reader, and not only of Jewish devotional texts. The Gratz household library included Hume's *History of England,* the collected works of Shakespeare, Milton's *Paradise Lost* and *Paradise Regained.* She read and apparently approved of

---

[10] Wolf and Whiteman, *History of the Jews of Philadelphia,* 42, 181.

[11] Chapter Three of Wolf and Whiteman's *History of the Jews of Philadelphia* is titled "The Gratzes Assume Leadership."

[12] William Weisberger, "Barnard and Michael Gratz," in *American National Biography,* vol. 9 (New York: Oxford University Press, 1999), 430–31.

[13] Ashton, *Rebecca Gratz,* 45.

Walter Scott's *Ivanhoe*—writing to a sister-in-law, "I ... felt a little extra pleasure from ... Rebecca's being a Hebrew maiden. ... I feel gratitude for [Scott's] justification of the Jewish character." There is, however, no evidence for the persistent claim that she served as the model for the Jewish character Rebecca of York.[14] Gratz enjoyed the theater. In 1834, she wrote to a friend that "Miss Kemble is in town ... she is really charming. I have seen her three times."[15]

Gratz never married. A widely circulated story suggests that she refused a proposal from a successful and otherwise eligible young Christian lawyer because she would not marry outside her faith.[16] After her sister, Rachel Gratz Moses, died in 1823, Rebecca took the youngest six of her children into her home and cared for them for the next two decades.

Gratz's significance lies in her tireless efforts to improve the lives of women and children, work underwritten by her family's resources, which led to her central role in Philadelphia's charitable activities. At the age of twenty, she co-founded the Female Association for the Relief of Women and Children in Reduced Circumstances. Over the following decades, she founded or co-founded with other women the city's first orphan asylum (1815), the Female Hebrew Benevolent Society (1819), the Hebrew Sunday School (1838), and the first Jewish foster home (1855). She took a leading role in the governance of all these institutions, repeatedly demonstrating both her commitment and her administrative skill.[17]

In the opinion of one historian, Rebecca Gratz "serves as the paradigm of the nineteenth-century Jewish volunteer."[18] She

---

[14] Cited in Judith Lewin, "Legends of Rebecca: Ivanhoe, Dynamic Identification, and the Portraits of Rebecca Gratz," *Nashim: A Journal of Jewish Women's Studies & Gender Issues* (Fall 5766/2005): 201. Scott's Rebecca of York has been described as the "most famous of the sympathetic portrayals of Jewish character in Regency literature." Montague Frank Modder, *The Jew in the Literature of England* (Philadelphia: The Jewish Publication Society of America, 1939/5700), 137.

[15] Cited in Ashton, *Rebecca Gratz*, 134.

[16] Wolf and Whiteman, *History of the Jews of Philadelphia*, p. 239.

[17] Somewhat surprisingly, Rebecca Gratz is never mentioned in Anne Firor Scott's otherwise comprehensive history, *Natural Allies: Women's Associations in American History* (Urbana: University of Illinois, 1991).

[18] Evelyn Bodek, "'Making Do': Jewish Women and Philanthropy," in *Jewish Life in Philadelphia, 1830–1940*, ed. Murray Friedman (Philadelphia: Institute for the Study of Human Issues, 1983), 145.

also exemplified a pattern that defined much of the societal work that women have performed and often led over the following decades. I once wrote of Jane Addams's creation of Hull House: "the settlement house translates to a larger context exactly the virtues traditionally associated with women's roles in the family. The values of domesticity are writ large and institutionalized in Hull House. Bustling and active and effective as it may have been, it was a 'feminine organization'; it enabled women to deal with their traditional constituents (the hungry and the sick, children in trouble) and to carry out their familiar tasks (feeding nursing, caring)."[19]

This does not diminish the value of the work that either Gratz or Addams (or countless other women) accomplished. When and where local and national governments failed, as they continue to do, female leadership designed, developed, managed, and sustained needful responses.

Throughout her life, while she defended her faith against insults and the missionary efforts of conversion, Gratz developed close friendships with many of Philadelphia's Christians. She felt especially close to the city's Unitarian minister, William Henry Furness, whose humanitarian, and frankly latitudinarian views, earned Gratz's admiration.

Though Thomas Sully didn't know it, he and Rebecca Gratz were connected before they met. In his reminiscence of Sully, published in 1918, Henry Budd wrote that Washington Irving made this recommendation: "A letter from Washington Irving to Miss Rebecca Gratz, dated November 4th, 1807, introduces Mr. Sully as one who 'purposes passing the winter in your city and as he will be a mere stranger and sojourner in the land,' Irving adds, 'I would solicit for him your good graces. He is a gentleman for whom I have a great regard, not merely on account of his professional abilities which are highly promising, but for his amiable character and engaging manners.'"[20]

Sully painted at least four portraits of Rebecca Gratz. The first, reproduced as Figure 7.2, was undertaken at the request of

[19] Peter Conn, *The Divided Mind: Imagination and Ideology in America, 1898–1917* (New York: Cambridge University Press, 1983), 162.
[20] Henry Budd, "Thomas Sully," *The Pennsylvania Magazine of History and Biography* 42, no. 2 (1918): 102.

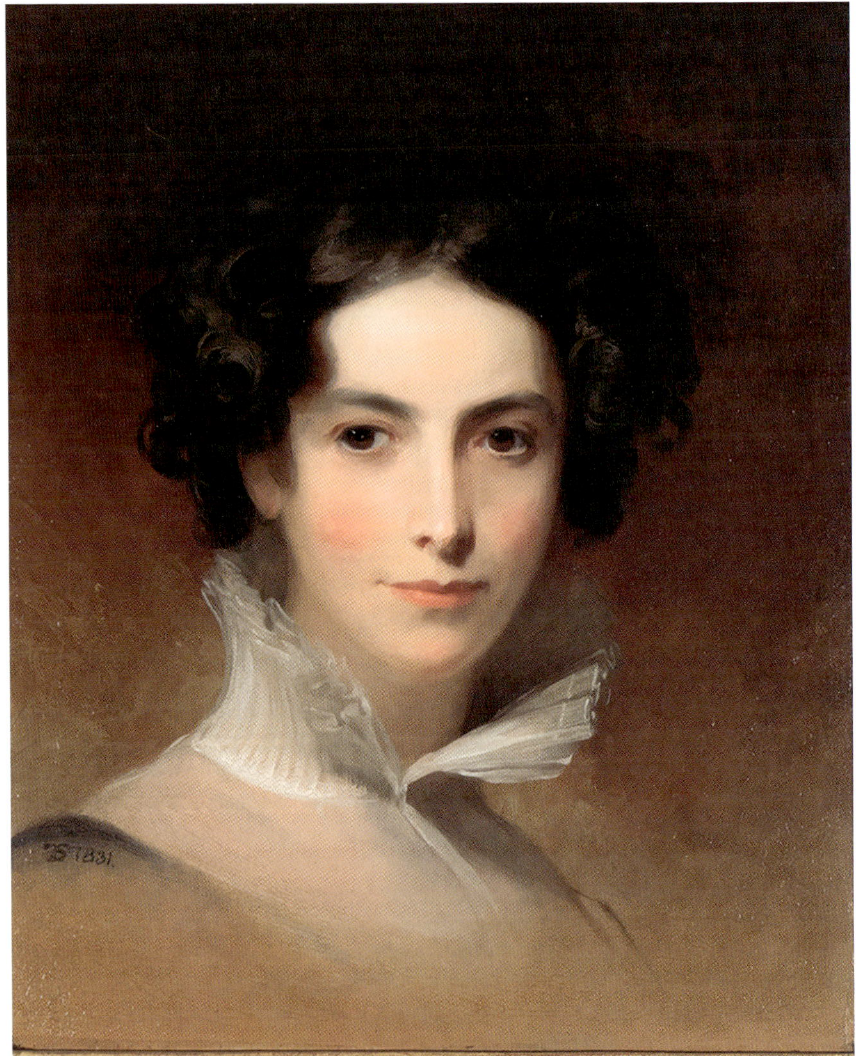

Figure 7.2 *Rebecca Gratz.*

Courtesy of the Rosenbach Museum and Library, 1954.1936.

her bother Benjamin and was completed in June 1831. Carol Soltis writes that Sully presents Gratz as "a glowing, stylish, and lively woman with a clear sense of self-command and undeterred by the proverbial designation 'spinster.' In this curvaceous and lush portrait, Sully captures her social persona as she directly but graciously greets the viewer."[21]

Sully's second portrait of Rebecca Gratz (Figure 7.3) was also completed in 1831. A romantically cloudy background, punctuated by a patch of blue, surrounds her. Glistening dark hair is topped by a splendid hat—almost provocatively heart-shaped—that encircles her face. Gratz emerges out of her elegant costume, looking past us, content with her own thoughts. This portrait has a different appeal, offering a visual record and reminder that the earnest and hard-working Gratz was also a social and sociable woman, a fine conversationalist, a frequent theatergoer, and a fashionably dressed guest at dinner parties and musical occasions.

[21] Carol Eaton Soltis, "Sully's Women: Real and Imagined," in William Keyse Rudolph and Carol Eaton Soltis, *Thomas Sully: Painted Performance* (New Haven, CT: Yale University Press, 2013), 40.

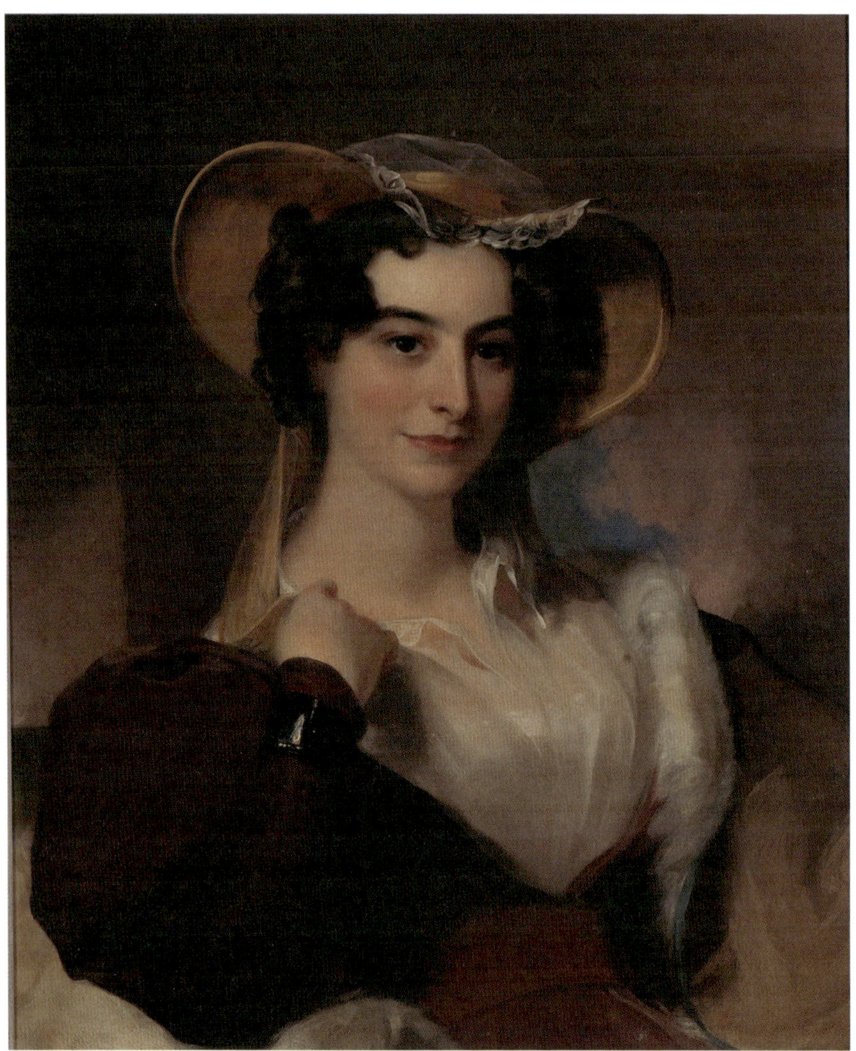

Figure 7.3 *Rebecca Gratz.*

Courtesy of the Rosenbach Museum and Library, 2010.0027.001.

8

The American Philosophical Society

IN 1743, BENJAMIN FRANKLIN PUBLISHED *A proposal for promoting useful knowledge among the British plantations in America*, a two-page pamphlet setting out the basis of what would become the American Philosophical Society (APS). Deploying a bit of optimistic overstatement, Franklin declared that "first drudgery of Settling New Colonies ... is now pretty well over." The time has come to turn America's attention toward improving "the common Stock of Knowledge ... for the Benefit of Mankind in general."

Given the enormous extent of Britain's American possessions, and the distances between those he called "Men of Speculation," many "useful particulars remain uncommunicated, die with their discoverers, and are lost to mankind." There should be a central society, "formed of Virtuosi or ingenious Men residing in the several Colonies, to be called *The American Philosophical Society*, who are to maintain a constant correspondence." The new organization would be located in Philadelphia, perhaps a somewhat self-interested decision, but a reasonable choice given the city's geographical, intellectual, and political centrality.

After a few procedural remarks, Franklin laid out what might be called the "research agenda," a list of subjects that exemplifies the scope of his insatiable curiosity about the workings of the physical world:

> All new-discovered Plants, Herbs, trees, roots, &c. their virtues uses &c. ... New Methods of Curing or Preventing Diseases. All-new discovered fossils ... New and useful improvements in any Branch of Mathematicks. New discoveries in Chemistry, such as Improvements in Distillation, Brewing, Assaying of Ores, &c. New Mechanical Inventions for saving labour; as Mills, Carriages, &c. and for Raising and Conveying of Water, Draining of Meadows, &c. All new Arts, Trades, Manufactures, &c. ... Surveys, Maps and Charts of particular Parts of the Sea-coasts or Inland Countries; Course and Junction of Rivers and great Roads, Situation of Lakes and Mountains, Nature of the soil, &c.

What holds the varied topics in this litany of practical tasks together is Franklin's Enlightenment belief in the power of human effort to both explain and improve the world. He concludes with an assertion of that belief. The proposed Society will support "all philosophical experiments that let light into the nature of things, tend to increase the power of man over matter, and multiply the conveniencies or pleasures of life."[1]

Several historians have suggested that the APS closely resembled the Junto, which dates to 1727, one of Franklin's earlier efforts to bring men together in the service of discussion and speculation, with the hope of discovering ideas useful to society. APS could be called "an intercolonial Junto," in Carl Van Doren's phrase.[2]

Franklin's proposal found initial support from men in Philadelphia and beyond. He was especially gratified by the enthusiasm of Cadwallader Colden, a New York polymath whose publications reached from medicine to geography, botany, moral philosophy,

---

[1] Benjamin Franklin, *Proposal for Promoting Useful Knowledge among the British Plantations in America*" (Philadelphia: printed by Benjamin Franklin, 1743).

[2] Carl Van Doren, *Benjamin Franklin* (New York: Viking Press, 1938), 138. See also, Gordon Wood, *The Americanization of Benjamin Franklin* (New York: Penguin Press, 2004), 72. This may be the place to mention the extended and sometimes heated debate that went on through much of the nineteenth century over the proper date that should be assigned to the founding of APS. The genealogical connection between the Junto and APS figured repeatedly in that debate. See, e.g., *An historical account of the origin and formation of the American philosophical society held at Philadelphia for promoting useful knowledge*, by Peter Stephen Du Ponceau (1841). In 1914, an APS committee reached the conclusion that "1727 was the date." APS itself uses the date of 1743.

and translations of Cicero's letters.[3] The charter members of the Society included botanist John Bartram; Thomas Bond, the physician with whom Franklin would later collaborate in founding Pennsylvania Hospital; and Thomas Hopkinson, a director of the Library Company.[4]

After its promising start, however, the Society's activities stuttered to a near stop. In a letter to Colden in 1745, Franklin complained that "The members of our Society here are very idle gentlemen. They will take no pains."[5] APS was more or less quiescent for the next two decades.

In the meantime, it found itself in competition with what might be called a copycat institution, the American Society for Promoting Useful Knowledge. The two groups agreed to a merger in 1769, the new entity to be called the *American Philosophical Society Held at Philadelphia for Promoting Useful Knowledge.*

More trouble soon followed. As political tensions rose, partisan divisions intruded on the Society's activities. Only a handful of meetings were convened between 1774 and 1776. An entry in the minutes, dated February 4, 1774, records that the members, "partaking with their countrymen in the distress and labors brought upon their country were obliged to discontinue their meetings for some months."[6] From 1776 to 1779 there were no meetings at all.[7]

The history of the Society from the late eighteenth through the first decades of the nineteenth century is dominated by Thomas Jefferson. He was elected to membership in 1780 and was almost continuously active in a variety of official and unofficial positions for forty-six years, until his death in 1826. He served

---

[3] Colden is also recognized for making the "first attempt to establish a systematic course of lectures on medical subjects in the colonies." Francis Randolph Packard, *The History of Medicine in the United States* (Philadelphia: J. B. Lippincott Company, 1901), 164.

[4] J. A. Leo Lemay, *Benjamin Franklin, Volume 2: Printer and Publisher, 1730–1747* (Philadelphia: University of Pennsylvania Press, 2006), 492.

[5] Cited in H. W. Brands, *The First American: The Life and Times of Benjamin Franklin* (New York: Doubleday, 2000), 170.

[6] Cited in William E. Lingelbach, "The Library of the American Philosophical Society," *The William and Mary Quarterly* 3, no. 1 (January 1946): 51.

[7] Henry M. Tinkum, "The Revolutionary City," in Russell Frank Weigley, Nicholas B. Wainwright, and Edwin Wolf, *Philadelphia: A 300-Year History* (New York: W. W. Norton, 1982), 149.

for many years on the governing board (the Council), was vice president from 1793 to 1795, and then president from 1797 to 1814, through the eight years of his presidency of the United States. After 1814, he continued to stay involved through a constant stream of letters and as an elected councillor.

According to the authors of the most thorough account of Jefferson's connection with APS, he and the Society shared several important convictions. These included an emphasis on America's distinctive natural history, along with a desire to compete successfully in scientific discoveries with Europe.[8] For Jefferson, as for Charles Willson Peale, Benjamin Rush, and other scientifically inclined patriots, the production of new knowledge was a weapon in the contest for international prestige.

The most significant scientific project Jefferson undertook during his dual presidency was the Corps of Discovery expedition that sent Meriwether Lewis and William Clark on a two-year journey, from May 1804 to September 1806, to explore and map the western portion of the newly acquired Louisiana Territory. Lewis, directed by Jefferson, prepared for the enterprise by coming to Philadelphia, consulting with APS members, and gathering medicine, equipment, and training. In 1817, Jefferson sent the journals and notebooks of the expedition to APS, acknowledging that there was no suitable depository for these valuable papers in Washington. He wrote that in the Society they would be useful "for the Historical Class."[9]

Jefferson called his election to APS—whether sincerely or with an eye to edifying the officers who sent the invitation—"the most flattering incident of my life." His decades of close affiliation undoubtedly raised the visibility and influence of the institution. At the same time, both before and during those years, the political party system was emerging, and his leadership of the Republican faction cast a partisan shadow over the intellectual endeavors that APS encouraged and sponsored. "With Jefferson as the symbol

[8] Patrick Spero, Abigail Shelton, and John Kenney, "The Other Presidency: Thomas Jefferson and the American Philosophical Society," *Proceedings of the American Philosophical Society* 162, no. 4 (December 2018): 324.

[9] J. G. Rosengarten, "The American Philosophical Society, 1743–1903," *The Pennsylvania Magazine of History and Biography* 27, no. 3 (1903): 330. These papers provided the materials for Nicholas Biddle's pioneering edition of the expedition journals.

of both the opposition party and the American Philosophical Society, the APS became, perhaps unwittingly, a part of the partisan environment that consumed the city."[10] That environment was often bitter and sometimes toxic. In short, along with the benefits Jefferson's conspicuous patronage conferred, his personal notoriety meant that the turbulence APS had experienced through most of its early history continued into the Early National years.

In addition, through the nineteenth century, the institution's finances frequently fell short of its aspirations. In a 1903 talk at the annual dinner, J. G. Rosengarten observed, presumably with a sigh, that it was "surprising that this venerable Society, the oldest scientific society in this country, and active and useful, has received so little recognition in the way of gifts." Later in his comments, Rosengarten referred to his hopes that Andrew Carnegie would respond to a fundraising appeal. This was a highly unusual and rather poignant signal of financial distress.

> It has been thought that Andrew Carnegie, a member of the American Philosophical Society, is so like Franklin in many ways that he would some day endow Franklin's and his Society with a fund large enough to enable it to enlist new recruits in the broad field covered by its purpose; "for promoting useful knowledge" is part of its title, and certainly both Franklin in his day and Carnegie in ours are the men who have given the world the best way of promoting useful knowledge.[11]

JOHN VAUGHAN

Carrying a letter of introduction from Benjamin Franklin, twenty-five-year-old John Vaughan moved to Philadelphia in 1782. The son of a prosperous London merchant, Vaughan brought with him the mercantile experience he had gathered in his father's business. He fairly quickly established a successful business in buying and selling wines. Vaughan also brought his family's com-

[10] Spero et. al., "The Other Presidency," 339.

[11] Rosengarten, "The American Philosophical Society," 333.

mitment to a liberal Christianity. He was for many years active in the First Unitarian Church and served a term as trustee of the Unitarian Society.

According to Elizabeth Geffen, Vaughan had a talent for friendship, establishing affectionate relations with a wide circle of Philadelphia's elite and middling citizens. He was proud of his connection to George Washington, who, on at least one occasion, dined at Vaughan's house in 1787, during the Constitutional Convention.[12] Washington was also a customer, placing his orders for wines exclusively with Vaughan.

Along with managing his business, Vaughan joined and sometimes led several of Philadelphia's philanthropic and cultural organizations. He was at one time or another during his long life president of both the Sons of St. George and the Pennsylvania Institution for the Instruction of the Blind, vice president of the Athenaeum of Philadelphia, a director of the Pennsylvania Academy of the Fine Arts, and a councillor of the Historical Society of Pennsylvania.

Vaughan's most extended and consequential service was his fifty-year association with the American Philosophical Society. He was elected a member of APS in 1784, elected secretary in 1789, became its treasurer in 1791, and its librarian in 1803. He held both of those positions until his death in 1841. A bachelor, Vaughan lived in the Society's building at the corner of Fifth and Chestnut Streets from 1822 until his death. He stored his wines in the basement.

Vaughan's contributions to APS were manifold. According to two historians who have studied the subject, when Vaughan assumed the position of Librarian there were only a handful of descriptive and theoretical books and articles on the nature and structure of language. "When he died in 1841 the Library of the APS held one of the richest collections in linguistics at that time. The main reason for this remarkable improvement must be sought in John Vaughan's linguistic, and broadly cultural, curios-

---

[12] Elizabeth Geffen, *Philadelphia Unitarianism, 1796–1861* (Philadelphia: University of Pennsylvania Press, 1961), 9. Geffen's book remains the most valuable source of biographical information on Vaughan.

ity and his organizational capacities."[13] Those organizational skills allowed Vaughan to bring order and utility to sprawling collections that had over the years often simply accumulated without arrangement.

Vaughan's friendships extended across the party lines that emerged during his years at APS. When Jefferson served as vice president and president, he often consulted with his Librarian. When he returned to Monticello, Jefferson's relationship with Vaughan "grew deeper even if they were separated by distance and party. Indeed, from 1816 until Jefferson's death in 1826 Vaughan was among Jefferson's most frequent correspondents. By 1818, Vaughan served as Jefferson's conduit for wine and books from Europe."[14]

Along with tireless exertions in the APS Library, Vaughan served as host and tourist guide to visitors from all over the Western world. In an 1818 letter, Harvard's president Jared Sparks called Vaughan "the most active member of the Philosophical Society, cicerone and friend to all the strangers who visit the city, occasional preacher in the Unitarian church and parish minister to all the poor of that society ... recommender-general of all schoolmasters, inventors, young men just entering their professions, and every sort of personage, whose characters are good, and who can be benefited by his aid."[15]

According to Elizabeth Geffen, Vaughan "became famous all over the world as an outstanding host in a city famous for its hospitality. A much-repeated opinion was that if Charles the 10th should be driven from France, he would be seen someday walking in Chestnut Street with John Vaughn."[16]

On one subject, Vaughan proved less collegial. He "could not bear to hear a word on the subject [of slavery]," when his minister at the Unitarian Church, William Henry Furness, began preaching abolitionism in 1839. The Athenaeum's reading room

---

[13] Roy Goodman and Pierre Swiggers, "John Vaughan (1756–1841) and the Linguistic Collection in the Library of the American Philosophical Society," *Proceedings of the American Philosophical Society* 138, no. 2 (June 1994): 254.

[14] Spero et. al., "The Other Presidency," 350.

[15] Ibid., 255.

[16] Geffen, *Philadelphia Unitarianism*, 11.

at the Philosophical Society's building "became a haunt of visiting southerners because Vaughan took many of them there as his guest."[17]

Sully's handsome portrait of Vaughan (Figure 8.1) was completed in 1815. Employing a favorite device, Sully directs the viewer to Vaughan's face and brightly lit forehead by the declarative contrast of the sitter's black coat and a white cravat topped by a high collar. Vaughan looks thoughtfully to his left, lips on the edge of a smile. The left side of the canvas is appropriately taken up with the large book Vaughan has been reading. The index finger of his superbly rendered hand holds his place while he pauses for reflection.

PETER STEPHEN DU PONCEAU

The son of a French military officer, Du Ponceau was born in June 1760 in the town of Saint Martins on the Isle of Ré, just off the Atlantic Coast of Brittany. Growing up in a French-speaking community, he began to display his gift for languages as a child. By his mid-teens, he had become competent in English and Latin. In the next few years, he would learn German, Italian, Danish, and some Greek. Poor eyesight ruled out a military career, and he refused to study for the Catholic priesthood. After two years of work as an assistant to minor Parisian officials, and a few months assisting philologist Antoine Court de Gébelin, Du Ponceau came to America in 1777 as secretary and military aide to Prussian army officer Baron Friedrich von Steuben.[18]

He served briefly in the Continental Army, after which he was appointed to the staff of Robert Livingston, the first American secretary for foreign affairs. While serving in that role from 1781 to 1783, Du Ponceau also studied law. The combination of his language abilities, his European connections, and his knowledge of both American and international law brought almost immedi-

[17] Gary B. Nash, *First City: Philadelphia and the Forging of American Memory* (Philadelphia: University of Pennsylvania Press, 2002), 192.

[18] Peter Stephen Du Ponceau and James L. Whitehead, "The Autobiography of Peter Stephen Du Ponceau," *The Pennsylvania Magazine of History and Biography* 63, no. 2 (April 1939): 189–227.

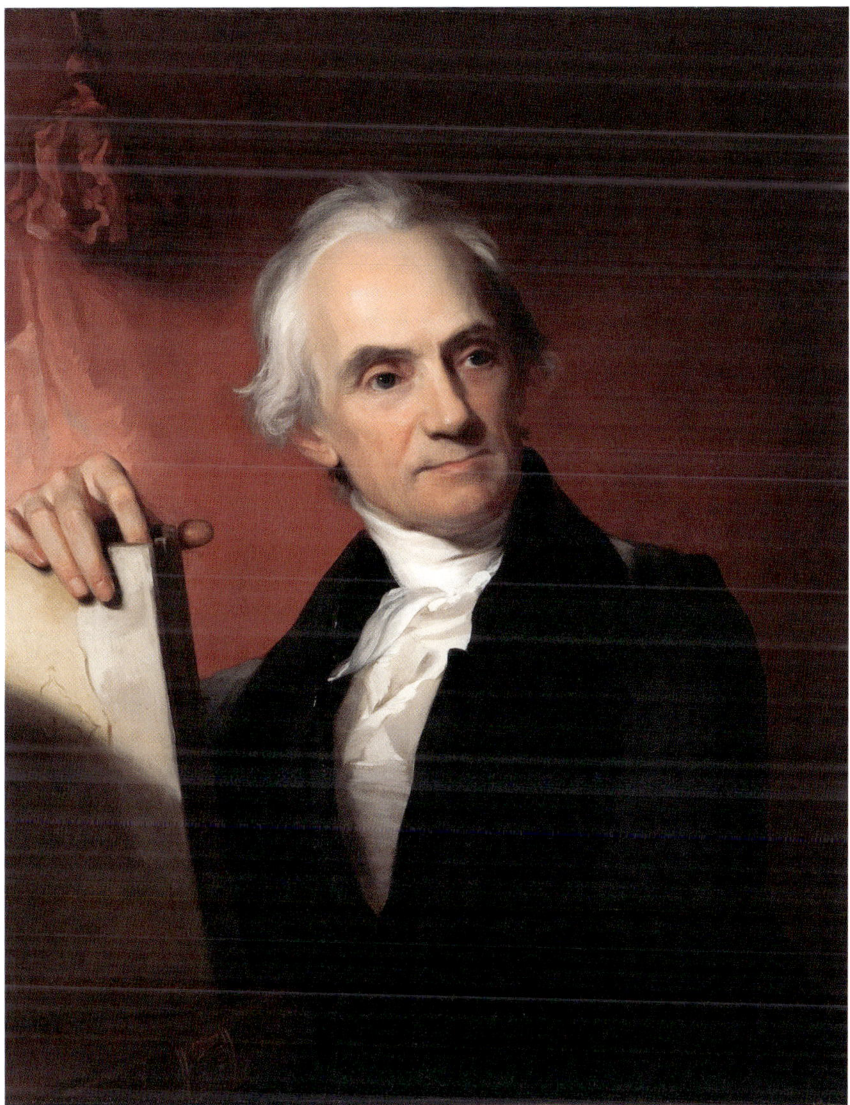

Figure 8.1 *Portrait of John Vaughan.*

Courtesy of the American Philosophical Society.

ate success and advancement. Within just a few years, Du Ponceau, who successfully tried several cases before the Supreme Court of the United States, was widely recognized as "one of the young nation's premier international lawyers and legal scholars."[19] He took American citizenship in 1787, writing to a friend: "I could never bear the despotism and the superstitions of the Old World."[20] He never returned to Europe.

During the Early National period, Philadelphia was the American city of choice for hundreds of French immigrants, fleeing in turn the ancien régime, the Terror, Napoleon, and the Restoration. Du Ponceau soon established himself as formal and informal counsel for many of these new arrivals.[21]

Beginning in his late twenties, and for the remainder of his life, Du Ponceau combined his lucrative law practice with a commitment to scholarship. His publications, which reflected his wide interests and prodigious scholarship, included a discussion of the jurisdiction of the courts of the United States, a brief history of early Pennsylvania, a discourse on the necessity of making America's national literature independent of Great Britain, and an essay on the prospects for American silk production. He also produced translations from French, Latin, and German, among which the most important was probably *A treatise on the law of war: translated from the original Latin of Cornelius van Bynkershoek.*

Du Ponceau's lifelong fascination with languages inspired his influential inquiries into both Native American languages and Chinese. Although linguistics had not yet been established as a recognized academic discipline, Du Ponceau is widely regarded today as the most distinguished linguist of the American nineteenth century.[22]

In March of 1815 the APS created a Historical and Literary Committee, naming Du Ponceau as its corresponding secretary.

---

[19] Edward G. Gray, *New World Babel: Languages and Nations in Early America* (Princeton, NJ: Princeton University Press, 2014), 142.

[20] Richard Heathcote Heindel and J. Marshall, "Some Letters of Peter Stephen Du Ponceau," *Pennsylvania History: A Journal of Mid-Atlantic Studies* 3, no. 3 (July 1936): 195.

[21] For a fine survey of the French emigré presence in Philadelphia, see François Furstenberg, *When the United States Spoke French: Five Refugees Who Shaped a Nation* (New York: Penguin Press, 2014).

[22] Du Ponceau used the term *philology* to describe his linguistic work.

For the next twenty years, the committee gathered information about Native American languages from dozens of correspondents, including Native informants. Thomas Jefferson was among Du Ponceau's regular contributors. "You will be pleased," Du Ponceau wrote to Jefferson in 1817, "to hear that our committee have particularly turned their attention to the languages of our Indian nations."[23]

Jefferson had collected hundreds of examples of Indian vocabulary. He believed that languages had histories, which might enable inferences about the origins and the relationships among the scores of Indian tribes. Du Ponceau was also convinced that languages could provide insight into Native history. Indeed, he proposed a more general premise: "The object of philology is from the variety of languages which exist on the Surface of the Earth, to trace, as far as possible, the history of Mankind."[24]

His method was comparative. "Data—vocabularies and grammars—and the conclusions drawn from their comparison, would replace armchair speculations."[25] The constantly growing APS collection enabled Du Ponceau to apply his method across increasing numbers of examples.[26]

In 1838, Du Ponceau published a five-hundred-page summation of his findings and conclusions: *Mémoire sur le système grammatical des langues de quelques nations indiennes de l'Amérique du Nord.* The book established Du Ponceau's international reputation. It won the prestigious Volney Prize, awarded by the Institut de France. Du Ponceau was the first American to receive the honor.[27]

Although Du Ponceau's contributions to the study of Native American languages were significant, his work on Chinese was seminal. In 1838, he published his *Dissertation on the Nature and Character of the Chinese System of Writing.* Stated briefly, Du Ponceau argued that Chinese writing is not ideographic: The characters

---

[23] Cited in Steven Conn, *History's Shadow: Native Americans and Historical Consciousness in the Nineteenth Century* (Chicago: University of Chicago Press, 2004), 86.

[24] Cited in Murphy D. Smith, "Peter Du Ponceau and His Study of Languages: A Historical Account," *Proceedings of the American Philosophical Society* 127, no. 3 (June 16, 1983): 149.

[25] Conn, *History's Shadow,* 89.

[26] The Native language documents at APS comprise one of the largest collections of such materials in the country.

[27] Du Ponceau's important *Memoire* has never been translated from the French.

do not represent ideas, but words; it is lexigraphic. Ignored or contradicted by most sinologists for more than a century, Du Ponceau's hypotheses are now recognized as pioneering and authoritative.

The prominent sinologist John DeFrancis, in his book *The Chinese Language: Fact and Fantasy*, explains that Du Ponceau's conclusions were decades ahead of their time and now represent the consensus view: "[O]bjections to describing Chinese writing as ideographic were anticipated by a century in a remarkable book by Peter S. Du Ponceau. ... For Du Ponceau, with an insight that is truly astonishing in view of the limited sources available to him, presents cogently reasoned arguments against the notion of Chinese as an ideographic script and against the whole concept of ideographic writing. His presentation ... constitutes what is probably the most extensive refutation yet written of the Ideographic Myth."[28]

In short, Du Ponceau showed that the "claims about the exotic, even bizarre, nature of the Chinese script, and its ostensible 'ideographic' basis, were naïve and untenable. ... Chinese writing, like writing everywhere, is simply a graphic device for representing speech."[29]

Recognizing his immense contributions to knowledge, Du Ponceau's colleagues elected him president of both the American Philosophical Society and the Historical Society of Pennsylvania, an unprecedented tribute.

Du Ponceau also served as a trustee of the University of Pennsylvania from 1818 through 1836.[30] During those years, he accepted two dozen assignments, among them to the committees on the library, the Grammar School, commencement, the Medical School, the printing of the college catalogue, and the sophomore and junior exam committees. In preparation for Lafayette's visit in 1824, Du Ponceau was part of the committee tasked with preparing a welcoming speech.[31]

---

[28] John DeFrancis, *The Chinese Language: Fact and Fantasy* (Honolulu: University of Hawaii Press. 1984), 145. The eighth chapter of DeFrancis's book is called "The Ideographic Myth."

[29] William G. Boltz, *The Origin and Early Development of the Chinese Writing System* (New Haven, CT: American Oriental Society, 1994), vii.

[30] The list of Penn's eleven hundred trustees includes twenty-two men whose portraits were painted by Sully in the years between 1810 and about 1840.

[31] University of Pennsylvania archives.

His reputation, on both sides of the Atlantic, was so great "that by the time of his death he had been granted membership in twenty-three American and nineteen foreign learned societies."[32]

Sully's likeness of Du Ponceau (Figure 8.2), completed in 1830, is another in his gallery of fine masculine portraits. As is often the case with Sully's portraits, the subject's face emerges from a dark background, contrasted with a glimpse of a white cravat under his chin. The eminent scholar gazes at us through his gleaming round spectacles. His high forehead is crowned with abundant and artfully tousled graying hair.

[32] Smith, "Peter Du Ponceau and His Study of Languages," 165.

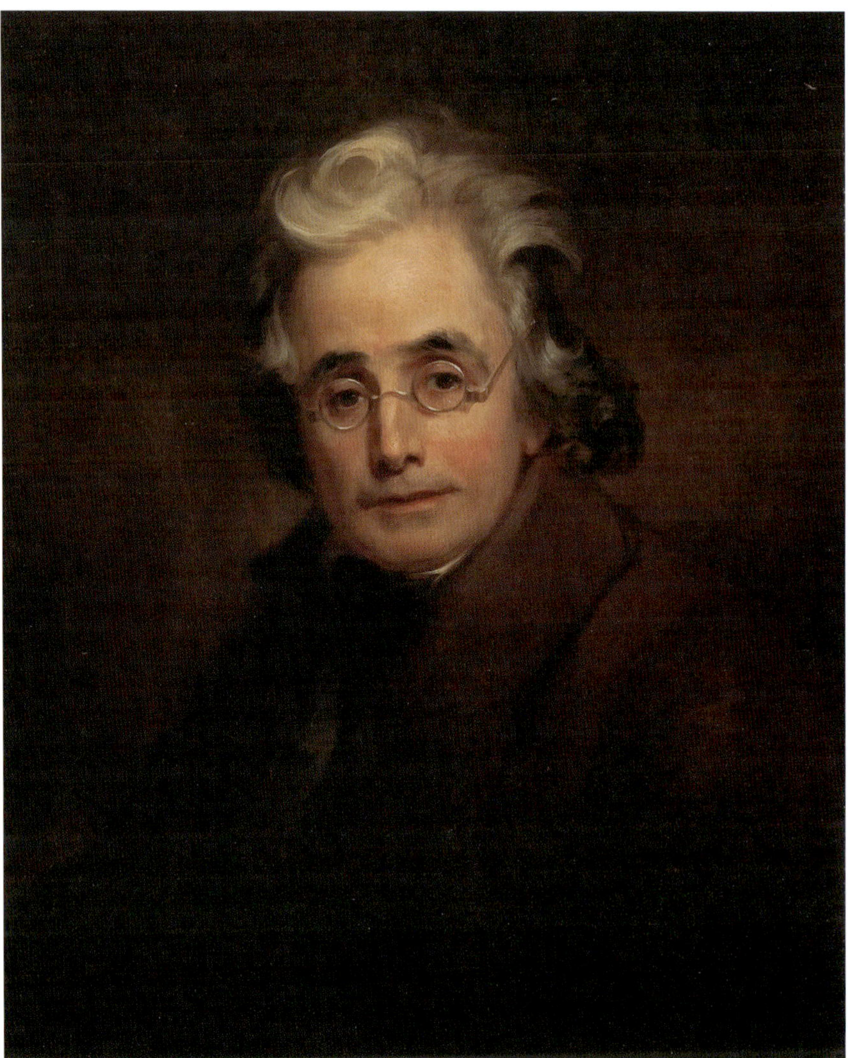

Figure 8.2 *Portrait of Peter Stephen Du Ponceau.*

Courtesy of the American Philosophical Society.

9

Lafayette Returns to Philadelphia

IN JULY 1824, THE MARQUIS DE LAFAYETTE stepped off the merchant ship *Cadmus* at Staten Island to begin a fifteen-month tour of the United States.[1] By all accounts, the tour proved to be one of the great national events of the first half of the nineteenth century.[2] Philadelphia was the centerpiece of Lafayette's sojourn; he visited twice, in September 1824 and again in July 1825. The parades and processions organized in his honor on both occasions attracted the largest crowds in the city's antebellum history. Men, women, and children turned out in their thousands "to honor, to see, to hear, and to shake the hand of this brother-in-arms of the immortal Washington."[3]

---

[1] Lafayette was invited by President Monroe to visit the United States as "the Nation's Guest." The invitation was taken as a personal insult by Louis XVIII, whose regime Lafayette strenuously opposed. Harlow Charles Unger, *Lafayette* (New York: John Wiley & Sons, 2002), 349.

[2] Lafayette's visit was a leading topic in American newspapers even before he embarked for the United States. A survey of *America's Historical Newspapers* includes contemporaneous stories from the *Baltimore Patriot*, the *Boston Commercial Gazette*, the *Daily National Intelligencer*, the *Saratoga Sentinel*, the *Charleston Courier*, the *New York Spectator*, the *Providence Patriot*, the *Washington Daily National Journal*, the *Trenton Federalist*, and *Poulson's American Daily Advertiser*, among many others. https://infoweb-newsbank-com.proxy.library.upenn.edu/apps/readex/welcome?p=EANX

[3] Edwin Wolf 2nd and Maxwell Whiteman, *The History of the Jews of Philadelphia from Colonial Times to the Age of Jackson* (Philadelphia: The Jewish Publication Society, 5717/1957), 300.

Most of us probably recall that Lafayette played a significant role in the American Revolution. Fewer of us recall what he actually did.

Born in 1757, Gilbert du Motier, Marquis de Lafayette was the only child of an aristocratic French family of great wealth and prestige. The deaths of both parents left him an orphan at three. Following in the footsteps of his family's men, the young Lafayette was commissioned as an officer at the age of thirteen. The title was ceremonial, but it pointed accurately toward the career Lafayette would follow, more famously in America than in France. In 1777, the twenty-year-old officer sailed to America in a ship he had purchased and joined Washington's staff as an honorary major-general. Franklin, who predicted that the young, high-born enthusiast would be useful in gaining French support for the Revolution, had encouraged this gesture of respect.[4]

While Lafayette lobbied for an immediate command, Washington judged that the young man's zeal outran his nonexistent military experience. The tension quickly gave way as Washington warmed to Lafayette's sincere commitment to the American cause, his more or less successful effort to learn English, and his humility—"I come to learn, not to teach."

Soon the two men, separated by a generation, embarked on a long-lasting friendship that blossomed into rare intimacy. Washington knew that many of the men who surrounded him were either sycophants or competitors. He gave his trust cautiously, but he gave it fully to Lafayette. The childless commander and the orphaned aristocrat began to refer to each other as father and son. On one occasion, with tears in his eyes, Washington declared that "I do not know a nobler, finer soul, and I love him as my own son."[5]

The bond was strengthened by Lafayette's courage and what proved to be his remarkable military skill. Just six weeks after taking the field, he was wounded at the Battle of Brandywine,

---

[4] Lloyd S. Kramer, "America's Lafayette and Lafayette's America: A European and the American Revolution," *The William and Mary Quarterly* 38, no. 2 (April 1981): 229.

[5] James R. Gaines, *For Liberty and Glory: Washington, Lafayette, and Their Revolutions* (New York: W. W. Norton, 2007), 8.

twenty miles west of Philadelphia. Writing to his wife, he spent more time on his affection for Washington than his injury. "His tender interest for me soon won my heart to him. ... When he sent me his personal surgeon, he told him to take care of me as if I were his son, because he loved me like one."[6] Lafayette shared the hardships of Valley Forge in the winter of 1777–78 and displayed conspicuous bravery at the Battle of Monmouth in June 1778.

Lafayette returned to France in January 1779, a year after the American colonies and France had signed a military treaty, an agreement that Lafayette had strongly supported in his transatlantic correspondence. Here was an unprecedented pledge of cooperation between an absolute monarchy and a collection of rebellious colonies. The treaty formalized France's financial and military support of the Revolutionary government in America and stipulated that "the essential and direct end of the present defensive alliance is to maintain effectually the liberty, sovereignty, and independence absolute and unlimited of the said United States, as well in Matters of Government as of commerce."[7]

Hailed as a hero in France, Lafayette met a similar welcome when he sailed back to America in April 1780, bringing with him six thousand French troops. He cemented his renown by commanding a division of American troops during the siege and surrender of Cornwallis on October 19, 1781, which effectively ended the war and secured American independence.[8]

After his return to France, and throughout the remaining years of his life, Lafayette would frequently refer to America as the nation in which the *Declaration of the Rights of Man* had been realized. At the same time, he argued strongly for the end of slavery, which he insisted violated the dictates of natural rights. In July 1789, after the storming of the Bastille, he was appointed

---

[6] Lynn H. Miller, "My Dear General: The Relationship between Lafayette and Washington," *France Revisited* (July 2009).

[7] "Treaty of Alliance with France (1778)," National Archives, https://www.archives.gov/milestone-documents/treaty-of-alliance-with-france.

[8] David A. Clary, *Adopted Son: Washington, Lafayette, and the Friendship that Saved the Revolution* (New York: Bantam Books, 2007). Clary provides a book-long, almost day-by-day account of the relations between Washington and Lafayette throughout the Revolutionary War.

commander-in-chief of France's National Guard. As the Revolution turned toward violence, he repeatedly tried and failed to promote more moderate alternatives.

He became, in biographer Olivier Bernier's phrase, a "hostage to revolution."[9] Denounced as an enemy of the people in 1792, Lafayette fled to the Netherlands where he was captured by Austrian troops and spent the next five years in prison. In Philadelphia, President Washington grieved over his dear friend's fate, but diplomatic imperatives prohibited his intervention. Eventually, Napoleon ordered Lafayette's release and invited him to join the new government. Lafayette declined.[10] Through the following tumultuous decades, both as a sometime liberal member of successive French assemblies and as a private citizen, Lafayette continued to speak, write, organize, and sometimes dangerously conspire on behalf of creating a more democratic France.

A divisive figure in France, Lafayette presumably relished the unanimous acclaim he received in 1824 and 1825 during his tour of all twenty-four American states. The impending fiftieth anniversary of the Declaration of Independence gave a special poignance to these occasions. One of the handful of surviving Revolutionary generals, he was greeted at every state border and county line by delegations of well-wishers.[11] *Niles' Weekly Register* noted that "no one like Lafayette has ever re-appeared in any country. To us he is like a venerated father, returned from the grave, to bless and receive the blessings of a mightily increased posterity."[12] Responding in English to the gratifying speeches he heard everywhere, he referred to himself as "an old American soldier."[13] He visited Jefferson at Monticello. As he approached Washington's Mount Vernon grave, he dismissed his companions and spent an hour alone with his adopted father.

---

[9] Olivier Bernier, *Lafayette: Hero of Two Worlds* (New York: E. P. Dutton, 1983), 203–41.

[10] For a detailed account of these events, see Paul Spalding, *Lafayette: Prisoner of State* (Columbia, SC: University of South Carolina Press, 2010).

[11] Scores of counties, towns, streets, and squares have been named for Lafayette, many of them during or shortly after his tour. "List of Places named for the Marquis de Lafayette," *Wikipedia*, https://en.wikipedia.org/wiki/List_of_places_named_for_the_Marquis_de_Lafayette.

[12] Cited in Fred Somkin, *Unquiet Eagle: Memory and Desire in the Idea of American Freedom* (Ithaca, NY: Cornell University Press, 1967), 153.

[13] Russell M. Jones, "The Flowering of a Legend: Lafayette and the Americans, 1825–1834," *French Historical Studies*, 4, no. 4 (Autumn 1966): 385.

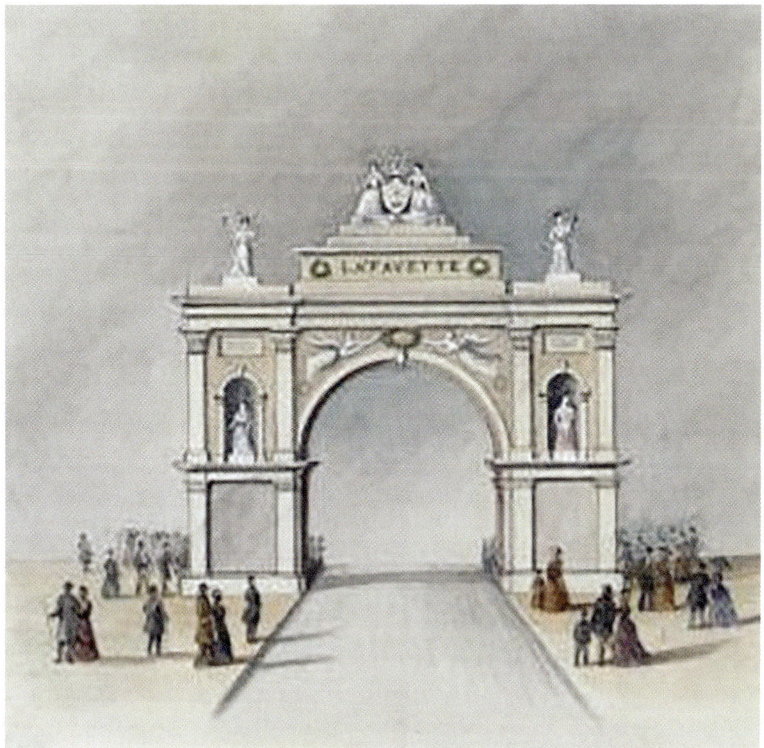

Figure 9.1 William Strickland, *Lafayette Arch.*

Lafayette arrived in Philadelphia on Monday, September 28, 1824, escorted by Governor John Shulze. Together they reviewed the Pennsylvania militia in Kensington and led a procession into the city. Their route took them through a series of triumphal arches. The largest—forty-five feet wide and twenty-four feet tall—was designed by architect William Strickland and was adorned with a copy of the coat of arms Thomas Sully had designed for the city, and with statues representing Liberty, Victory, Independence, and Plenty (Figure 9.1).[14]

[14] The details of Lafayette's fall 1824 visit to Philadelphia are taken from Marian Klamkin, *The Return of Lafayette, 1824–1825* (New York: Charles Scribner's Sons, 1975), 76–85; and J. Bennett Nolan, *Lafayette in America Day by Day* (Baltimore, MD: Johns Hopkins University Press, 1934).

An estimated 160,000 people lined the procession route. On Tuesday, which had been proclaimed "Lafayette Day," the Marquis attended a reception in his honor hosted by Nicholas Biddle. "For one week ... the city abandoned itself to festivities. There were military processions. ... There were civic processions ... printers, cordwainers, weavers, rope makers, coopers, blacksmiths, firemen and butchers vying with the militia."[15]

The *Saturday Evening Post* comically captured Lafayette's galvanic effect on Philadelphians: "We wrap our bodies in La Fayette coats during the day, and repose between La Fayette blankets at night. ... We have La Fayette bread, La Fayette butter, La Fayette beef and La Fayette vegetables. ... Even the ladies distinguished their *proper* from *common* kisses under the title La Fayette *smooches.*"[16]

Lafayette remained in Philadelphia until October, enjoying and sometimes merely enduring dozens of receptions, concerts, dinners large and small, and individual meetings, including a breakfast with soon-to-be-President-elect John Quincy Adams. Over two thousand tickets were sold for a grand ball on October 4, the day before Lafayette's departure.

As part of the preparation for Lafayette's visit, members of the Committee of Arrangement began a subscription for a portrait of the French general. The subscription prospectus, dated August 20, 1824, declares the intention to have "a correct resemblance of the excellent and early friend of their country ... a Full Length Portrait of His Excellency Major General La Fayette to be painted by Mr. Sully."[17]

Sully was only able to arrange one sitting with Lafayette, an hour in Washington, during which the artist made a drawing of the marquis's head.

Sully's composition (Figure 9.2) clings to the conventions of neoclassical portraiture. He has trimmed quite a few of the

---

[15] Hampton L. Carson, *A History of the Historical Society of Pennsylvania* ... vol. 1 (Philadelphia: Published by the Historical Society of Pennsylvania under the special centennial publication fund, 1940), 44–45.

[16] Cited in Gary B. Nash, *First City: Philadelphia and the Forging of Historical Memory* (Philadelphia: University of Pennsylvania Press, 2002), 6–7.

[17] Doris Devine Fanelli and Karie Diethorn, *History of the Portrait Collection, Independence National Historical Park* and *Catalog of the Collection* (Philadelphia: American Philosophical Society, 2001), 21.

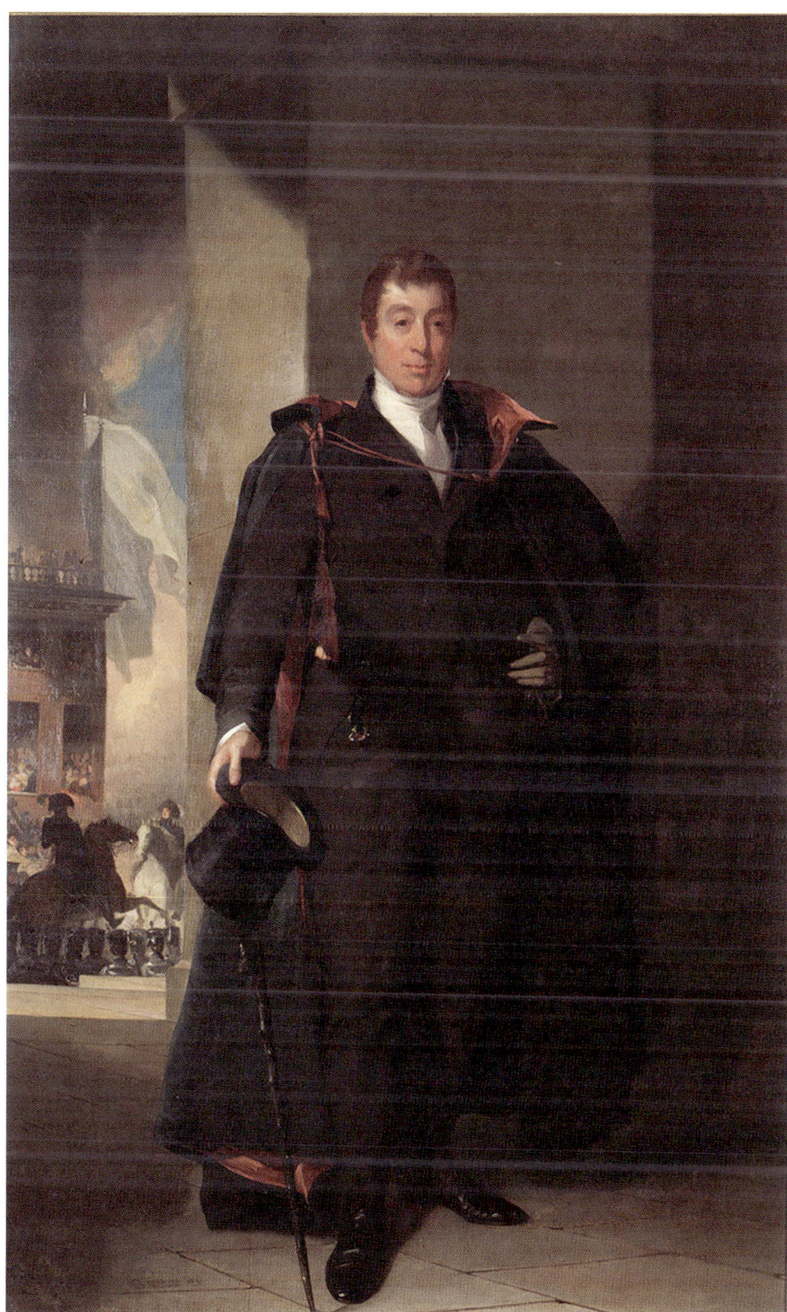

Figure 9.2 *Marquis de Lafayette.*

Courtesy of Independence National Historical Park.

general's years and pounds and added some hair. But he captured Lafayette's steady gaze, and something of the charisma that had attracted the admiration of almost everyone he met.

Lafayette stands in front of Strickland's triumphal arch. The general's dignified solidity is contrasted to the busyness of the background scene. The troops of Philadelphia's Washington Grays, who had provided Lafayette's military escort through the city, can be glimpsed marching in the background. Behind them stands Independence Hall. Crowds cheer from the windows of the now iconic building. An American flag flies proudly over the scene.[18]

[18] For further comment on the painting and its creation, see Monroe H. Fabian, *Mr. Sully, Portrait Painter: The Works of Thomas Sully (1783–1872)* [exhibition cat.] (Washington, DC: Smithsonian Institution Press, 1983), 78.

10

The Historical Society of Pennsylvania

WILLIAM RAWLE

During the first quarter of the nineteenth century, Americans began to take an increasing interest in their national history. "Historical societies were founded, sites were honored, documents preserved, historical writings published, and the historical theme found expression in orations, art, the theatre, and literature."[1] Philadelphia, which had played a more central part in that history than any other city, responded to the memorial impulse most visibly and permanently in the founding of the Historical Society of Pennsylvania.

The story begins with the American Philosophical Society (APS). The bylaws that APS adopted in 1796 identified six committees:

> 1. Geography, Mathematics, Natural Philosophy, and Astronomy.
> 2. Medicine and Anatomy.

---

[1] Nicholas B. Wainwright, "The Age of Nicholas Biddle," in *Philadelphia: A 300-Year History*, ed. Russell F. Weigley (Philadelphia: W. W. Norton, 1982), 301.

3. Natural History and Chemistry.
4. Trade and Commerce.
5. Mechanics and Architecture.
6. Husbandry and American Improvements.[2]

Two decades later, in 1815, the directors of APS apparently realized that these categories, with their single-minded focus on the scientific and the practical, left out entire domains of intellectual activity. In response, the directors created a Committee on History, Moral Science, and General Literature. The new committee was charged to gather "a collection of original documents, such as official and private letters, Indian treaties, ancient records, ancient maps" to "throw light on the history of the United States, but more particularly of this state."[3] As with Charles Willson Peale's conception of natural history, the historical paintings of John Trumbull, and poetry such as Joel Barlow's *The Columbiad*, the APS committee conceived of its task as patriotic, a means of codifying and preserving the progress of the new American nation.

The work of collecting fell almost wholly on the shoulders of the indefatigable Peter Stephen Du Ponceau, the committee's secretary. He sent personal and often detailed letters to nearly two hundred individuals over the next dozen years. Thomas Jefferson received quite a few of them.

Not long after its ambitious initial exertions, the committee's efforts began to decline, "attendance at the meetings perceptibly dwindling, the older members being irregular, and the newer members fitfully appearing and disappearing. Finally, in August 1820 the minutes ceased."[4] Presumably not by coincidence, these were the years when Du Ponceau was devoting more and more of his time and energy to his linguistic explorations.

William Rawle, a prominent attorney and a member of APS as well as the Library Company, devoted the next several years

---

[2] Edward C. Carter II, *"One Grand Pursuit": A Brief History of the American Philosophical Society's First 250 Years, 1743–1993* (Philadelphia: American Philosophical Society, 1993), 6–7.

[3] J. Stephen Catlett, ed., *A New Guide to the Collections in the Library of the American Philosophical Society* (Philadelphia: American Philosophical Society, 1987), xiii.

[4] Hampton L. Carson, *A History of the Historical Society of Pennsylvania*, vol. 1 (Philadelphia: Published by the Society under the special centennial publication fund, 1940), 41.

to the creation of a new organization that would continue the work of collection. Lafayette's visit of 1824, along with the impending fiftieth anniversary of the Declaration of Independence, provided a catalyst.[5] By the end of the year, a group of Philadelphians had met, agreed to establish what would be called *The Historical Society of Pennsylvania* (HSP), and elected Rawle as the first president. HSP first met in the room of the Phrenological Society in Carpenters' Hall. Like other newly founded cultural and scientific organizations in the eighteenth and early nineteenth century, HSP spent its first sixty years searching for a suitable home.

Rawle was sixty-seven years old when he accepted the HSP presidency. He brought to the job a long and successful legal career. Rawle Law Offices, the firm he founded in 1783, remains in business today; Rawle and Henderson is the oldest law firm in the United States. In 1791, President Washington appointed Rawle US attorney for Pennsylvania. He held the office for more than eight years, "during which time the Whiskey Insurrection [of 1791–94] occurred, and it fell to him to prosecute the authors, for which purpose the court followed the military to the western part of the state."[6] He was elected as the first chancellor of the newly founded Philadelphia Bar Association in 1822, a position he held until his death. He was a member of the American Philosophical Society, a trustee of the University of Pennsylvania, and counsel for the First Bank of the United States.

A man of wide interests, Rawle published books and articles on Native Americans, Pennsylvania history, religion ("An Essay Upon Angelic Influences"), and the law. *A view of the constitution of the United States of America* (1825) was among the earliest book-length analyses of that founding document. The book's most controversial section, in a commentary on Article Four, Section Four, argued that the Union was constitutionally dissoluble—"The states, then, may wholly withdraw from the Union"—and should the Union be dissolved, the allegiance of individuals would revert to the separate states. According to one group of scholars,

[5] Gary B. Nash, *First City: Philadelphia and the Forging of Historical Memory* (Philadelphia: University of Pennsylvania Press, 2002), 16.

[6] Allen Johnson and Dumas Malone, eds., "William Rawle," in *Dictionary of American Biography,* vol. 18 (New York: Charles Scribner's Sons, 1928), 401.

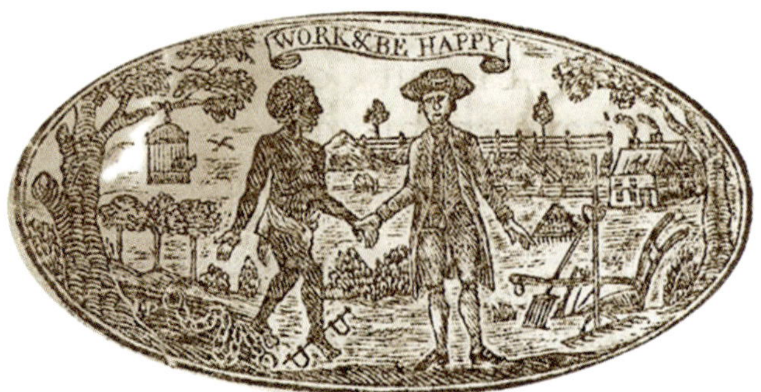

Figure 10.1 Seal of the Pennsylvania Abolition Society. Today, the Pennsylvania Abolition Society "continues its work through grants to organizations and programs that seek to improve conditions of African Americans throughout Pennsylvania." PAS also continues to display the organization's eighteenth-century medallion on its website.

Rawle's book continued to be assigned at West Point until at least 1840. Cadet Fitzhugh Lee, later a Confederate general, was among the students who read it. Fitzhugh's uncle, Robert E. Lee, supposedly once said: "Had it not been for the instruction from Rawle's textbook at West Point, [he] would not have left the Union and joined the southern Confederacy."[7]

Along with his other memberships and leadership positions, Rawle served from 1818 to 1836 as president of the Pennsylvania Abolition Society (PAS). Founded in 1775 as the Pennsylvania Society for Promoting the Abolition of Slavery, and for the Relief of Free Negroes Unlawfully Held in Bondage," it was the first such organization in the world (Figure 10.1). A revised charter in 1787 added a third goal: "for Improving the Condition of the African Race." In that same year, Benjamin Franklin accepted the position of honorary president. He would be followed as president by Benjamin Rush.

In the early nineteenth century, PAS pressed the case for abolition in courts and legislatures, earning a few individual suc-

[7] John Sickles, Michael J. Winey, and John Mills Bigham, "Southern Soldiers," *Military Images* 21, no. 3 (November–December 1999): 30.

cesses, and keeping the subject of slavery in the public consciousness. Bishop Richard Allen wrote that PAS was "the friend of those who hath no helper."[8] Through the antebellum years, however, PAS found itself in conflict with more militant organizations and individuals, among them Frederick Douglass, Lydia Maria Child, and William Lloyd Garrison. The history of the abolition movement is now told by scholars without much reference to PAS.

William Rawle's contributions to the antislavery struggle included personal advocacy. In 1815, he accepted the case of an enslaved woman known only as Kitty, who had escaped from slavery in Virginia about 1808 and had three children born in Pennsylvania. Rawle wrote in favor of the freedom of her children. Though his claim would have been supported by Pennsylvania law, the record of the outcome of the case has apparently not survived.

The story of the Historical Society in its early years is to a large extent a record of William Rawle's exertions. He gave his "inaugural discourse" on the 5th of November 1825, in what was still called *The President's House*, at Market and Ninth Streets.[9] In the first few pages, he makes his patriotic intentions clear. "Why," he asks, "does the peasant in Pennsylvania in her early days deserve a higher place in history than the peasant of England or of France?" Because they were the forebears of "that success which almost uniformly has accompanied our progress." This was the New World, whose ordinary citizens had built the nation.

Although HSP shared some of its purposes with APS, the two organizations were in many respects quite unlike, especially in their membership criteria. Gary Nash offers a commentary that concludes with an egalitarian insult to HSP's conception of itself:

> After its reorganization in 1769 the Philosophical Society's self-selected membership was primarily composed of weighty intellectuals, men of science, literature, linguistics, medicine, law, and philosophy, who were selected nationally and internationally ... The Historical Society of Pennsylvania from the beginning

---

[8] Cited in Richard S. Newman, "The Pennsylvania Abolition Society: Restoring a Group to Glory," *Pennsylvania Legacies* 5, no. 2 (November 2005): 7.

[9] William Rawle, *An inaugural discourse delivered on the 5th of November 1825, before the Historical Society of Pennsylvania*, in *Memoirs of the Historical Society of Pennsylvania* (Philadelphia: M'Carty and Davis, 1826), 25–81.

> was very different. It was composed almost entirely of local residents, many of whom were related and traced to their families back to early settlers; it grew by internal nomination of new members ensuring that it would be a gentleman's club; it made the collection of historical materials its singular priority; it was policy driven rather than intellectually thirsty; it created an aloofness that kept out the unwashed; and it was self-conscious about cultivating a reverence for particular aspects of the past in order to counteract the acids its members saw eating at their community.[10]

Relations between the two institutions were sometimes frosty. In 1824, even before HSP had completed creating its own organization, Roberts Vaux sent a letter to John F. Watson soliciting the important collection of early Pennsylvania manuscripts and pamphlets that Watson had gathered in preparing his *Annals of Philadelphia* (1830). Learning that Watson intended to deposit his collection with APS, Vaux wrote: "I wish to be understood as entertaining great respect for the Philosophical Society, but I know it is unequal to the department of History."[11] Watson donated his materials to HSP.

In his "Inaugural Discourse," Rawle outlined in detail the committee structure that he established immediately after his inauguration. These were:

1. On the national origin, early difficulties, and domestic habits of the first settlers
2. On the biography of the founder of Pennsylvania, his family, and the early settlers
3. Biographical notices of persons distinguished among us in ancient and modern times
4. On the Aborigines of Pennsylvania, their numbers, names of their tribes, intercourse with Europeans, their language, habits, character, and wars
5. On the principles to which the rapid population of Pennsylvania may be ascribed

[10] Nash, *First City*, 16.

[11] *The Formal Opening of the New Fireproof Building of the Historical Society of Pennsylvania, April 6–7, 1910* (Philadelphia: Historical Society of Pennsylvania, 1910), 7.

6. On the revenues, expenses, and general policy of the provincial government
7. On the judicial history of Pennsylvania
8. On the literary history of Pennsylvania
9. On the medical history of Pennsylvania
10. On the progress and present state of agriculture, manufactures, and commerce in Pennsylvania

Describing the work of each committee, Rawle devoted half of the total pages to the fourth committee: on Native Americans. Beyond insisting on the need for more complete histories of these tribes and individuals, Rawle engaged in vigorous advocacy. "The natives of this continent," he argued, "were utterly ignorant of such a place as Europe, till we poured upon them our adventurers, our refinements, and our vices." Their lands were taken from them without justification. The various defenses of those expropriations are specious: that they did not till the soil or live in cities, and Rawle rejected the "still less founded allegation that the extension of the Christian religion would justify the seizure of the property, and the destruction of the persons of the natives."[12]

To each of the ten committees Rawle also appended the names of the five or six men who would be tasked with carrying out the research and reporting. He eagerly awaited results.

At the conclusion of his inaugural address, Rawle expressed the "ardent hope that this Society will not, like too many others, be marked only by vivacity of inception, apathy of progress, and prematureness of decay." Alas, Rawle soon learned that his ambitious agenda did not seem to be finding an echoing response from his members. There was, writes Hampton Carson, "frequent want of a quorum in 1829, 1830, 1831, and 1832. … The venerable president once or twice found himself alone, at other times with but Roberts Vaux, Doctor James, and Mr. Wharton in attendance."[13]

Despite these early disappointments, Rawle soldiered on, eventually laying a solid foundation for an institution that has grown into one of the nation's most important collections of

---

[12] Rawle, "Inaugural Discourse," 21, 50.

[13] Carson, *A History of the Historical Society of Pennsylvania*, 105.

Early American books, pamphlets, maps, photographs, manuscripts, and ephemera.

Among the earliest of his Philadelphia portraits (Figure 10.2), Sully completed this painting in February 1808. Rawle emerges dramatically from the dark background, indifferent to the viewer, his gaze intently focused on the book he is holding. Equally skillful in modeling his subject's face and rendering his hands, Sully has created another image of a mind intently at work.

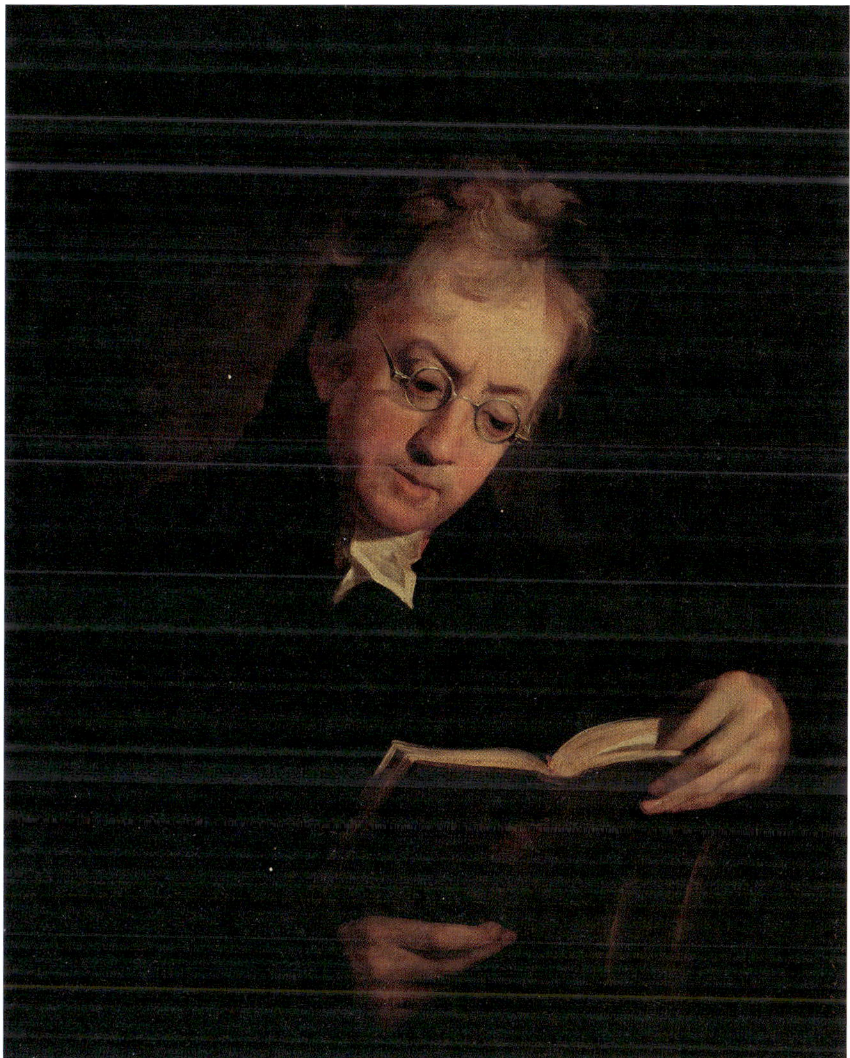

Figure 10.2 *Portrait of William Rawle.*

Courtesy of the Philadelphia History Museum at the Atwater Kent, the Historical Society of Pennsylvania Collection/Bridgeman Images.

11

Natural History

PROLOGUE: RALPH WALDO EMERSON AND CHARLES WILLSON PEALE

Natural history has often been described as the oldest of the sciences. Ralph Waldo Emerson evidently agreed. On November 5, 1833, Emerson delivered a lecture called "The Uses of Natural History." The lecture, the first he gave after resigning from his Unitarian pulpit in Boston, was the introduction to a course sponsored by the Natural History Society in Boston.

As he often did, Emerson began with a strong assertion: "It seems to have been designed, if anything was, that men should be students of Natural History. Man is, by nature, a farmer, a hunter, a shepherd and a fisherman, who are all practical naturalists and by their observations the true founders of all societies for the pursuit of science."[1] The earth, he continued, "is a museum" from which we can learn to understand the "amazing puzzle" of the universe.

Emerson had recently visited "that celebrated Repository of Natural Curiosities," the Jardin des Plantes in Paris. As he would do a few years later, in his small but permanently influential

[1] Ronald A. Bosco and Joel Myerson, eds., *Ralph Waldo Emerson: The Major Prose* (Cambridge, MA: Belknap Press, 2015), 13.

volume *Nature* (1836), Emerson emphasized the moral lessons that nature teaches, and the harmony that union with nature's creatures could ensure. Entranced by the seemingly inexhaustible fecundity and variety of nature, Emerson recalls his exhilarated response: "I am moved by strange sympathies. I say I will listen to this invitation. I will be a Naturalist."

Charles Willson Peale did not share Emerson's transcendental enthusiasm, but he did concur with the idea that nature was a teacher. His museum's admission ticket was stamped with the declaration: "NATURE. The Birds and Beasts will teach thee." Peale had pragmatic and nationalist motives in mind when he founded America's first museum of natural history—indeed the nation's first museum of any importance. Europe had by this time seen the founding of many museums and what were called "cabinets of curiosities."

The museum began as a picture gallery. An enthusiastic supporter of American independence, Peale rose to the rank of captain in the Pennsylvania army early in the Revolutionary War. Following the war, and to honor its heroes, Peale produced dozens of portraits of such leading figures as Benjamin Franklin, Alexander Hamilton, Thomas Jefferson, and George Washington. He installed the pictures in his Lombard Street home and in 1782 opened the collection to the public. His purpose was patriotic: to keep America's recent history continuously in the minds of its citizens.

Four years later, Peale began to include preserved animal specimens, geologic examples, and fossils in his displays. The museum collections began with "a dried paddlefish from the Allegheny River and a badly preserved Angora cat. By 1831, the museum contained 250 quadrupeds, 1,310 birds, more than 4,000 insects, 8,000 minerals, 1,044 shells, several hundred fish, more than 200 snakes, lizards, turtles and tortoises and the major American collection of fossil bones; it had become *the* primary resource for American natural history."[2] Eventually, Peale accumulated

---

[2] Robert E. Schofield, "The Science Education of an Enlightened Entrepreneur: Charles Willson Peale and His Philadelphia Museum, 1784–1827," *American Studies* 30, no. 2 (Fall 1989): 21.

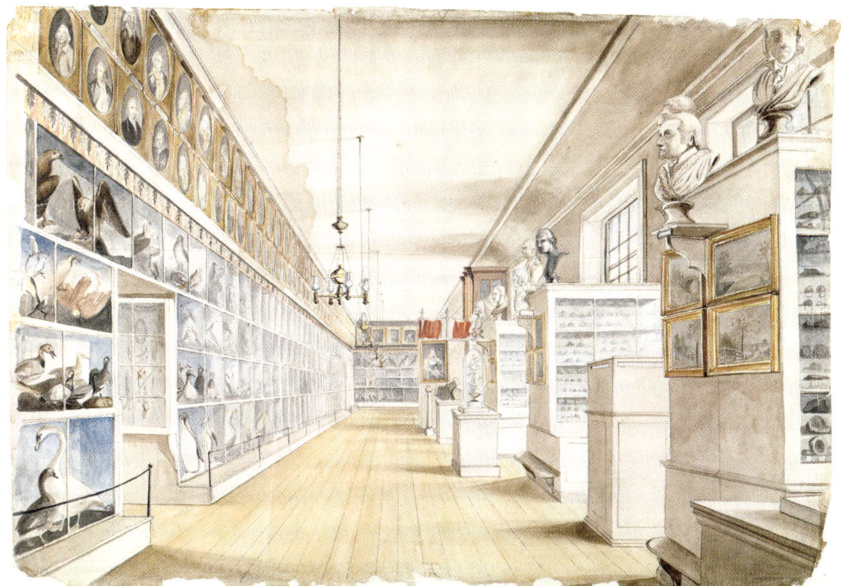

Figure 11.1 Charles Willson Peale and Titian Ramsay Peale, *The Long Room, Interior of Front Room in Peale's Museum* (1822).

Courtesy of the Detroit Institute of Arts, Founders and Society Purchase, Director's Discretionary Fund/Bridgeman Images.

more than 100,000 artifacts. With some justice, he referred to his museum as "a world in miniature."

The museum became Peale's full-time occupation. On April 24, 1794, a few years after the doors opened, Peale "respectfully" informed the public that "he should bid adieu to Portrait Painting."[3] He would occasionally accept a portrait commission, but for the next three decades he devoted nearly all his time and energy to managing and funding his museum.

Peale did his best to organize the dizzying array of objects (Figure 11.1). He modeled his categories on the Linnaean system: every item contributed its part to an orderly and interconnected

[3] Sidney Hart and David C. Ward, "The Waning of an Enlightenment Ideal: Charles Willson Peale's Philadelphia Museum," *Journal of the Early Republic* 8, no. 4 (Winter 1988): 389.

world. The museum was an extraordinary achievement. Peale was right to boast that his collection offered a greater look at "the wonderful works of nature" than had ever before been possible.[4]

Peale also began to give lectures, offering a view of natural history that connected it to the growth of the new republic. Like Emerson, he emphasized the importance of natural history for the farmer, the merchant, and the mechanic. Knowledge would be put to practical ends and would thereby enhance American prosperity.[5] Rising prosperity, in turn, would strengthen the nation's democracy.

Although Peale always insisted that education was the museum's primary mission, he also knew that many of his customers were more engaged by the curiosities than the high-minded ideas that organized them. And he was himself a bit of a promoter: "he attracted his audience by highlighting the entertainment value of his displays and demonstrations in language that he shared with promoters of the theaters, circuses, waxworks, and itinerant amusements in the city."[6] To see Peale himself, whether slyly or inadvertently, declaring his showmanship, we need look no further than the famous self-portrait in which he lifts the velvet curtain and invites the viewer into the gallery's space.

Peale spent years trying to persuade city and state officials that his museum served a public good and should receive public funding. No support was forthcoming. In the two decades after he died, in 1827, dwindling ticket sales and increasing maintenance costs forced his sons to sell the collection (except for the portraits).[7] In a transaction that could serve as an emblem for the shift from Enlightenment idealism to Jacksonian populism, one of the buyers was Phineas T. Barnum.

---

[4] Cited in Gary B. Nash, *First City: Philadelphia and the Forging of Historical Memory* (Philadelphia: University of Pennsylvania Press, 2002), 136.

[5] Steven Conn, *Museums and American Intellectual Life, 1876–1926* (Chicago: University of Chicago Press, 1998), 37.

[6] David Brigham, *Public Culture in the Early Republic: Peale's Museum and Its Audience* (Washington, DC: Smithsonian Institution Press, 1995), 13.

[7] For the most detailed account of the museum's decline and fall, see Charles Coleman Sellers, *Mr. Peale's Museum: Charles Willson Peale and the First Popular Museum of Natural Science and Art* (New York: W. W. Norton, 1980), 307–35.

WILLIAM WAGNER

Born in 1796 into a prosperous Philadelphia family—his father was a successful cotton merchant—William Wagner displayed from early childhood a keen and precocious interest in science. Although he determined to embark on a scientific career, under some paternal pressure, he accepted an apprenticeship with Stephen Girard, the French-born merchant who had reputedly become the richest man in the country. And one of the most philanthropic.[8]

Working for Girard taught Wagner a great deal about commerce; the job also provided exceptional opportunities for the young naturalist. He traveled widely across Europe, the Middle East, and Asia, organizing shipments of coffee, cotton, and other products for Girard. In each country, he began gathering specimens of natural history. During those years, working for Girard and then independently, he accumulated a substantial fortune, enough money to retire from business in his mid-forties. From that time until his death in 1885, at the age of ninety-one, Wagner was engaged full time in his collection, which would eventually grow into an estimated thirty thousand objects.

Wagner married Louisa Binney, daughter of a prominent Philadelphian, in 1841. The couple spent a two-year honeymoon in Europe, buying and trading artefacts, and visiting natural history museums. He was exceptionally impressed with the Jardin des Plantes, but he was gratified that the Berlin Museum of Natural History charged no admission fee: "The Museum is open for free to every one bravo! every day from 10-4."[9] A few years after the couple returned to Philadelphia, Wagner began giving free lectures based on objects in his collection. His first venue was Elm Grove, his large suburban home. When attendance outgrew the house, Wagner moved to Municipal Hall on Spring Garden Street.

---

[8] Wagner is not included in *American National Biography*. Biographical information can be found in the *Dictionary of American Biography*; *The National Cyclopaedia of American Biography*, vol. 6 (New York: James T. White & Company, 1896), 16; and Susan Glassman, "Wagner Free Institute of Science" (1990).

[9] Cited in Matthew A. White, "Science for All: The Wagner Free Institute of Science of Philadelphia," *Pennsylvania Legacies* 15, no. 1 (Spring 2015): 14.

In 1865, he moved into a building of his own design, large enough to hold his collection and to provide space for lectures.

Like Charles Willson Peale, Wagner considered education to be his primary task. Unlike Peale, Wagner aspired to offer formal coursework leading to college degrees. And for free. In 1855, the Wagner Free Institute of Science received its charter, specifically identifying the "practical, busy, laboring people" of Philadelphia as prospective students. Women as well as men were welcome. Subjects included geology, anatomy, biology, botany, chemistry, and civil engineering. The University of Pennsylvania and Princeton University provided many of the faculty.

The Institute's "First Annual Announcement" included a lengthy "Plan" for the work to be undertaken. This manifesto opens with the promise that "Every branch of the natural sciences will receive attention, and be duly taught." Then, before describing the details of instruction, Wagner delivered a rhapsodic celebration—possibly indebted to Alexander von Humboldt's hugely influential *Cosmos*—on the grand underlying assumptions that motivated his endeavors:

> While these sciences have each their separate spheres, they nevertheless are all inseparably connected, and form in fact but one great science. All are engaged in making known the great fabric of creation, which is one vast indivisible system, its several parts depending on each other, and interweaving and moving together in the most wonderful harmony. The field of operations for this Institution will therefore be as wide as the great creation, and as beautiful and grand as the glories that everywhere garnish the earth and the skies.[10]

Descending from those heights, the rest of the document lays out the subjects to be taught and the resources to be employed.

Following Wagner's death in 1885, the Institute's trustees hired Joseph Leidy, the brilliant professor of anatomy at the University of Pennsylvania, to serve as president of the faculty

---

[10] Wagner Free Institute archives. The first English translations of *Cosmos: A Sketch of a Physical Description of the Universe*, were published in the late 1840s and early 1850s.

and curator.[11] Along with establishing an important scientific journal, and sponsoring expeditions, Leidy systemically reorganized the entire collection. Leidy was Charles Darwin's first major American ally. He arranged fossil organisms in the presumed order of their evolutionary development. A case containing a group of skeletons, human and monkey, was intended to illustrate Darwin's theory (Figure 11.2). "Looking at the monkey and human bones, a visitor would first notice their similarities and then focus on the subtle variations on which Darwin's law of natural selection acted."[12]

By the time of Wagner's death, his institute had already become professionally obsolete. Museums of natural history were replacing their rows of glass cases with quasi-realistic arrangements of objects and large-scale dioramas of colorful habitats. In addition, by the end of the nineteenth century, the scientific study of natural history was moving from museums to university departments of biology.

Over time, and almost inadvertently, the Wagner Free Institute was transformed from a place of scientific research into a rare surviving repository of Victorian science. As such, it continues to play an important role, more than a hundred and sixty years after its founding. The many visitors who tour the building today, or attend its excellent free lectures, the historians of science who consult its archive, the artists and architects who are drawn to the building and its collections, are all the beneficiaries of William Wagner's philanthropic exertions.

This portrait (Figure 11.3), completed in 1836, is organized along the compositional lines Sully often employed. Wagner's face emerges from a variously dark and darker background, an emphatic contrast with the crisp and high-collared shirt that Sully renders with a few broad strokes of white paint. The strong light that illuminates the right side of Wagner's face modulates skillfully into the shadows on the left. The blue and yellow lining of the

[11] There are several biographies of Leidy. The best is Leonard Warren's *Joseph Leidy: The Last Man Who Knew Everything* (New Haven, CT: Yale University Press, 1998). The title is only a small overstatement.

[12] Morris J. Vogel, *Cultural Connections: Museums and Libraries of Philadelphia and the Delaware Valley* (Philadelphia: Temple University Press, 1991), 85.

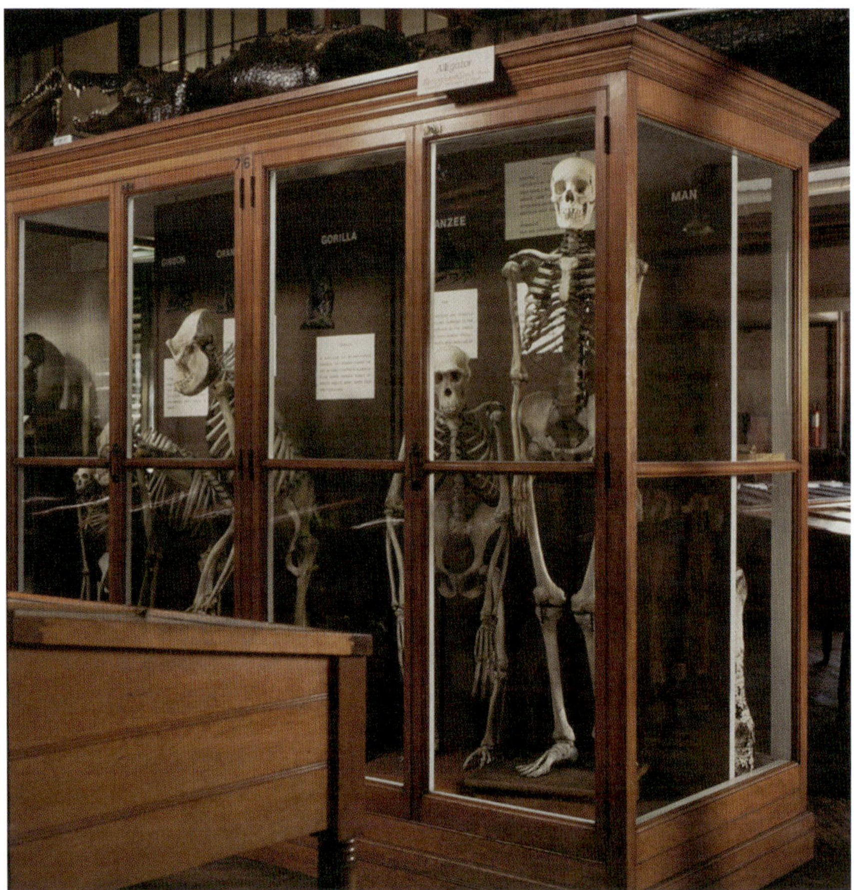

Figure 11.2 Display case at the Wagner Free Institute of Science.

Tom Crane, Courtesy of the Wagner Free Institute of Science.

subject's black coat (a couple of buttons indicated with simple dabs of white) lends vitality to the scene. What the scholar Michael Lewis describes as a "casual straying lock of hair" infuses this quite formal portrait with just a touch of informality.[13]

[13] Michael Lewis, "Thomas Sully and the Studious Subjects," *Nineteenth Century* 38, no. 1 (Spring 2018): 33.

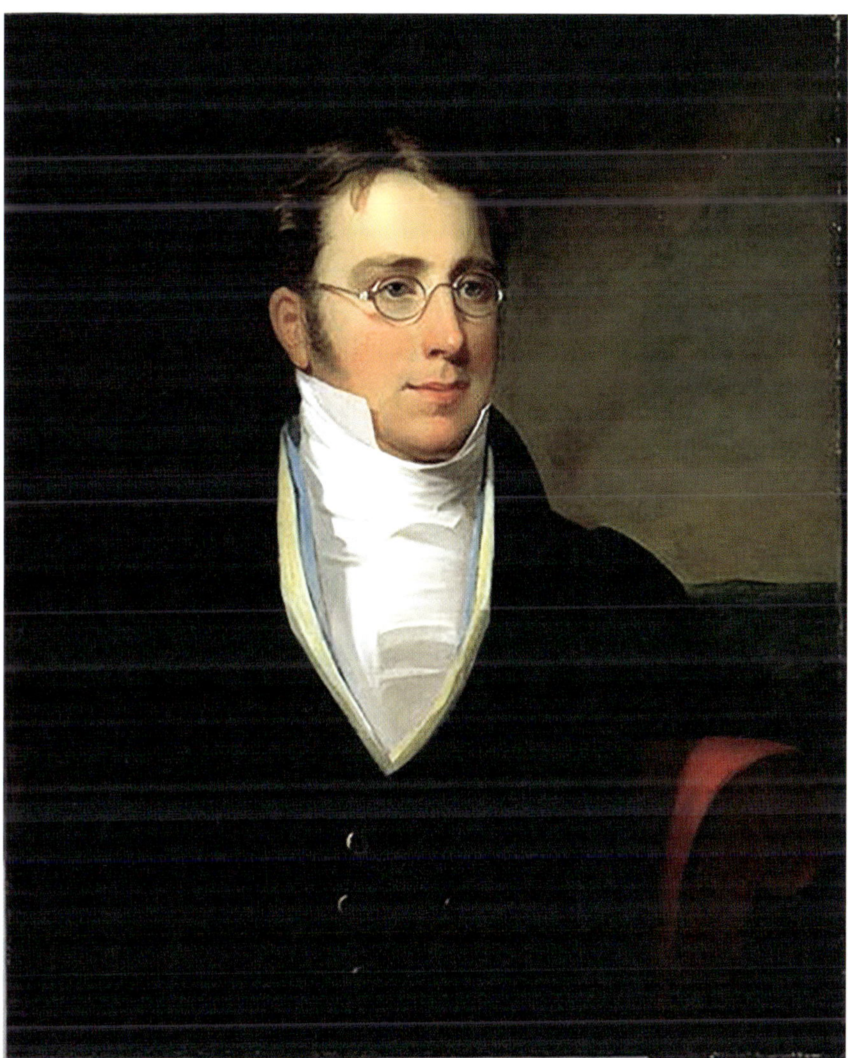

Figure 11.3 *Portrait of William Wagner.*

Courtesy of the Wagner Free Institute of Science.

WILLIAM MACLURE

Unlike the Wagner Free Institute, the Academy of Natural Sciences, founded in 1812 on nineteenth-century principles, has adapted over the past two centuries. Now a part of Drexel University, the Academy continues to produce original biological and ecological research.[14]

The seven men who founded the Academy, friends of English, Dutch, French, and Irish backgrounds, described themselves as "gentlemen, friends of science," who intended "to occupy their leisure, in each other's company, on subjects of natural science, interesting and useful to the country and the world."[15] Their principal aim would be "the advancement and diffusion of useful, liberal human knowledge." The repeated use of the word *useful* suggests the pragmatic motive that inspired the undertaking. They also shared with Emerson and Peale a nationalist view of their work: Young America was ready to compete with Europe in the conduct of science.

The collection grew through a combination of Academy-sponsored expeditions and from specimens solicited by way of a wide-ranging correspondence—with other natural history museums and with individuals, including ship captains. The additions included "a box of insects from China, 'a small flying-fish' from a Captain Kitty, the skin of a bird of paradise from the East Indies, a group of tarantulas and their nests from Jamaica, a robe from the northwest coast of America made from skins of the Diver duck and edged with ermine, and a Captain Craycroft's collection of shells from the West Indies." Artifacts, fossils, agricultural products, minerals, and more were coming to the Academy from Austria, France, India, Australia, Ireland, South America, and every region of the United States. Public lectures were on offer on a regular schedule; women were welcome to attend, at no cost. Two hundred women signed up.

---

[14] Patricia Tyson Stroud, "The Founding of the Academy of Natural Sciences of Philadelphia in 1812 and Its Journal in 1817," *Proceedings of the Academy of Natural Sciences of Philadelphia* 147 (1997): 227–36. Most of the quotations in the following paragraphs are taken from Stroud's essay.

[15] Cited in Simon Baatz, *Patronage, Science, and Ideology in an American City: Patrician Philadelphia, 1800–1860* (PhD diss., University of Pennsylvania, 1986), 55.

At about this point: Enter William Maclure. Born in Scotland in 1763, he earned a mercantile fortune and, in 1796, took American citizenship and settled in Philadelphia. Maclure would prove to be the most important figure in the Academy's early history. Like William Wagner, his wealth enabled him to retire from business and pursue his scientific interests, especially in mineralogy and geology. His mainly self-taught command of geology secured his appointment to produce the first systematic geological survey of the eastern half of the United States. "Observations on the Geology of the United States, Explanatory of a Geological Map" established his reputation. Several sources refer to him as "The Father of American Geology."[16]

In 1818, Maclure settled permanently in Philadelphia and became an active member of the Academy. His influence and his philanthropy were soon apparent. The members of the Academy had realized that, if they wanted to earn credibility with other institutions, they needed to publish a journal. Funds were insufficient. Maclure purchased a printing press, installed it in his home, and supervised the publication of the *Journal of the Academy of Natural Sciences*. The *Journal* was received with respect both in the United States and abroad. Thomas Jefferson sent a note of congratulations. Academy member George Ord wrote from Paris that the publication had impressed the renowned scientists at the Jardin des Plantes: "You may meet, and specify, and confabulate, and elect members, and enlarge your collections, and beautify your domicile, but if you publish not, down goes your character to the tomb of the Capulets."[17]

In addition to the printing press and the costs of printing the *Journal*, Maclure also funded the third of the succession of buildings that housed the Academy, and he donated over five thousand of his books to the library. He was a member of the Academy for twenty-eight years, seventeen as president, until his death in 1840. Maclure's patronage helped the Academy become the most important scientific society in America, until the creation of the Smithsonian Institution.[18]

---

[16] Archibald Geikie, *The Founders of Geology* (London: Macmillan, 1905), 458.

[17] Stroud, "The Founding of the Academy of Natural Sciences," 231.

[18] Simon Baatz, "William Maclure," in *American National Biography*, vol. 14 (New York: Oxford University Press, 1999), 273–75.

Along with his commitment to science, Maclure was deeply interested in education, especially the education of young children. On a trip to Switzerland, he had visited Johann Pestalozzi. For the rest of his life, he spoke and wrote in support of Pestalozzi's progressive methods, with its emphasis on the development of the whole individual without the harsh discipline and rote learning typical of most nineteenth-century schools on both sides of the Atlantic.

In the 1820s, Maclure invested heavily in Robert Owen's utopian community, New Harmony, in Indiana. When the experiment collapsed, Maclure remained in Indiana, repurposing the buildings as a campus for scientific research. He also laid out plans for a school based on Pestalozzian principles, with a curriculum designed around the daily experiences of children, and books as supplementary. Here are some of the roots of what would later be called progressive education.

In 1831, with Joseph Neef, Maclure organized an institution to which they gave the unwieldy name, the Manual Labor School for Promoting Manual Labor in Literary Institutions. Whether consciously or not, the school promoted educational principles rather like those of Benjamin Franklin, as we will see in the chapter on the University of Pennsylvania. Academic study would be combined with farming or industrial work. By emphasizing the practical value of their learning, students would be more inclined to embrace school assignments. Beyond that, they would acquire "habits of industry, independence, health and cooperation."[19]

During his early years at New Harmony, Maclure also founded another journal, *The Disseminator of Useful Knowledge*, in which he published scores of articles on scientific, pedagogical, and political subjects. Many of these were collected into two volumes under the title, *Opinions on Various Subjects, Dedicated to the Industrious Producers.*

Those opinions, often inflammatory, declare Maclure's populist allegiance to the working men and women of America, in his view the victims of an unjust economic and political system.

---

[19] R. Freeman Butts and Lawrence A. Cremin, *A History of Education in American Culture* (New York: Henry Holt and Company, 1953), 277.

A few excerpts capture the tone of his judgments, repeated and elaborated at enormous length through his publications.

> It is high time to check the growing abuses of a monied aristocracy.[20]
>
> All property is produced by labor: even the wild fruits and animals are gathered and caught by the labor and industry of some part of the society, before they can be a property useful to man. Those who labor produce all and those who do not labor produce nothing, but live on the produce of others' labor. (p. 114)
>
> In our southern states slavery has annihilated equality and monopolized all freedom to the master who is of the nonproductive and consuming class. The life persons and property of the producers are possessed as a lawful inheritance by their owners. (p. 125)[21]
>
> The two greatest obstructions to useful improvements have been church and state, religion and politics. The great ruling members of both, having more than their share of good things by the present distribution, fear a smaller share by the least approach to equality, and oppose every change. (p.189)
>
> Politics and religion have always secluded in the dark corners of monopoly, masked by the impenetrable curtain of hypocrisy superstition and mystery. (p. 346)

Sully completed this portrait in December 1825 (Figure 11.4). The composition is dramatically orchestrated, with the right side of Maclure's face brightly lit, the left in shadow. His receding hair exposes a high forehead, emphasized by the almost uniform darkness of both background and clothing. His right arm is resting on a group of books, his head pensively poised on his hand and casting a shadow on his white collar. Sully has given us another image of a man preoccupied with his own thoughts.

---

[20] William Maclure, *Opinions on Various Subjects, Dedicated to the Industrious Producers* (New Harmony, IN: 1837), 4.

[21] For a discussion of abolitionist activity at New Harmony, see Sean Griffin, "Antislavery Utopias," *Journal of the Civil War Era* 8, no. 2 (June 2018): 243–68.

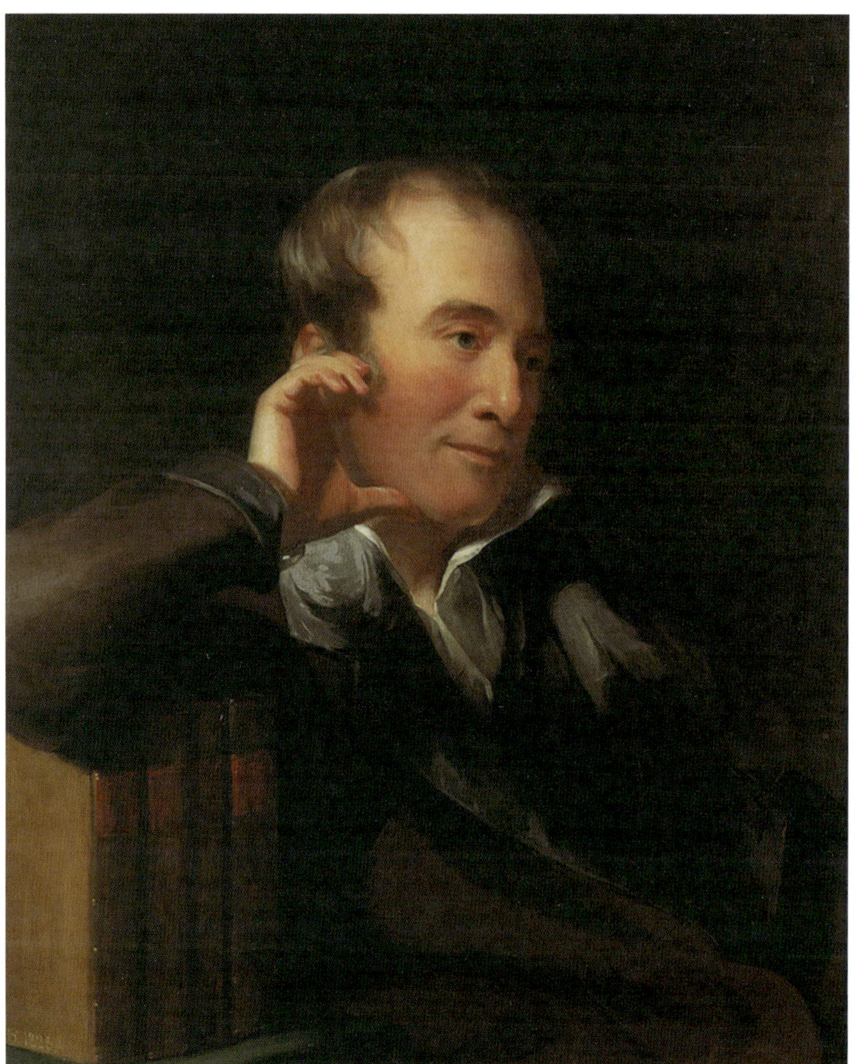

Figure 11.4 *Thomas Sully Painting of William Maclure.*

Courtesy of the Academy of Natural Sciences of Drexel University.

12

The University of Pennsylvania

OF THE EIGHT COLLEGES FOUNDED before the Revolution, the University of Pennsylvania undoubtedly has the most complicated origin story.[1] It begins in 1740, with the creation of the Academy. Housed at Fourth and Arch in the city's largest building—100 by 70 feet—the Academy was designed for two purposes (Figure 12.1). It would serve as a charity school devoted to the education of poor children. At that time, while "boys and girls whose parents were able to pay for private teaching were obtaining the rudiments of an education, the great body of the poor here, as elsewhere, were growing up in absolute ignorance."[2]

The building's second purpose was to provide a venue for George Whitefield, the British evangelical firebrand whose sermons attracted thousands of Philadelphians on each of his several visits to the city. Not surprising, the Academy was often called

[1] In addition to Penn, and in chronological order: Harvard (1636), College of William and Mary (1693), Yale (1701), Princeton (1746), Brown (1764), Rutgers (1766), and Dartmouth (1769). Nearly a dozen colleges and universities had been established in Spanish America before Harvard was founded. Russel B. Nye, *The Cultural Life of the New Nation, 1776–1830* (New York: Harper & Row, 1963), 171.

[2] Edward Potts Cheney, *History of the University of Pennsylvania, 1740–1940* (Philadelphia: University of Pennsylvania Press, 1940), 15. Cheney's book remains the most comprehensive history of Penn's founding and early development.

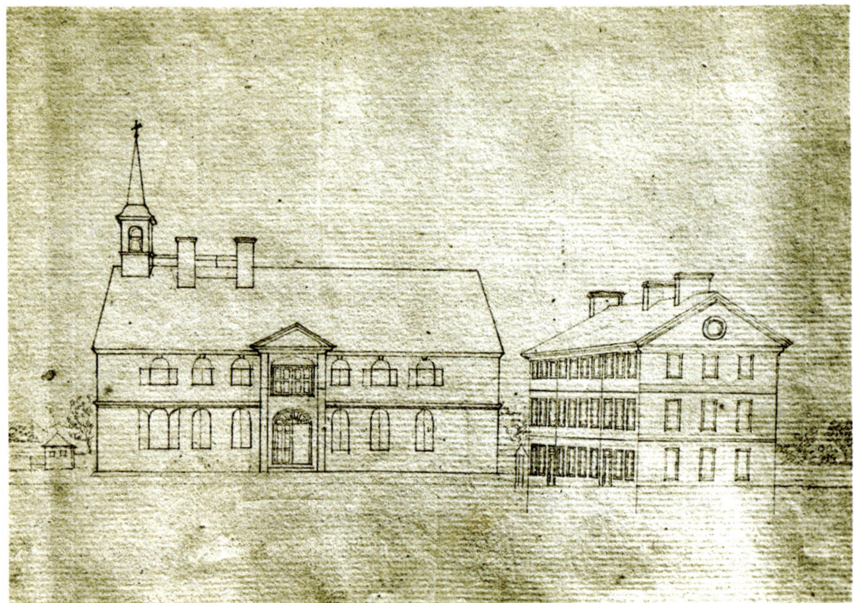

Figure 12.1 A 1918 sketch of the Academy's Fourth Street Campus. The dormitory was added in 1759.

Whitefield's *New Building*. Over the next several years, far more preaching than teaching took place, and the building was vacant more often than occupied.

In 1749, after consulting with a number of friends—"of whom the junto furnished a good part"—Franklin published a pamphlet titled *Proposals Relating to the Education of Youth in Pensilvania* (Figure 12.2).[3]

Franklin's recommendations reflected his egalitarian and pragmatic inclinations. Students should learn "*every Thing* that is useful, and *every Thing* that is ornamental: but Art is long and their Time is short," so it is proposed that they learn "those Things that are likely to be *most useful* and *most ornamental*. Regard being

[3] Both a complete transcript of *The Proposal*, along with a digital facsimile, can be found at the University of Pennsylvania archives: https://archives.upenn.edu/digitized-resources/docs-pubs/franklin-proposals.

PROPOSALS

RELATING TO THE

EDUCATION

OF

YOUTH

IN

PENSILVANIA.

PHILADELPHIA:
Printed in the Year, M.DCC.XLIX.

Figure 12.2 Title page of Franklin's pamphlet.

had to the several professions for which they are intended." Here is Franklin's implicit but unmistakable rebuke to the received conception of higher education's purposes. Having Oxford and Cambridge in mind as bad models, he envisioned education for practical use rather than for refinement and the mastery of ancient languages and literature. To buttress his arguments, and his own authority, he scattered references to Locke, Milton, the "learned and ingenious Dr. *George Turnbull*, Chaplain to the present Prince of Wales," among many others. Quite a few of the supportive citations were helpfully altered to suit Franklin's purposes.[4]

He met predictable resistance from some of the conservative supporters he needed, and grudgingly allowed for the possibility of including Greek and Latin in the curriculum. Nonetheless, in the words of one of his biographers: "his curriculum differed drastically from the standard education available in other colonial and English academies and colleges."[5]

The bulk of Franklin's pamphlet provides extended descriptions of the subjects to be covered in the new Academy. To begin with, "All should be taught to write a *fair Hand*, and swift, as that is useful to All." Arithmetic and accounting should be taught, and at least "some of the first Principles of *Geometry* and *Astronomy.*"

Geography and agriculture are to be taught, both tied to potential uses and careers. History, both ancient and modern, would be valuable mainly for providing models of good and bad behavior. (This was of course a fairly ancient and durable rationale for the study of history.)

Rhetoric and logic—both of which were included in older curricular systems—are maintained because of their obvious utility. Franklin includes the study of natural history, but predictably urges that theoretical study be informed by the practical: "While they are reading Natural History, might not a little *Gardening, Planting, Grafting, Inoculating,* &c. be taught and practised; and now and then Excursions made to the neighbouring Plantations

[4] The twenty-nine lengthy and closely printed notes take up more pages than the text.

[5] J. A. Leo Lemay, *The Life of Benjamin Franklin, Volume Three: Soldier, Scientist, and Politician, 1748–1757* (Philadelphia: University of Pennsylvania Press, 2009), 183.

of the best Farmers." Commerce, inventions, and manufactures are also proposed as subjects, probably for the first time in a curricular prospectus.

Perhaps the most striking section of the *Proposals* is Franklin's three-and-half-line comment on the place of religion. "*History* will also afford frequent Opportunities of showing the Necessity of a *Publick* Religion, from its Usefulness to the Publick; the Advantage of a Religious Character among private Persons; the Mischiefs of Superstition, *&c.* and the Excellency of the CHRISTIAN RELIGION above all others antient or modern." Aside from that perfunctory final salute to Christianity—undoubtedly inserted, and in capital letters, to placate the less deistical men he hoped to engage—the study of religion is recommended for its utility.

After publishing his proposals, Franklin moved quickly to secure the support and especially the contributions of several dozen of the city's leading citizens. He appointed a group of trustees and called the first meeting on November 13, 1749, at which he was elected president of the board. The first order of business was to find a suitable home. After a brief negotiation, the trustees were able to buy the under-used Academy by assuming the building's debt (amounting to nearly £800). The deed was transferred in February 1750.

Franklin secured some initial support from the city's Common Council. In the spring of 1750, the Council voted £200 toward completing the Academy building, along with £50 a year for five years "towards supporting a Charity School for the Teaching of poor Children Reading, Writing and Arithmetick."[6] That statement of purpose underscores the egalitarian focus of the institution, a point to which I will return. Classes began in the spring of 1751, first in a warehouse near the river, and then in the Academy when renovations were completed.

In April 1753, the colony's proprietors granted a charter for the new school. Two years later, the charter was amended to grant the trustees power to grant degrees. Accordingly, the institution's title was changed; it was now called *The College, Academy, and*

[6] "Paper on the Academy [31 July 1750]," *Founders Online*, National Archives, https://founders.archives.gov/documents/Franklin/01-04-02-0007.

Charitable School of Philadelphia.[7] Two years after that, Franklin stepped down from the board and left for England as Pennsylvania's representative to the Crown.

The first provost of the college was an Anglican clergyman, William Smith, with Franklin serving as the first president of the board of trustees.[8] Working together, they created a curriculum that focused on the sciences, history, logic, mathematics, and geography.[9] Edward Cheney described the course of study as the first curriculum in America that offered "a group of college studies not following medieval tradition and not having a specifically religious object."[10]

In the second half of the eighteenth century, the histories of the nation and the College were closely linked. During the occupation of Philadelphia by British troops, the "confusions of the Revolution put an end for a while to all degree giving and taking."[11] Those same confusions led to administrative upheaval at the College. As one of Franklin's biographers summarized the situation: "The College of Philadelphia, which had evolved out of Franklin's Academy, gradually grew away from its egalitarian roots, so that by the start of the Revolutionary era it was often seen as a nest of aristocracy and Anglicanism."[12]

This is barely an exaggeration. Provost William Smith and most of the trustees were vocally conservative, Anglican, and monarchist. In 1779, in a bitter confrontation, they were ushered out

---

[7] William L. Turner, *The Charity School, the Academy, and the College Fourth and Arch Streets*, Transactions of the American Philosophical Society, n.s., 43, pt. 1 (Philadelphia: American Philosophical Society, 1953), 182.

[8] Unlike most other American colleges and universities, Penn continued to use the title of "provost" for its senior officer rather than "president" until the 1930s.

[9] Smith was Franklin's choice. Within a few years, the arrogant and conservative provost had become one of Franklin's relatively few enemies. In 1763, Franklin wrote of Smith: "I made that Man my Enemy by doing him too much Kindness. Tis the honestest Way of acquiring an enemy." Franklin added, with characteristic humor: "And since 'tis convenient to have at least one Enemy, who by his Readiness to revile one on all Occasions may make one careful of one's Conduct, I shall keep him an Enemy for that purpose." "From Benjamin Franklin to Mary Stevenson, 25 March 1763," *Founders Online*, National Archives, https://founders.archives.gov/documents/Franklin/01-10-02-0123.

[10] Cheney, *History*, 134.

[11] Ibid., 103.

[12] H. W. Brands, *The First American: The Life and Times of Benjamin Franklin* (New York: Doubleday, 2000), 662.

of office by American patriots, many of them Presbyterian.[13] These insurgents received a revised charter, which bestowed yet another new title: The University of the State of Pennsylvania.

In the late 1780s, as the political winds shifted in their favor, Smith and his allies were re-installed in the College. When they in turn tried to replace the men who had replaced them, the ensuing stalemate meant that, for two years, 1789–91, "while the city was only dubiously capable of supporting a single college, Philadelphia now had two rival colleges within a few blocks of each other."[14]

In September 1791, after lengthy but surprisingly cordial negotiations, the two institutions agreed on a merger, under the title "The University of Pennsylvania."

Despite the administrative instability and the financial struggles that it continuously faced, Penn, in one or another of its incarnations, could boast a faculty of considerable distinction. Francis Alison, who taught Latin and Greek and served for several years as vice provost, was called by Ezra Stiles (later president of Yale) "the greatest classical scholar in America, especially in Greek."[15] His Doctor of Divinity (DD) degree from Glasgow is likely the first doctorate granted an American by a European university. James Wilson, the nation's first professor of law, was among the first six justices of the United States Supreme Court. He played an important (if ultimately dubious) role in the writing of the Constitution.[16]

[13] Often described as secular, the early College should more accurately be described as nonsectarian. Christianity was taken for granted. Eight of the first ten Penn provosts were clergymen, seven of them ordained in the Church of England and its American successor, the Episcopal Church. See Russell Nye, *The Cultural Life of the New Nation, 1776–1830* (New York: Harper & Row, 1963), 177. Furthermore, despite its nonsectarian identity, the College was often the scene of religious controversy, pitting Anglicans against Presbyterians. See Richard Hofstadter and Walter P. Metzger, *The Development of Academic Freedom in the United States* (New York: Columbia University Press, 1955), 115ff.

[14] Harry M. Tinkcom, "The Revolutionary City, 1765–1783," in *Philadelphia: A 300-Year History*, ed. Russell F. Weigley (New York: W. W. Norton, 1983), 161.

[15] Allen Johnson and Dumas Malone, eds., "Francis Alison" in *Dictionary of American Biography*, vol. 1 (New York: Charles Scribner's Sons, 1995), 181.

[16] Wilson's contributions included the notorious "three-fifths clause," a concession to slave-holding states, which declared that "any person who was not free would be counted as three-fifths of a free individual for the purposes of determining congressional representation."

Benjamin Rush, America's most celebrated physician, was installed as the nation's first professor of chemistry. Theophilus Grew, professor of mathematics, predicted a solar eclipse and served on the commission that established the boundary between Pennsylvania and Maryland. Benjamin Barton, professor of natural history and botany, won the prestigious Magellanic Premium in 1804, awarded by the American Philosophical Society, of which he was vice president. David Rittenhouse, professor of astronomy, was also a mathematician and instrument maker, and is widely regarded as one of the leading American scientists of the eighteenth century, second only to Benjamin Franklin.

Following the union of college and university in 1791, "It was determined that, besides the charity schools, there should be three departments; those of the arts, of law, and of medicine."[17] In other words, in line with Franklin's vision, the University of Pennsylvania confirmed its commitment to the education of the city's poor children at the very moment of its formal reincorporation.

However, the commitment proved to be more rhetorical than substantive. From its earliest days, and like most other major private institutions, then and now, Penn had been led by trustees who represented Philadelphia's economic and social elite. According to one study, in the years immediately following the Revolution:

> There were twenty-four trustees, of whom three quarters were Anglicans. At least fourteen were wealthy from investments in trade or land or a combination of the two, and many inherited such wealth. Four were lawyers, four physicians, one an ex-clergyman turned to public service and the Indian trade, and one, Benjamin Franklin, was a scientist, inventor, author, and diplomat, as well as a man of business. No fewer than twenty-one held public offices at one time or another; most of them held multiple offices during their lives including many of the highest positions in the provincial government and the municipal government of Philadelphia. Fourteen of the trustees were closely related to

[17] George B. Wood, *Early History of the University of Pennsylvania, From Its Origins to the Year 1827*, 3rd ed., with supplementary chapters by Frederick D. Stone (Philadelphia: J. B. Lippincott Company, 1896 [1827]), 111.

> other trustees, either directly or through their siblings or children.[18]

Perhaps not surprising, given the influence of such individuals, Franklin's conception of education for the poor slowly but inevitably evaporated. The charity school lingered into the second half of the nineteenth century, but the university's energy, planning, capital investments, and fundraising were all directed toward collegiate and professional education. Medicine and law were organized in the late eighteenth century, to be joined over the next decades by engineering, dentistry, and Wharton, the nation's first school of business.

JOHN ANDREWS

John Andrews graduated from the College of Philadelphia in 1765. While still an undergraduate, he served as a tutor in the Academy. Loyal to the Crown, and concerned for his safety in patriotic Philadelphia, Andrews left the city at the start of the Revolutionary War. He settled in western Pennsylvania for the duration of the war, where he opened the first classical school west of the Susquehanna River. The school eventually evolved into the York County Academy. Andrews received the DD degree from Washington College in Maryland in 1785. He returned to Philadelphia in that year and served until 1789 as headmaster of the Academy of the Protestant Episcopal Church of Philadelphia.

In 1789, Andrews resigned from the Episcopal Academy and returned to the College as a professor of moral philosophy and, for twenty years, served as vice provost. In December of 1810, he was unanimously elected the fourth provost of the university, succeeding Dr. John McDowell, who had resigned. Andrews was regarded as one of the greatest classical scholars in the country and was reputed to be a successful and popular teacher. Aside from his many printed sermons, Andrews published some of his addresses to graduating classes in the university. His publications included *Elements of Logic* (1800) and *Elements of Rhetoric and Belles*

[18] Hofstadter and Metzger, *The Development of Academic Freedom*, 150n75.

Lettres (1813), the books that earned his election to the American Philosophical Society in 1786.

One of his pupils, John McAllister, described Andrews as "tall and dignified and courteous, honest in opinions, of good judgment, benevolent, cheerful, and a fine conversationalist."[19] His election as provost confirmed his academic achievements, but it also reflected the conservative tenor of the board in the years after the Revolution. Although his academic career was not as distinguished as those of some of his colleagues, he left a proud record of accomplishment.

Sully's portrait (Figure 12.3), completed not long before Andrews's death, is another example of the artist's mastery. The dark background, together with Andrews's black ministerial robe and sash, draw our attention to the provost's rubicund face, which shows some of the wear and tear of his sixty-seven years. The contrast of dark and light is dramatically accented by the bright-red cape that frames Andrews's face. Wisps of gray hair, along with a slight tilt in his pose, add a homely accent to the handsome portrait.

[19] "John Andrews, 1746–1813," Penn Archives, https://archives.upenn.edu/exhibits/penn-people/biography/john-andrews.

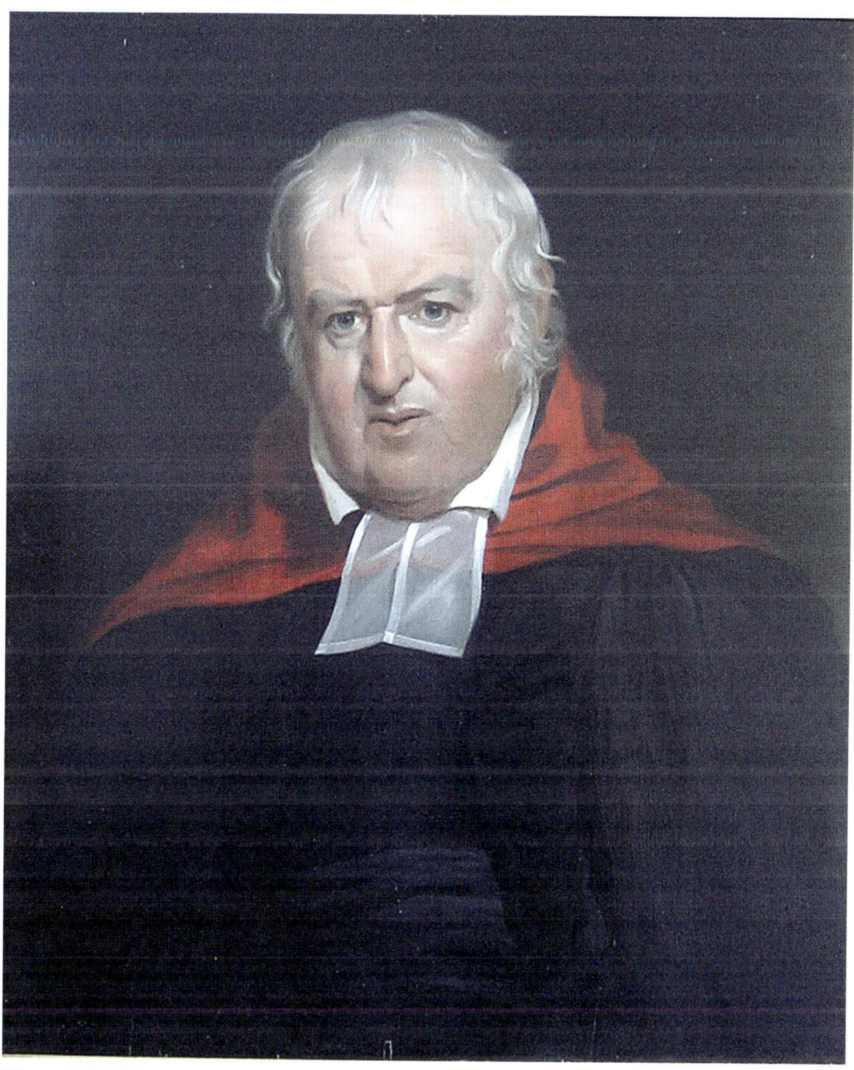

Figure 12.3 *Rev. John Andrews, D.D.*

Courtesy of the University of Pennsylvania Art Collection.

13

The Debate over Slavery

In the late eighteenth and early nineteenth centuries, Philadelphia had the country's largest population of Black people, free and enslaved. Free Black people had lived in Philadelphia since at least as early as 1717, when the Anglican Church recorded the baptism of a free Black woman.[1] The numbers of free Blacks may have reached 250 by 1775. The number of enslaved Black people was much larger, perhaps about 1,400 in the same year. Local census figures recorded that about 16 percent of the city's taxpayers owned enslaved persons.[2] (By contrast, 30 percent of the families in Newport, Rhode Island, home to America's largest slave trading fleet, owned slaves.)[3]

In part because of its Quaker roots, the earliest formal protests against slavery emerged in Philadelphia in the late seventeenth century. In 1688, Francis Daniel Pastorius and three of his fellow Quakers drafted the first anti-slavery resolution in the colonies. The resolution raised objections to slavery on both moral and practical grounds during a period when Pennsylvania Quak-

[1] Edward Raymond Turner, "The Abolition of Slavery in Pennsylvania," *The Pennsylvania Magazine of History and Biography* 36, no. 2 (1912): 132.

[2] These data are tabulated in Gary B. Nash, "Slaves and Slaveowners in Colonial Philadelphia," The *William and Mary Quarterly* 30, no. 2 (April 1973): 223–56.

[3] James Oakes, "Ships Going Out," *The New York Review of Books* (September 21, 2023): 60.

ers were nearly unanimous in their acceptance of the practice.[4] Five years later, the Philadelphia Monthly Meeting released the first printed protest in America against slavery.[5] Although not a Quaker, and the owner of at least two enslaved persons, Benjamin Franklin persuaded the members of the Junto, which he had organized in 1727, to take a stand against slavery.[6]

The Pennsylvania Society for Promoting the Abolition of Slavery, for the Relief of Free Negroes, unlawfully held in Bondage, and for Improving the Condition of the African Race was organized in Philadelphia in 1775. It was the first anti-slavery society in America; one of its founders, the tireless Quaker abolitionist campaigner Anthony Benezet, emerged as the leading figure in the anti-slavery movement. In 1776, he succeeded in convincing the Philadelphia Yearly Meeting to declare that all members who refused to free their slaves would be expelled.

Benezet also worked to secure the passage of the Gradual Abolition Act of 1780, the first more or less comprehensive abolition law in the western hemisphere.[7] "To appease slave owners, the act created a schedule for the emancipation of enslaved people without making slavery immediately illegal. The Act permitted Pennsylvania slaveholders to keep the enslaved individuals they already owned unless they failed to register them annually. At the same time, the Act provided for the eventual freedom of individuals who were newly born into slavery, though these individuals had to wait until they were twenty-eight-years old.[8]

Though it was rightly assailed by anti-slavery activists for caving in to the compromises that pro-slavery legislators de-

---

[4] Among other sources, see "The Journey to Emancipation: The Germantown Protest, 1688," National Museum of African American History & Culture, https://nmaahc.si.edu/explore/stories/journey-emancipation-germantown-protest-1688.

[5] Edward Raymond Turner, "First Abolition Society in the United States," *Pennsylvania Magazine of History and Biography* 36, no. 1 (1912): 92–109.

[6] Merle Curti, *The Growth of American Thought* (New York: Harper & Bros., 1943), 125.

[7] "After [Anthony] Benezet's death [in 1784], Benjamin Rush became the most important liaison between the black community and its white supporters, most of them members of the Pennsylvania Abolition Society." Gary B. Nash, *Forging Freedom: The Formation of Philadelphia's Black Community, 1720–1840* (Cambridge, MA: Harvard University Press, 1988), 41.

[8] For a detailed account of the Act's legislative history and its consequences, see Gary B. Nash and Jean R. Soderlund, *Freedom by Degrees: Emancipation in Pennsylvania and Its Aftermath* (New York: Oxford University Press, 1991).

manded, the Act was important in establishing the principle that Pennsylvania had the authority to regulate and perhaps ultimately abolish slavery in the Commonwealth.[9] And, unlike the British Parliament's 1833 legislation abolishing slavery, the Pennsylvania law provided no compensation for slave holders.

Philadelphia's leading position in abolition activism made it a natural meeting place for national organizations, and "of the twenty-four antislavery conventions held in the United States from 1794 to 1828, twenty were held in Philadelphia. William Lloyd Garrison organized the American Anti-Slavery Society there in 1833."[10] In the same year, a group of Black and white women launched The Philadelphia Female Anti-Slavery Society, the first racially integrated anti-slavery organization.[11] The founding members included Lucretia Mott and Angelina Grimké. In the late 1830s, according to Sean Wilentz, "abolitionism became a genuine popular movement," with membership in the American Anti-Slavery Society reaching three hundred thousand men and women.[12] In Ira Berlin's summary phrase, Philadelphia had become "the world capital of abolition."[13]

However, as Wilentz also acknowledges, the movement attracted more opposition than support, not just in the South, but in the North as well. In Philadelphia, to give the most pertinent example, many of the merchants who depended on the cotton and tobacco produced by enslaved labor supported the slave regime, sometimes tacitly, in other cases vocally. Recall that Philadelphia was the most southern of the northern cities and,

---

[9] One of the rancorous debates that divided antebellum abolitionists pitted the gradualists against the immediatists, who insisted that the moral outrage of slavery should be extinguished at once.

[10] Elizabeth M. Geffen, "Violence in Philadelphia in the 1840's and 1850's," *Pennsylvania History: A Journal of Mid-Atlantic Studies* 36, no. 4 (October 1969): 383.

[11] Emily Hatcher, "The Philadelphia Female Anti-Slavery Society and the Civil War," *The Pennsylvania Magazine of History and Biography* 135, no. 4 (October 2011): 528.

[12] Sean Wilentz, *The Rise of American Democracy: Jefferson to Lincoln* (New York: W. W. Norton, 2005), 403.

[13] Ira Berlin, "Slavery, Freedom, and Philadelphia's Struggle for Brotherly Love, 1685 to 1861," in *Antislavery and Abolition in Philadelphia: Emancipation and the Long Struggle for Racial Justice in the City of Brotherly* Love, eds. Richard Newman and James Mueller (Baton Rouge: Louisiana State University Press, 2011), 19.

as several historians have pointed out, many families in the city had Southern relatives.

Abolitionist agitation proved to be one cause, among many, for the frequent and often vicious attacks on Philadelphia's Black residents in the early nineteenth century. Black people found themselves confronted by the rising immigration of Irish Catholics, who saw Blacks as competitors for jobs in a city beset by widespread unemployment during the periodic hard times of the 1820s and 1830s. Eighteenth-century white tolerance, even sometimes sympathy, was replaced by nineteenth-century hostility.[14] At least "six large-scale race riots targeted Black people between 1829 and 1854."[15] Thousands were injured, and hundreds died.

The mobs that attacked Philadelphia's Black people insisted on their patriotism, often invoking the Sons of Liberty and the Minute Men of the 1770s as their antecedents. The men who led the bloody assaults of 1835 re-enacted the Boston Tea Party, tearing up hundreds of abolitionist pamphlets and throwing the pieces into the Delaware River.[16]

The year 1838 witnessed a double assault on the lives and dignity of Philadelphia's Black people. The state's Constitutional Convention added the word *white* to the list of qualifications for voting and thus, with the stroke of a pen, disenfranchised free Black men of a right they had been able to exercise since 1790.

And in May of that year, a mob of enraged white men destroyed Pennsylvania Hall, a large and handsome building opened as a meeting place for abolitionists to convene. Sarah Forten had led a fundraising effort that raised over $40,000 for the building's construction. At the inaugural session, just a few days after the hall opened, Angelina Grimké was speaking to an auditorium filled with hundreds of white and Black men and women. A mob of white men broke into the hall and set it ablaze (Figure 13.1). No lives were lost, but Pennsylvania Hall was completely demol

---

[14] W. E. B. Du Bois, *The Philadelphia Negro: A Social Study* (Philadelphia: University of Pennsylvania Press, 1996 [1899]), 26–31.

[15] Priscilla Ferguson, *Welfare and the Poor in the Nineteenth-Century City: Philadelphia, 1800–1854* (Madison, NJ: Fairleigh Dickinson University Press, 1985), 33.

[16] Leonard L. Richards, *"Gentlemen of Property and Standing": Anti-Abolition Mobs in Jacksonian America* (New York: Oxford University Press, 1970), 69.

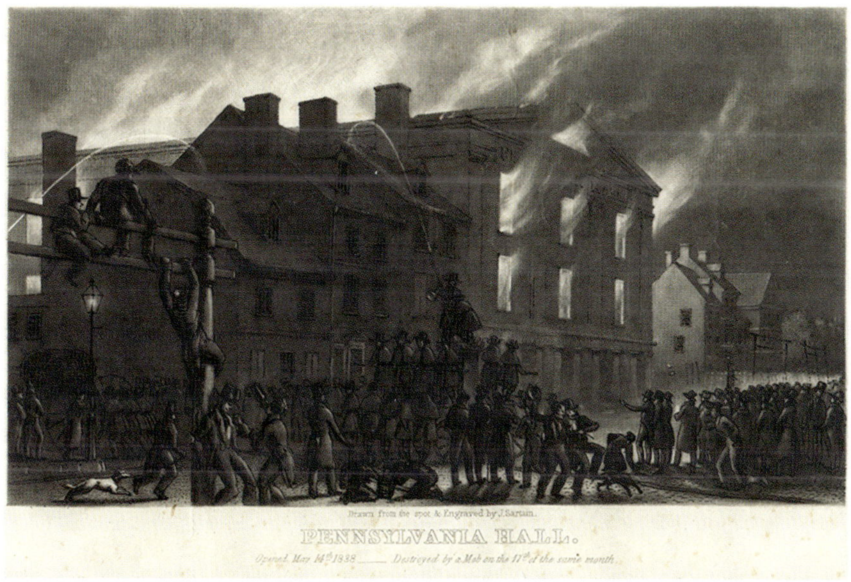

Figure 13.1 This print of the destruction of Pennsylvania Hall was produced and published by the artist John Sartain, who was an eyewitness to the fire.

Courtesy of the Historical Society of Pennsylvania Collection.

ished.[17] For Black people in Philadelphia, the arc of history seemed to be bending inexorably backward.

After 1835 or thereabouts, in spite of the heroic efforts of men and women, such as David Walker, the Grimké sisters, Frederick Douglass, William Lloyd Garrison, and Sojourner Truth, the abolitionist cause was losing influence and stamina. The combined opposition of violent thugs and pro-slavery politicians seemed sadly to confirm the despairing opinion that anti-slavery activism brought more pain than progress to Black people.[18]

---

[17] Among the many accounts of this event, one of the most vivid will be found in the History Making Production film, "Disorder: 1820–1854," an episode in the series *Philadelphia: The Great Experiment*, https://www.youtube.com/watch?v=lTOUquhPKWc&list=PLwEWxvgiPVsXPeZVV0erTz83OyYjD8yjF&index=6.

[18] Presumably in response to the ubiquitous and continuous violence Blacks suffered in the 1830s and 1840s, Philadelphia's Black population declined from 1840 to 1850. Du Bois, *The Philadelphia Negro*, 28–30.

In addition, beginning in the 1810s, the movement also found itself competing with a quite different response to America's racial conflicts. The American Colonization Society (ACS) emerged out of decades of intermittent discussion among both Northern and Southern politicians, journalists, and clergymen. The most significant of the precursors of ACS was Thomas Jefferson, who often and eloquently denounced slavery as a "moral depravity" and a "hideous blot," but neither freed his own enslaved Black people, nor supported emancipation. He reasoned that the ineradicable differences between the white and free Black populations would lead to ceaseless conflict. The best course, accordingly, would be to separate the two groups, removing free Black people to some distant and unspecified location, perhaps in the western territories of America, perhaps in Haiti or Africa.[19]

After gestating for years, the idea of colonization was brought to organizational birth in 1816 by an energetic Presbyterian clergyman named Robert Finley, director of the Princeton Theological Seminary. He yearned to demonstrate his benevolence, decided on colonization, and quickly gathered both financial and political support. Among the great and the good who endorsed the scheme were Francis Scott Key, the author of "The Star-Spangled Banner"; Dr. Lyman Beecher, celebrated Presbyterian theologian and reformer; Bushrod Washington, George's nephew and an associate justice of the US Supreme Court; former president James Madison; and the incumbent president, James Monroe. Aside from Monroe, the ACS's most prominent political ally was Henry Clay, Speaker of the House for three terms between 1811 and 1825, who would serve as ACS president from 1836 to 1849. Abraham Lincoln, too, endorsed the project until the middle of the Civil War.

Slaveholders were among the most vocal supporters. Local branches emerged in every state; by 1832, there were 105 local societies in northern states, and 251 in the South.[20] The Pennsylvania Colonization Society was established in 1826. Churchmen

[19] The organized colonization project was preceded by the efforts of Paul Cuffe, a Boston ship owner of Native American and African parentage. In 1815, a group of free Blacks took passage with him to Freetown, Sierra Leone. Cuffe died two years later.

[20] Margaret Hope Bacon, "Quakers and Colonization," *Quaker History* 95, no. 1 (Spring 2006): 29.

were particularly rapturous in their messages, one of them referring to ACS as "a most glorious Christian enterprise."[21] In 1819, the federal government appropriated $100,000 to support the cause, an enormous sum at that date, and at a time of economic disruption nationally. That money, along with contributions from hundreds of individual donors, launched the Society's project. In negotiations that were almost certainly coercive, ACS secured the rights to large parcels of territory in West Africa, carving out a state that would eventually be called *Liberia.* In February 1820, the first ship carried ACS agents and 86 Black emigrants to the place.[22]

According to Sean Wilentz, the American Colonization Society "merged two distinct, and in some ways contradictory, points of view: a philanthropic antislavery reformism that aimed to eliminate slavery gradually and allow the ex-slaves the chance to return [*sic*] voluntarily to Africa, and second, a growing fear among slaveholders that the nation's two hundred thousand free blacks were potential fomenters of slave rebellion."[23]

In fact, the founders and supporters of the campaign acted out of a wide range of motives. Some were undoubtedly sincere in believing that Africa could offer a better alternative than the slavery of the South and the lethal bigotry that both northern and southern whites shared. Others, especially some of the clergy, saw the Black emigrants as engines of religious conversion, bringing the saving grace of Christianity to the benighted African natives. Still others endorsed the project in economic terms, anticipating increased trading opportunities across the Atlantic. And some were moved strictly by racial hatred. Henry Clay declared that the transportation of Black people to Africa would rid our country of "a useless and pernicious, if not a dangerous portion of its population."[24]

---

[21] Benjamin Platt Thomas, *Theodore Weld, Crusader for Freedom* (New Brunswick, NJ: Rutgers University Press, 1950), 277.

[22] Among the dozens of books devoted in whole or part to the colonization project, Eric Burin's *Slavery and the Peculiar Solution: A History of the American Colonization Society* (Gainesville: University Press of Florida, 2005) provides the most thoughtful and thorough account.

[23] Wilentz, *The Rise of American Democracy*, 331. I have inserted [*sic*] after "return" because few if any of the intended voluntary emigrants would have been born in Africa.

[24] Cited in Henry Louis Gates Jr., ed., *Lincoln on Race and Slavery* (Princeton, NJ: Princeton University Press, 2009), 31.

Although colonization initially attracted the attention of free Black Americans, the movement eventually provoked their almost universal rejection. In January 1817, in a famous meeting at Richard Allen's Mother Bethel Church on South Sixth Street in Philadelphia, shouts of "No!" met the proposal that Black people embrace colonization. The influential Black businessman James Forten, who had supported the project for several years, turned defiantly and eloquently against it. America, he declared, where he had been born and lived his life, was his only home.[25]

Colonization propaganda met its most outspoken opposition in a belligerent, relentless, two-hundred-and-forty-page book published by William Lloyd Garrison in 1832 (Figure 13.2). *Thoughts on African Colonization* argued that, despite whatever humanitarian claims made in its defense, the project was in fact a tool of proslavery interests. It was, he wrote, in an aria of invective, "a creature without heart, without brains, eyeless, unnatural, hypocritical, relentless, unjust."[26] Along with his scathing moral accusations, Garrison underlined the sheer stupidity of the scheme: The idea of transporting hundreds of thousands of men, women, and children across three thousand miles of ocean, settling them in a place they had never seen, was nothing more than a fever dream.

In 1833, the Quaker poet and abolitionist John Greenleaf Whittier published a pamphlet, *Justice and Expediency*, in which he wrote that since the founding of ACS a decade-and-a-half earlier, only about six hundred manumitted slaves had been sent to Africa; in those same years, "nearly one million human beings have died in slavery."[27]

By the 1840s, the American Colonization Society was in decline.[28] It would linger on paper until its formal dissolution in the 1960s (not a typo), but it was a spent force more than a

---

[25] For the most detailed account of Black Philadelphians' response to the colonization movement, see Julie Winch, *A Gentleman of Color: The Life of James Forten* (New York: Oxford University Press, 2002).

[26] William Lloyd Garrison, *Thoughts on African Colonization* (Boston: Garrison and Knaff, 1832), 11.

[27] John Greenleaf Whittier, "Justice and Expediency," in *Anti-Slavery Reporter* 1, no. 4 (September 1833): 52.

[28] The movement continued to find influential support, most famously from Harriet Beecher Stowe. Near the conclusion of *Uncle Tom's Cabin* (1852), George Harris and his family leave America, moving first to Canada, then France, and finally to Liberia.

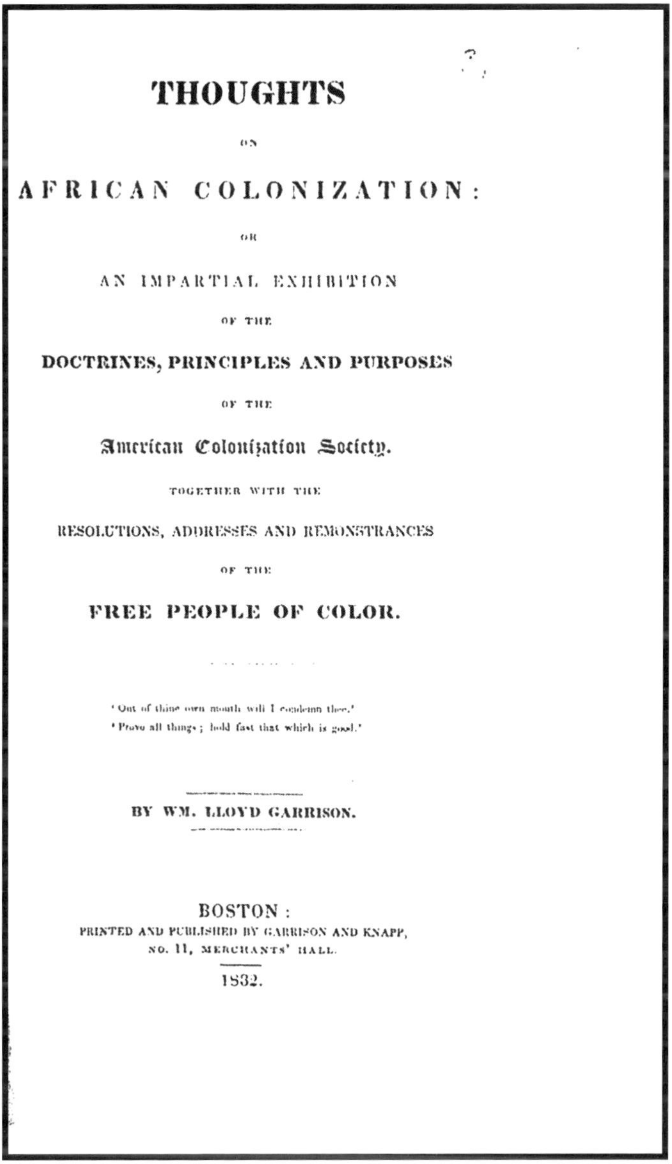

THOUGHTS

ON

AFRICAN COLONIZATION:

OR

AN IMPARTIAL EXHIBITION

OF THE

DOCTRINES, PRINCIPLES AND PURPOSES

OF THE

American Colonization Society.

TOGETHER WITH THE

RESOLUTIONS, ADDRESSES AND REMONSTRANCES

OF THE

FREE PEOPLE OF COLOR.

'Out of thine own mouth will I condemn thee.'
'Prove all things; hold fast that which is good.'

BY WM. LLOYD GARRISON.

BOSTON:
PRINTED AND PUBLISHED BY GARRISON AND KNAPP,
NO. 11, MERCHANTS' HALL.

1832.

Figure 13.2 Title page of William Lloyd Garrison's *Thoughts on African Colonization.*

century earlier. In the eighty-two years between its founding and 1899, fewer than sixteen thousand colonists had moved to Liberia. In those years, "many more black Americans in search of a better life would move to Canada than to Liberia."[29]

WILLIAM HENRY FURNESS

In 1872, William Still published *The Underground Railroad*, which remains the most significant source of information about the activities of that legendary anti-slavery enterprise. Still, the corresponding secretary of the Railroad's Vigilance Committee offered this opinion of the anti-slavery exertions of the Unitarian minister William Furness: "Among the abolitionists of Pennsylvania no man stands higher than Doctor Furness and no antislavery minister enjoys more universal respect. For more than thirty years he bore faithful witness for the black man, in season and out of season, contending for his rights. When others deserted the cause he stayed firm; when associates in the ministry were silent he spoke out."[30]

Furness served as minister of Philadelphia's First Unitarian Church from 1825, when he was still in his twenties, to 1875, and as senior pastor until his death in 1896 at the age of ninety-three. Unitarians were regarded with moderate to active hostility by other Protestants, who charged that the Unitarian rejection of the trinity insulted the divinity of Jesus. (Unitarians were sometimes condemned as "deists.") Comprising a small congregation when Furness arrived, membership in the church more than doubled during the decades of his leadership.

He was passionate in his devotion to Jesus, about whom he wrote several books, but impatient with the dogmatic and humorless pronouncements of many of his clerical contemporar-

---

[29] Daniel Walker Howe, *What Hath God Wrought: The Transformation of America, 1815–1848* (New York: Oxford University Press, 2007), 266.

[30] Cited in Elizabeth M. Geffen, "William Henry Furness: Philadelphia Antislavery Preacher," *The Pennsylvania Magazine of History and Biography* 82, no. 3 (July 1958): 259.

ies.[31] He was good company, and his friendships extended ecumenically. As I mentioned earlier, Rebecca Gratz admired Furness's generosity and saw a likeness between Unitarianism and her own Jewish beliefs. She often attended Furness's sermons and grew close both to him and his wife.[32]

Furness and Ralph Waldo Emerson, friends since childhood, sustained a warm correspondence that lasted for decades. They touched on many subjects, their shared opposition to slavery among them.[33] The correspondence is the record of a mutual admiration society. Furness repeatedly saluted Emerson as the finest thinker and writer in the country. For his part, Emerson summarized his feelings about Furness in a letter to one of his daughters: "The minister," he wrote, "has a face like a benediction, and a speech like a benefaction, and his stories are more curative than the Phila. Faculty of Medicine."[34]

The letters Furness and Emerson exchanged were by turns serious and mordantly funny. This from Furness to Emerson, just before the General Conference of the Methodist Church in September 1859: The Methodist Church faces "a serious time," Furness wrote. Many delegates to the conference will vote to declare slavery a sin. "Think of it! A majority of a Christian body in this age and country will probably adjudge slavery to be a sin." And this, from Furness, in the middle of the Civil War: "I wonder

---

[31] Furness maintained an ecumenical outlook through the five decades of his Unitarian pastorate. In a "discourse" on the fiftieth anniversary of his Philadelphia ministry, he insisted that "it is not all bearing the same religious name but all bearing different religious names and yet each respecting in others the right of everyone to think for himself—this is what illustrates most impressively the broad spirit of our common Christianity." *Exercises at the Meeting of the First Congregational Unitarian Society, January 12, 1875: Together with the Discourse Delivered by Rev. W. H. Furness, Sunday, Jan. 10, 1875, on the Occasion of the Fiftieth Anniversary of his Ordination, January 12, 1825* (Philadelphia: Sherman & Co., 1875), 13–14.

[32] Dianne Ashton, *Rebecca Gratz: Women and Judaism in Antebellum America* (Detroit: Wayne State University Press, 1997), 98.

[33] Emerson's "Emancipation of the Negroes in the British West Indies," a two-hour speech delivered in Concord on August 1, 1844, "remains his most extensive and most important anti-slavery statement." Len Gougeon, "Militant Abolitionism: Douglass, Emerson, and the Rise of the Anti-Slave," *The New England Quarterly* 85, no. 4 (December 2012): 622.

[34] Horace Howard Furness, ed., *Records of a Lifelong Friendship, 1807–1882: Ralph Waldo Emerson and William Henry Furness* (Boston: Houghton Mifflin Company, 1910), 132.

at the taste of the Upper Powers in tolerating such monstrous stupidity in mankind. Just think of the New England folks petitioning Congress to let the Negro alone. Petition the mouse under the cat's paw to let the cat alone."[35]

For the first two decades of his ministry, Furness was moderate in his comments on slavery. Starting in 1839, however, and almost certainly in reaction to the burning of Pennsylvania Hall, he became increasingly outspoken. From then until the end of the Civil War, Furness preached relentlessly, eloquently, and controversially on the evils of slavery. Some members of his congregation objected, some petitioned for his removal, some abandoned the Church. He never backed down, and most of his congregation remained loyal.[36]

Furness was enraged by the Fugitive Slave Act of 1850, and especially by the inability or unwillingness of Philadelphia's citizens and officials to resist the law's enforcement. His vocal opposition to the law, and his repeated promise that he would disobey it, brought federal scrutiny. There were reports that President Buchanan had consulted with his Cabinet about the possibility of indicting Furness for treason.[37]

Although scholars have often referred to Furness's oratorical power, his sermons are rarely quoted extensively, and often not at all. Here is one example, from a sermon he delivered in May 1854, continuing his attack on the Fugitive Slave Act. His method, as with all Protestant preaching, is to move from a biblical text to the lessons that the text conveys. Christ told his disciples: "Feed my lambs. Feed my sheep."

> Who are the lambs! Who are his sheep! Behold that great multitude, more than three millions of men and feeble women and children wandering on our soil,—no, not wandering, but chained down, not allowed to stir a step at their own free will,

---

[35] These are among the letters exchanged by Furness and Emerson in the University of Pennsylvania Archives, Ms. Coll 1356.

[36] The merchant Joseph Sill was among Furness's strongest supporters. His diary refers to scores of the minister's sermons on slavery. In each entry, Sill provides a summary of the sermon's contents, after which he usually adds a comment, almost invariably positive. On November 25, 1849, for example, Furness argued that slavery was not merely a political issue; it was "connected with our highest and holiest feelings." Sill's response: "I thought his views perfectly sound and good." Joseph Sill, *Diary*, vol. 9, Pennsylvania Historical Society, Mss. collection # 600, p. 104.

[37] Geffen, "William Henry Furness," 287.

> crushed and hunted, with all the power of one of the mightiest nations that the world has yet seen wielded to keep them down in the depths of the deepest degradation into which human beings can be plunged. These that we despise are our neighbors, the poor stricken lambs of Christ.[38]

The sermon continues at this pitch of intensity, for about forty-five minutes.

Completed in 1830, shortly after Furness began his service as minister of the First Unitarian Church, Sully's portrait (Figure 13.3) presents a young, serious, and confident man. No flattery was necessary: According to Elizabeth Geffen, "he was impressive in stature, graceful in bearing, with a handsome face and a wonderfully winning smile."[39] As with so many of Sully's portraits, in this the subject is animated and lively: Furness seems to be engaged in a conversation—as he so frequently was. He gestures casually with his right hand, the curled fingers leading us up through the bright white V of his waistcoat to that attractive face.

Sully and Furness were close friends for two decades, and Furness makes frequent appearances in Sully's *Journal.* Sully, a member and sometime trustee of the Unitarian Church, records that on "August 4, 1828, Last Sunday, 27th, I borrowed a M.S. sermon from Mr. Furness." On January 16, 1837: "Last Sunday sent Furness anonymously $10 to distribute to charity." December 4, 1838: "Attended a lecture of genius by Rev'd Furness, delivered for the Franklin Institute."

However, Sully eventually ended the friendship over the issue of slavery. On June 21, 1846, Sully writes, "I can no longer go to our Church; Mr. Furness has driven me away with his abolition sermons."

BENJAMIN COATES

In 1835 or thereabouts, the twenty-something Quaker Benjamin Coates (1808–87) became active in both the Pennsylvania Aboli-

[38] W. H. Furness, "Christian duty," in *Three Discourses Delivered in the First Congregational Unitarian Church of Philadelphia May 28th, June 4th and June 11th, 1854, with Reference to the Recent Execution of the Fugitive Slave law in Boston and New York* (Philadelphia: Merrihew & Thompson's Steam Power Press, 1854), 8.

[39] Geffen, "William Henry Furness," 262.

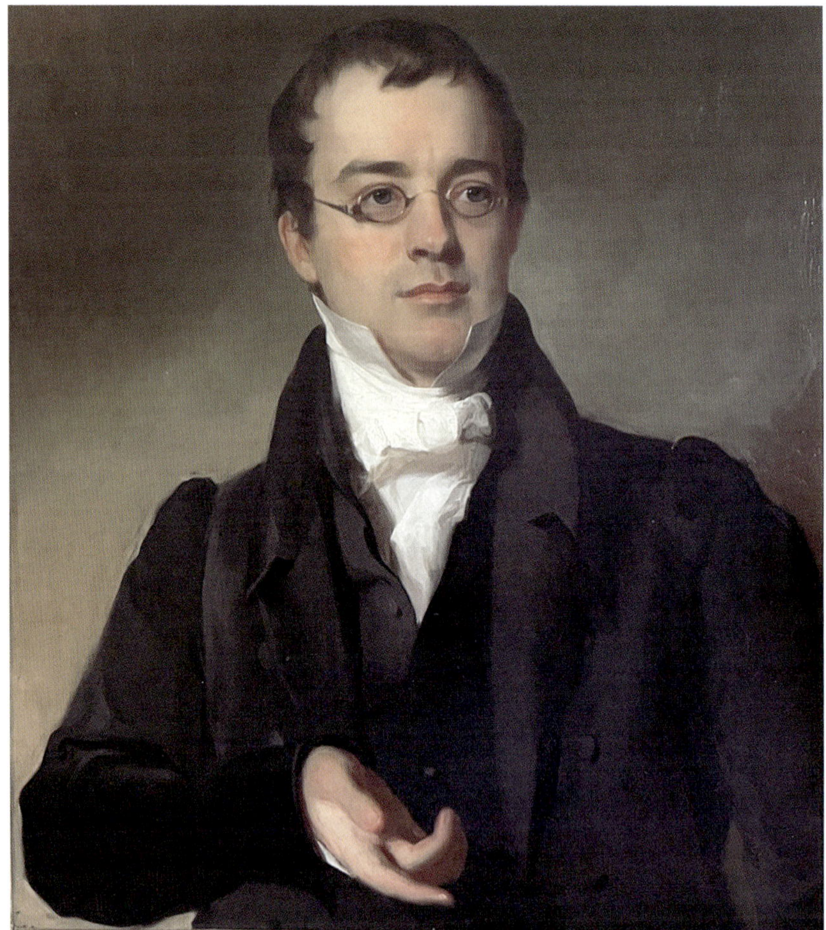

Figure 13.3 *William Henry Furness.*

Private collection.

tion Society (PAS) and the ACS.[40] The rising young merchant, who dealt in cotton goods, was already troubled by the conflict between his anti-slavery sentiments and his reliance on the en-

[40] Coates's multiple allegiances were not unusual. Several scholars have traced the overlapping memberships of Pennsylvania's several anti-slavery organizations. Coates would eventually become a vice president of both of these groups.

slaved labor that underwrote his prosperity. As a resident of Philadelphia in the 1830s, he was surrounded by a city embroiled in both nonstop and often furious debate over slavery and violence, much of it directed against Black residents.

Emma Lapansky-Werner and Margaret Bacon describe Coates's moral dilemma: "As southern cotton crop prices rose to more than half the dollar value of American exports, Coates's struggle to separate his own need for cotton from the brutality of the slavery that produced it became almost an obsession."[41]

Coates had become engaged in charitable work some years earlier, when he joined the Union Benevolent Association. Founded by businessmen in 1831, the Union provided food, fuel, and clothing to the poor of both races while educating them to become self-supporting.[42] Education for the poor would remain one of Coates's philanthropic concerns. When Philadelphia Quakers opened the Institute for Colored Youth, Coates quickly joined the effort and remained an active member until the 1870s.

Throughout his long life, Coates devoted most of his energy and fundraising to African colonization. An orthodox Quaker, he was opposed to violence, and stayed clear of immediatist abolitionism. For him, colonization offered a different and peaceful pathway to Black emancipation. Those more confrontational abolitionists, including Garrison as we have seen, denounced colonization as a crutch for slavers to lean on rather than a strategy for the elimination of slavery. Coates summed up his contrary view in a sentence he frequently used: "A thorough abolitionist could not be such without being a colonizationist."[43]

In 1854, Coates laid out his defense of colonization in a short book, *Cultivation of Cotton in Africa in Reference to the Abolition of Slavery in the United States*. The title page of this twenty-eight-page pamphlet identifies Coates's intended audience: "the friends of

---

[41] Emma J. Lapsansky-Werner and Margaret Hope Bacon, eds., *Back to Africa: Benjamin Coates and the Colonization Movement in America, 1848–1880* (University Park: Pennsylvania State University Press, 2005), 3.

[42] Now under Black leadership, the Union continues to provide financial support to impoverished Philadelphians of all races.

[43] Beverly C. Tomek, *Colonization and Its Discontents: Emancipation, Emigration, and Antislavery in Antebellum Pennsylvania* (New York: New York University Press, 2010). Tomek uses the sentence as the title of her excellent chapter on Coates.

emigration among the colored population of the northern states." More specific, in the opening pages of the essay, Coates calls on "the intelligent and energetic among the free colored population of the United States" to embrace his vision.[44] In the following pages, Coates summarizes the arguments that he had been making for two decades.

Black Americans who moved to Africa would free themselves from the oppression that all of them, both enslaved and free, experienced. They would enjoy opportunities for leadership, opportunities denied to all Black people in America. They would take their place as equals among the nations of the world. Their cotton production—Coates was convinced that West African climate and soil would support superior cotton production—would accomplish two goals: It would underpin the Liberian economy, priced more cheaply than American cotton, and it would undermine slavery by outcompeting the plantation system of the South. Finally, Coates contended that Black Americans who emigrated to Africa would bring with them both Christianity and—a synonym for Coates—civilization.

The book attracted some attention internationally. One of its readers, Henry Harland Garnet, a Black New York minister, publicized Coates's ideas and joined in his emigration efforts. Joseph Jenkins Roberts, an emigrant who became Liberia's first president when the country declared its independence in 1847, corresponded with Coates for over twenty years, from 1848 to 1869. When Roberts visited Philadelphia during those years, he stayed at Coates's home.[45] On the other hand, Coates's repeated overtures to Frederick Douglass were consistently rejected.

When the eighty-year-old Sully completed this elegant portrait of Benjamin Coates (Figure 13.4) in 1863, he was serving as one of the several vice presidents of the Pennsylvania Colonization Society. Sully's *Register* includes fifteen PCS portraits, all of them donated to the African Colonization Gallery, housed in a building at 609 Walnut Street. Along with Coates, the subjects included James Washington Lugenbeel, a physician who went to

[44] Coates's focus on the Black elite anticipates, though it did not directly influence, W. E. B. Du Bois's early reliance on "the talented tenth" as the engine of African American progress.
[45] Lapsansky-Werner and Bacon, eds., *Back to Africa*, 21.

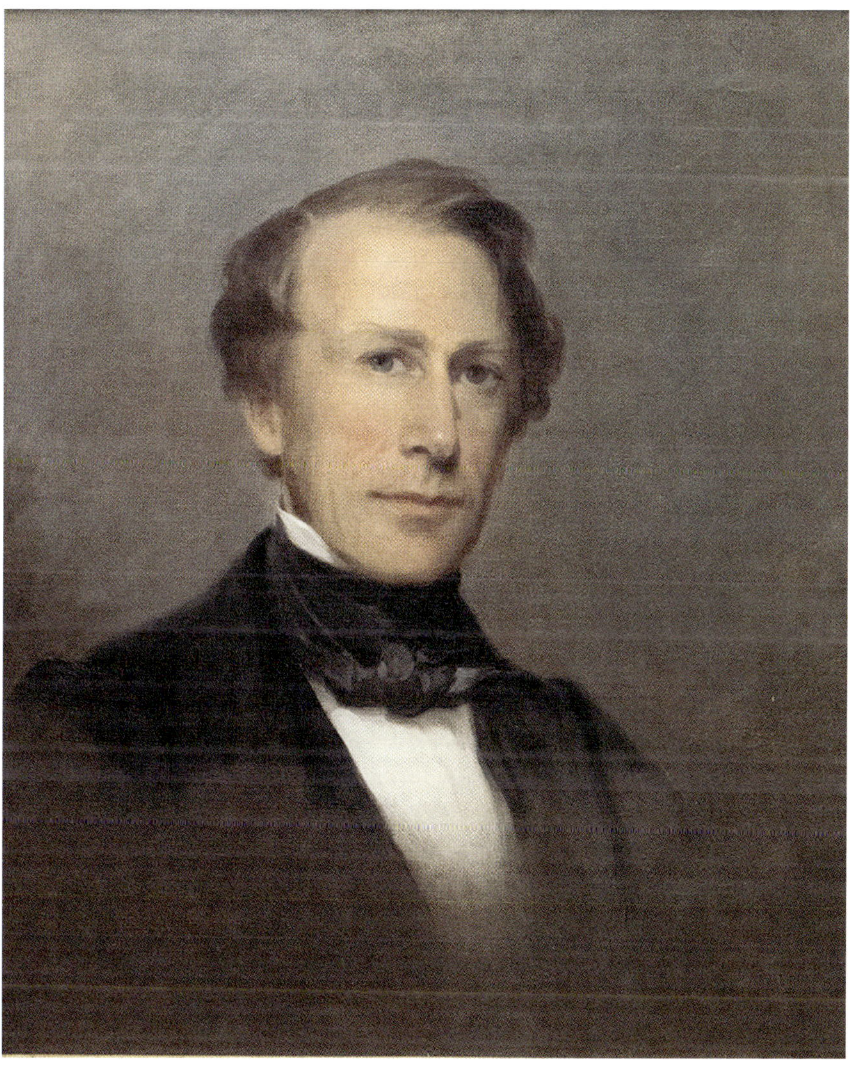

Figure 13.4 *Benjamin Coates.*

Courtesy of the Philadelphia History Museum at the Atwater Kent/courtesy of Historical Society of Pennsylvania Collection/Bridgeman Images.

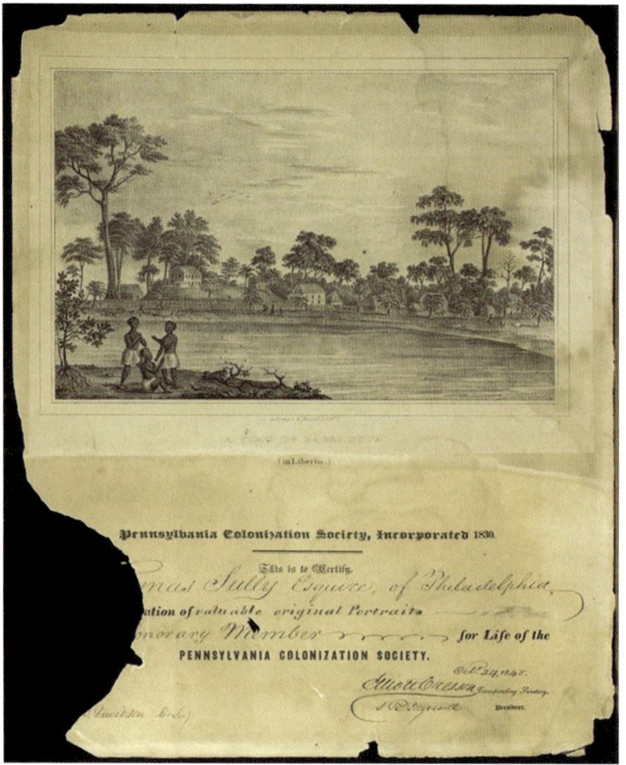

Figure 13.5 Sully's certificate of lifetime membership in the Pennsylvania Colonization Society.

Liberia; Margaret Mercer, a Maryland woman who freed her slaves and sent them to Liberia; and Mrs. Lydia H. Sigourney, a widely published Connecticut poet. An essay in *The African Repository and Colonial Journal,* published in January 1866, salutes the collection as "a perfect gallery of those eminent in the foundation and growth of African Colonization and Liberia."[46]

Sully was awarded this certificate (Figure 13.5), with its image of Bassa Cove in Liberia, when he was granted a lifetime membership in the Pennsylvania Colonization Society. The certificate was issued in 1848.

[46] *The African Repository and Colonial Journal* (Washington, DC: Colonization Society Building, January 1866), 20–21.

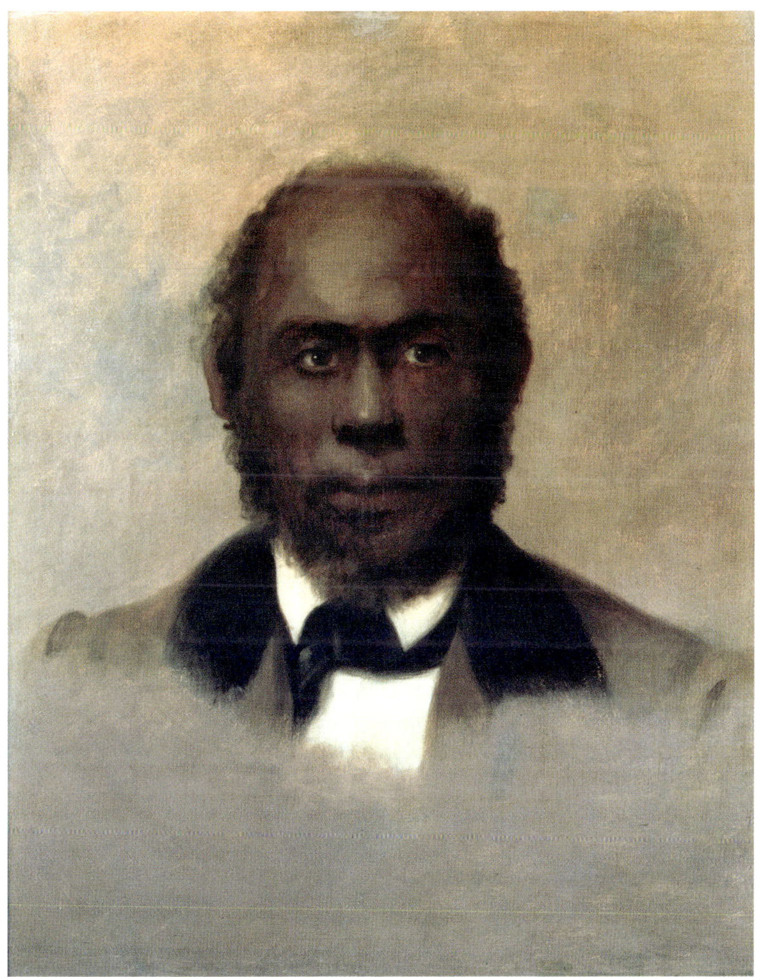

Figure 13.6 *Daniel Bashiel Warner.*

Courtesy of Philadelphia History Museum at the Atwater Kent/courtesy of Historical Society of Pennsylvania Collection.

DANIEL BASHIEL WARNER AND EDWARD JAMES ROYE

Sully's portraits of Daniel Bashiel Warner (Figure 13.6) and Edward James Roye (Figure 13.7), both completed in 1864, are two

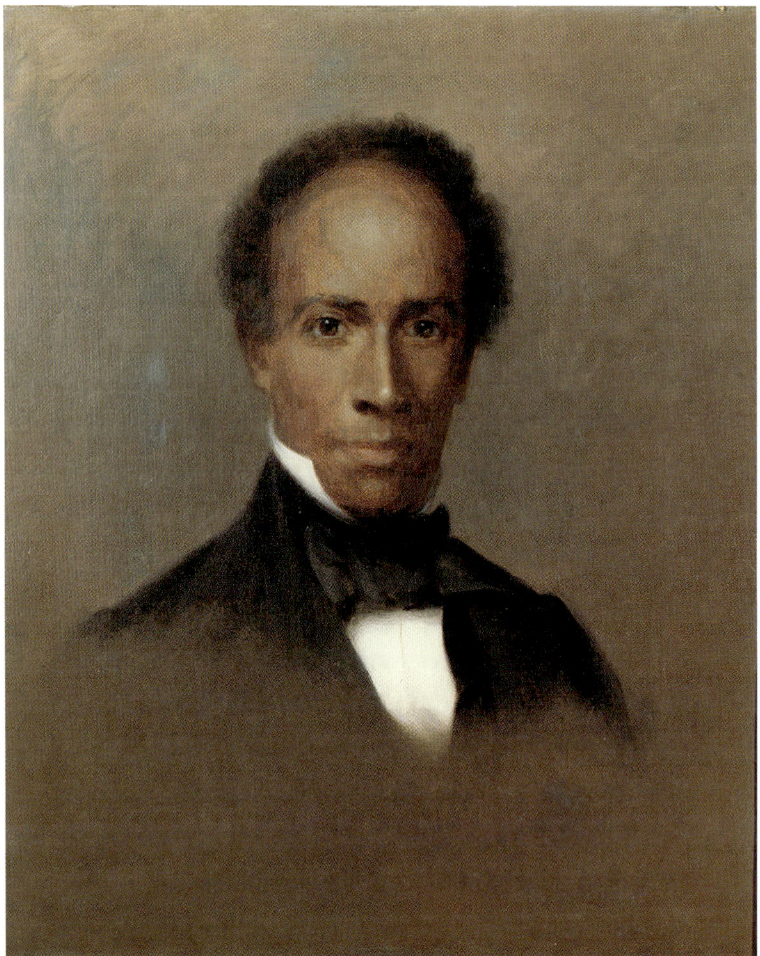

Figure 13.7 *Edward James Roye.*
Courtesy of Philadelphia History Museum at the Atwater Kent/courtesy of Historical Society of Pennsylvania Collection.

of the three known likenesses of Black subjects in the artist's oeuvre.[47]

Daniel Bashiel Warner (1815–80) served as the third president of Liberia from 1864 to 1868. Prior to this, he served as the

[47] A Black man named William Lee, George Washington's enslaved valet during the Revolutionary War, is included in the group of men around the general in Sully's *The Passage of the Delaware.* Sully called the painting "a historical portrait."

third secretary of state in the Cabinet of Joseph Jenkins Roberts from 1854 to 1856 and the fifth vice president of Liberia under President Stephen Allen Benson from 1860 to 1864.

Edward James Roye (1815–72) served as the fifth president of Liberia from 1870 to his overthrow in 1871 and subsequent death. He had previously served as the fourth chief justice of Liberia from 1865 until 1868.

There is no evidence that either Daniel Warner or Edward Roye ever set foot in Philadelphia. In his *Register,* Sully records that the portraits were based on photographs taken in New York and given to him by the Colonization Society.[48]

[48] The daguerreotype of Edward James Roye on which Sully almost certainly based his portrait can be found in the Prints and Photographs division of the Library of Congress, https://tile.loc.gov/storage-services/service/pnp/cph/3g00000/3g03000/3g03500/3g03594r.jpg.

14

Epilogue: Thomas Sully and His Critics

THIS PROJECT GREW OUT OF MY interest in the history of Early National Philadelphia and in Thomas Sully's portraits. Beyond that, I also hope to underscore the strengths of Sully's paintings. To be sure, he has not been neglected in histories of American art. On the first pages of this book's introductory chapter, I quoted several strong statements attesting to his talent. I could have included others.

After reading scores of the essays and reviews of Sully's work published over the past two centuries, however, I have concluded that Sully has often been misrepresented, both by his admirers (the majority) and his critics. Specifically, a substantial share of those notices assert that Sully's reputation derives primarily from his portraits of women. The comments that follow often lean toward condescension. Sully's son-in-law John Neagle "divid[ed] the best patronage with Sully, who 'painted the pretty women,' while Neagle saw to 'the virile men.'"[1] "His delicate pencil has for years been employed in portraying that peculiar type of female

[1] C. H. Collins Baker, review of H. L. Ehrich and W. L. Ehrich, *One Hundred Early American Paintings*, *The Burlington Magazine for Connoisseurs* 35, no. 197 (August 1919): 82–83.

beauty which is identified with Philadelphia."[2] "His women were almost uniformly insipid, idealized, and pretty."[3]

Many of Sully's portraits of women are in fact superb, demonstrating both his technical skill and his emotional power. In my view, however, most of Sully's best pictures, including quite a few in this book, are those that populate his gallery of male subjects.[4] Here are two more.

JONATHAN WILLIAMS

Jonathan Williams, whose portrait (Figure 14.1) Sully completed in 1815, has a place in my account of Philadelphia, if admittedly only edgewise, since he lived for just a few years in the city. He was born in 1750 in Boston. In 1770, after attending Harvard College, he went to London to learn about the ways of business from his great-uncle, Benjamin Franklin. He later served as Franklin's private secretary in Paris, where he also studied military engineering. Later Williams served as a commercial agent in Nantes. In the course of that assignment, his fractious relations with another agent, William Lee, each accusing the other of malfeasance, led to a duel in 1779, from which both men emerged unscathed.[5]

Williams returned to the United States with Franklin in 1785. His scientific publications earned him election to the American Philosophical Society in 1787; he would later serve APS as secretary, vice president, and councillor. In 1799, he published *Thermometric Navigation,* which remained a reference work for decades. Several of his publications appeared in the Transactions of the American Philosophical Society. During his residence in Philadel-

---

[2] Henry T. Tuckerman, "Art in America," *Cosmopolitan Art Journal* 3, no. 1 (December 1858): 2.

[3] Robert Hughes, *American Visions: The Epic History of Art in America* (New York: Alfred A. Knopf, 1997), 130. See also, among many others, Robert William Torchia, *American Paintings of the Nineteenth Century, Part II* (Washington, DC, National Gallery of Art, 1998), 136–137.

[4] I should add this qualification. Neither I nor any other writer who has offered opinions about Sully's work has ever seen more than a fraction of those two thousand portraits. Most of them have disappeared, some into family and other private collections, more into oblivion.

[5] Biographical information is taken from *American National Biography*, the Member History of the American Philosophical Society, and the United States Military Academy.

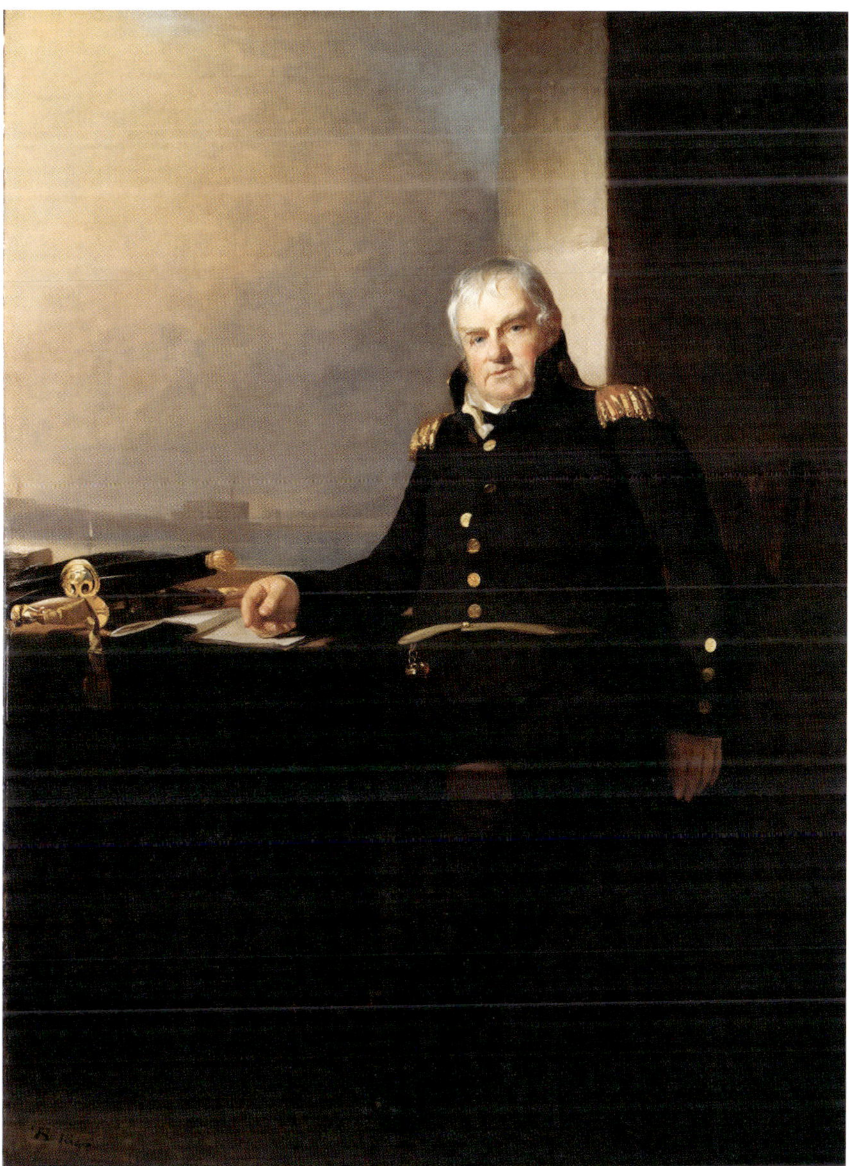

Figure 14.1 *Portrait of Colonel Jonathan Williams (1750–1815).*

Courtesy of the Philadelphia Museum of Art.

phia, he also served as a judge in Philadelphia's Court of Common Pleas.

In 1801, President Jefferson named Williams the first superintendent of West Point, with the rank of lieutenant colonel; a year later, Williams was also appointed the first commander of the Army Corp of Engineers. In September 1810, Williams sent a long letter to Jefferson, telling the former President: "I could not deny myself showing you another instance of the usefulness of the thermometer in navigation. When science comes in aid of humanity, it must be particularly pleasing to you." In fact, the letter is mainly taken up with Williams's complaints about disappointing developments at West Point: "I wish I could make your influence advantageous to the military academy: you planted it, but now it withers."[6]

From 1807 to 1812 Williams designed and completed the construction of Castle Williams in New York Harbor, the first casemated battery in the United States. He founded the US Military Philosophical Society and devised its motto, "Science in War is the Guarantee of Peace." After resigning from the Army in 1812, following a dispute with the secretary of war, he organized a group of volunteer engineers to build fortifications around Philadelphia. He was in his last years a well-known figure in the city, his prominence confirmed by his election to the US Congress in 1814. He died before taking his seat.

Sully's splendid portrait captures an old and weary soldier resting from his long labors. He addresses us directly, his bright, blue eyes assessing us even as we assess him. His full and indeed rather fleshy face is framed by the high collar of his uniform. One button on his tunic has become undone; he no longer needs to stand inspection. Behind him, an atmospheric, almost smoky sky, and in the distance a view of New York's Fort Williams, which he designed to defend the city in the War of 1812.

GEORGE MIFFLIN DALLAS

George Mifflin Dallas was the son of Alexander James Dallas, a wealthy lawyer who served as secretary of the treasury and acting

---

[6] "Jonathan Williams to Thomas Jefferson, 17 September 1810," *Founders Online,* National Archives, https://founders.archives.gov/documents/Jefferson/03-03-02-0056.

secretary of war under James Monroe. His father's money and connections provided the younger Dallas with financial security along with entry into the upper reaches of Philadelphia society. Tacking first toward and then against the Jacksonian upheavals of the 1820s and 1830s, Dallas held a long list of political offices: mayor of Philadelphia from 1828 to 1829; US senator from 1831 to 1833; attorney general of Pennsylvania, 1833–35; US minister to St. Petersburg in 1837–39, and to the United Kingdom from 1856 to 1861.[7] The capstone of his career was his election as the eleventh vice president of the United States, under James K. Polk, from 1845 to 1849.[8]

Although Dallas was probably the most significant politician in Philadelphia's history, his biographer acknowledges that his accomplishments were few and his subsequent obscurity is well deserved. Along with his elected and appointed offices, he played a modest but malign role in the city's debate over slavery. In 1850, at a Great Union Meeting organized to defend slavery and resist abolition, Dallas denounced the "imported fanaticism" of the abolitionists.[9] A few years later, during his tenure as Minister to Great Britain, Dallas used his authority to deny a passport to Frederick Douglass. Invoking the Supreme Court decision in *Dred Scott*, Dallas ruled that Douglass was not a citizen.[10]

Sully completed this portrait (Figure 14.2) in 1810, the year Dallas graduated with highest honors from the College of New Jersey (Princeton). As in many of his other portraits, Sully directs our attention upward from the elaborately arranged shirt front and wide collar. The future politician can be discerned from the

[7] Susan Dallas, ed., *Diary of George Mifflin Dallas, while United States Minister to Russia 1837 to 1839 and to England 1856 to 1861* (Philadelphia: Lippincott, 1892).

[8] John M. Belohlavek, *George Mifflin Dallas: Jacksonian Patrician* (University Park: The Pennsylvania State University Press, 1977). Belohlavek's slender volume remains the only full-length biography. Additional information can be found in Phyllis F. Field, "George Mifflin Dallas," in *American National Biography*, vol. 6 (New York: Oxford University Press, 1999), 31–33.

[9] Gary B. Nash, *First City: Philadelphia and the Forging of American Memory* (Philadelphia: University of Pennsylvania Press, 2002), 192.

[10] In his third autobiography, *The Life and Times of Frederick Douglass* (1882), Douglass wrote that Dallas "is now dead and generally forgotten … but I have lived to see myself everywhere recognized as an American citizen" (Hartford, CT: Park Publishing Company, 1882), 327. Sidney George Fisher, who loathed Dallas, commented with relish on the episode in his diary. Nicholas B. Wainwright, ed., *A Philadelphia Perspective: The Diary of Sidney George Fisher Covering the Years 1834–1871* (Philadelphia: The Historical Society of Pennsylvania, 1967), 358–59.

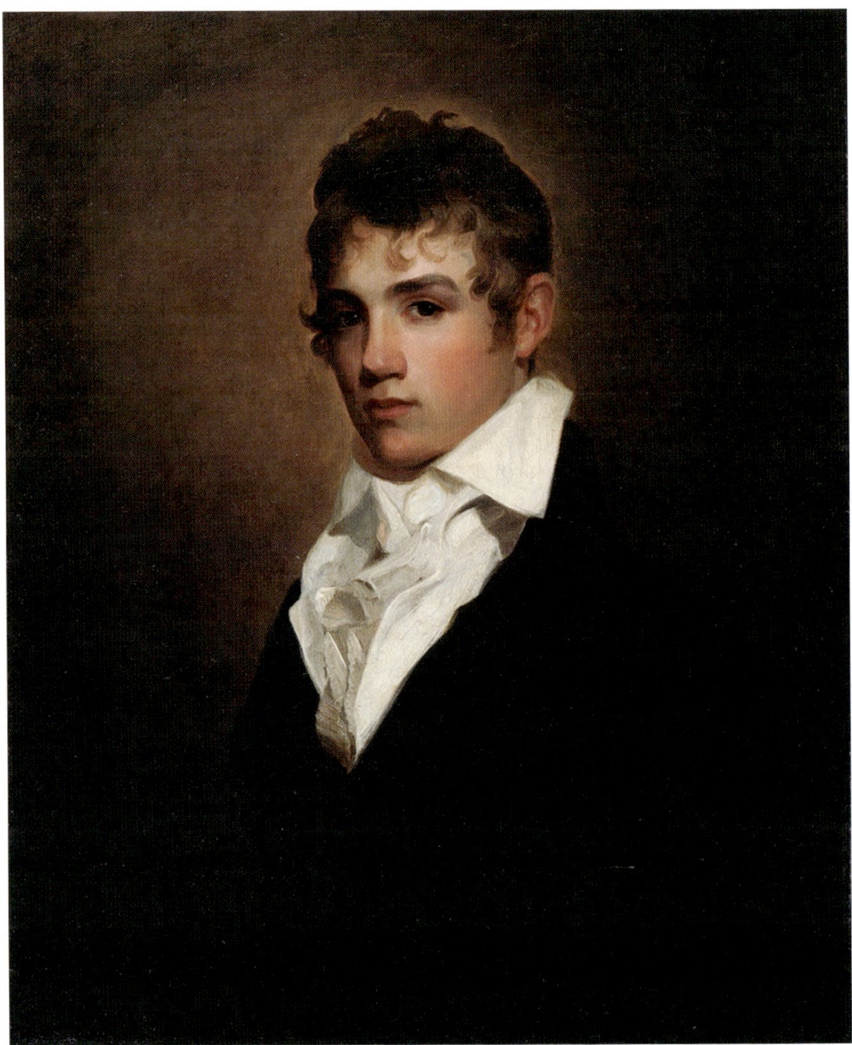

Figure 14.2 *George Mifflin Dallas, Class of 1810 (1792–1864).*
Courtesy of the Princeton University Art Museum.

elegant image. The young man turns toward us, his handsome face radiating the self-confidence that will propel his career. There is more than a hint of aristocratic hauteur in his glance. A thin halo of lighter paint thrusts Dallas's head forward from the darker background. The evidence of later photographs suggests that Dallas's good looks are his own, not Sully's contrivance.

Bibliography

Abbot, George Maurice. *A Short History of the Library Company*. Philadelphia: Published by order of the Board of Directors, 1913.

Altick, Richard. *Paintings from Books: Art and Literature in Britain, 1760–1900*. Columbus: The Ohio State University Press, 1985.

Altschuler, Sari, and Christopher J. Bilodeau. "The Republics of Benjamin Rush." *Early American Studies* 15, no. 2 (Spring 2017): 233–51.

American Philosophical Society. *A Catalogue of Portraits and Other Works of Art in the Possession of the American Philosophical Society*. Philadelphia: American Philosophical Society, 1961.

Anderson, John G. T. *Deep Things out of Darkness: A History of Natural History*. Berkeley: University of California Press, 2013.

Armstrong, Margaret. *Fanny Kemble: A Passionate Victorian*. New York: Macmillan, 1938.

Ashby, Clifford. "Fanny Kemble's 'Vulgar' Journal." *Pennsylvania Magazine of History and Biography* 98 (1974): 58–66.

Ashton, Dianne. *Rebecca Gratz: Women and Judaism in Antebellum America*. Detroit: Wayne State University Press, 1997.

"At the Instance of Benjamin Franklin": A Brief History of the Library Company of Philadelphia, rev. enlarged ed. York, PA: Printed for the Library Company of Philadelphia by York Graphic Services, 1995.

Baatz, Simon. *Patronage, Science, and Ideology in an American City: Patrician Philadelphia, 1800–1860*. PhD diss., University of Pennsylvania, 1986.

———. "William Maclure." In *American National Biography*. New York: Oxford University Press, 1999.

Bacon, Margaret Hope. "Quakers and Colonization." *Quaker History* 95, no. 1 (Spring 2006): 29.

Bailyn, Bernard, ed. *The Great Republic*. Boston: Little, Brown, 1977.

Baltzell, E. Digby. *Philadelphia Gentlemen: The Making of a National Upper Class*. Glencoe, IL: The Free Press, 1958.

Barratt, Carrie Rebora. "Faces of a New Nation: American Portraits of the 18th and Early 19th Centuries." *Metropolitan Museum of Art Bulletin* LXI (Summer 2003): 1–56.

———. *Queen Victoria and Thomas Sully*. Princeton, NJ: Princeton University Press, 2000.

Barratt, Carrie Rebora, and Ellen G. Miles. *Gilbert Stuart*. New Haven, CT: Yale University Press, 2005.

Bayeck, Rebecca. "Robert Douglass Jr., 19th Century African American Artist." New York Public Library. https://www.nypl.org/blog/2020/05/22/robert-douglass-jr-african-american-artist.

Bell, Whitfield J. *The Art of Philadelphia Medicine*. Philadelphia: Philadelphia Museum of Art, 1965.

Belohlavek, John M. *George Mifflin Dallas: Jacksonian Patrician*. University Park, PA: The Pennsylvania State University Press, 1977.

Berger, Harry, Jr. "Fictions of the Pose: Facing the Gaze of Early Modern Portraiture." *Representations* 46 (Spring 1994): 87–120.

Berkowitz, Julie S., ed. *The College of Physicians of Philadelphia: Portrait Catalogue*. Philadelphia: College of Physicians, 1984.

Berlin, Ira. "Slavery, Freedom, and Philadelphia's Struggle for Brotherly Love, 1685 to 1861." In *Antislavery and Abolition in Philadelphia: Emancipation and the Long Struggle for Racial Justice in the City of Brotherly Love*, edited by Richard Newman and James Mueller, 19. Baton Rouge: Louisiana State University Press, 2011.

Bernier, Olivier. *Lafayette, Hero of Two Worlds: The Art and Pageantry of His Farewell Tour of America, 1824–25*. New York: E. P. Dutton, 1983.

Biddle, Edward, and Mantle Fielding, eds., *The Life and Works of Thomas Sully*. Philadelphia: The Wickersham Press, 1921.

"Biddle, Nicholas." Papers of Abraham Lincoln Digital Library. https://papersofabrahamlincoln.org/persons/BI47179.

Binger, Carl. *Revolutionary Doctor: Benjamin Rush, 1746–1813.* New York: W. W. Norton, 1966.

Blumin, Stuart. *The Emergence of the Middle Class: Social Experience in the American City, 1760–1900.* New York: Cambridge University Press, 1989.

Bobbé, Dorothie. *Fanny Kemble.* New York: Minton, Balch, & Co., 1931.

Bodek, Evelyn. "'Making Do': Jewish Women and Philanthropy." In *Jewish Life in Philadelphia, 1830–1940,* edited by Murray Friedman, 141–60. Philadelphia: Institute for the Study of Human Issues, 1983.

Boltz, William G. *The Origin and Early Development of the Chinese Writing System.* New Haven, CT: American Oriental Society, 1994.

Bosco, Ronald A., and Joel Myerson, eds., *Ralph Waldo Emerson: The Major Prose.* Cambridge, MA: The Belknap Press of Harvard University Press, 2015.

Brandon, Edgar Ewing, ed. *Lafayette: Guest of the Nation,* vol. II. Oxford, OH: The Oxford Historical Press, 1954.

Brands, H. W. *The First American: The Life and Times of Benjamin Franklin.* New York: Doubleday, 2000.

Brigham, Clarence S. *History and Bibliography of American Newspapers, 1690–1820,* vol. 2. Worcester, MA: American Antiquarian Society, 1947.

Brigham, David. *Public Culture in the Early Republic: Peale's Museum and Its Audience.* Washington, DC: Smithsonian Institution Press, 1995.

Brilliant, Richard. *Facing the New World. Jewish Portraits in Colonial and Federal America.* New York: Jewish Museum, 1997.

———. *Portraiture.* Cambridge MA: Harvard University Press, 1991.

Bristol, Michael D. *Shakespeare's America, America's Shakespeare.* New York: Routledge, 1990.

Brodsky, Alyn. *Benjamin Rush: Patriot and Physician.* New York: St. Martin's Press, 2004.

Bronson, Steven Eric. *Thomas Sully: Style and Development in Masterworks of Portraiture, 1783–1839.* PhD diss., University of Delaware, 1986.

Brown, David Paul. *Eulogium upon William Rawle, L.L.D. delivered on the 31st of December, 1836.* Philadelphia: E. L Carey & A Hart, 1837.

Brown, Milton W. *American Art to 1900.* New York: Harry N. Abrams, 1977.

Budd, Henry. "Thomas Sully." *Pennsylvania Magazine of History and Biography* 42 (1918): 97–126.

Burin, Eric. "Rethinking Northern White Support for the African Colonization Movement: The Pennsylvania Colonization Society as an Agent of Emancipation. " *The Pennsylvania Magazine of History and Biography* 127, no. 2 (April 2003): 197–229.

———. *Slavery and the Peculiar Solution: A History of the American Colonization Society.* Gainesville: University Press of Florida, 2005.

Burt, Nathaniel. *The Perennial Philadelphians: The Anatomy of an American Aristocracy.* Boston: Little, Brown, 1963.

Butler, Jon. *Awash in a Sea of Faith: Christianizing the American People,* Cambridge, MA: Harvard University Press, 1992.

Butler, Willliam. "Peter Stephen Du Ponceau: Pennsylvania Lawyer Extraordinaire." *The Pennsylvania Bar Association Quarterly* LXXXIX, no. 4 (October 2018): 156–65.

Butterfield, Lyman Henry, ed. *Letters of Benjamin Rush, Volume II, 1793–1813.* Princeton, NJ: Princeton University Press, 2019 [1951].

Butts, R. Freeman, and Lawrence A. Cremin. *A History of Education in American Culture,* New York: Henry Holt, 1953.

Byvanck, Valentijn. "Public Portraits and Portrait Publics." *Pennsylvania History: A Journal of Mid-Atlantic Studies,* 65, *Explorations in Early American Culture* (1998): 199–242.

Caldwell, John, and Oswaldo Roque. *American Paintings in the Metropolitan Museum of Art. Volume 1, A Catalogue of Works by Artists born by 1815.* New York: Metropolitan Museum of Art, 1994.

Carson, Hampton L. *A History of the Historical Society of Pennsylvania.* 2 vols. Philadelphia: Published by the Society under the special centennial publication fund, 1940.

Carter, Edward C. *"One Grand Pursuit": A Brief History of the American Philosophical Society's First 250 Years, 1743–1993.* Philadelphia: American Philosophical Society, 1993.

Catalog of the Memorial Exhibition of Portraits by Thomas Sully. Philadelphia: Pennsylvania Academy of Fine Arts, 1922.

Catlett, J. Stephen, ed. *A New Guide to the Collections in the Library of the American Philosophical Society.* Philadelphia: American Philosophical Society, 1987.

Cheney, Edward Potts. *History of the University of Pennsylvania, 1740–1940.* Philadelphia: University of Pennsylvania Press, 1940.

Churchill, George B. "Shakespeare in America." *Jahrbüch der Deutschen Shakespeare-Gesellschaft* 42 (1906). Reprinted in Rawlings, Peter. *Americans on Shakespeare, 1776–1914,* 418–448. Aldershot, UK: Ashgate, 1999.

Clary, David A. *Adopted Son: Washington, Lafayette, and the Friendship that Saved the Revolution.* New York: Bantam Books, 2007.

Clement, Priscilla Ferguson. *Welfare and the Poor in the Nineteenth-Century City: Philadelphia, 1800–1854.* Rutherford, NJ: Fairleigh Dickinson University Press, 1985.

Clepp, Susan E. "The Demographic Characteristics of Philadelphia, 1788–1801: Zachariah Poulson's Bills of Mortality, 1788–1801." *Pennsylvania History: A Journal of Mid-Atlantic Studies* 53, no. 3 (July 1986): 201–21.

Clinton, Catherine. *Fanny Kemble's Civil Wars.* New York: Simon & Schuster, 2000.

Clubbe, John. *Byron, Sully and the Power of Portraiture.* Aldershot, UK: Ashgate, 2005.

Coben, Stanley, and Lorman Ratner, eds. *The Development of an American Culture,* New York: St. Martin's Press, 1983.

Cohen, Naomi W. *Jews in Christian America: The Pursuit of Religious Equality.* New York: Oxford University Press, 1992.

Conn, Peter, ed., *The Autobiography of Benjamin Franklin.* Philadelphia: University of Pennsylvania Press, 2006.

———. *The Divided Mind: Imagination and Ideology in America, 1898–1917.* New York: Cambridge University Press, 1983.

Conn, Steven. *History's Shadow: Native Americans and Historical Consciousness in the Nineteenth Century.* Chicago: University of Chicago Press, 2004.

———. *Museums and American Intellectual Life, 1876–1926.* Chicago: University of Chicago Press, 1998.

Corner, George W., ed. *The Autobiography of Benjamin Rush: His "Travels Through Life" Together With His Commonplace Book for 1789–1813.* Princeton, NJ: Princeton University Press, 1945.

Craven, Wayne. *American Art: History and Culture.* New York: H. N. Abrams, 1994.

———. *Colonial America Portraiture: The Economic, Religious, Social, Cultural, Philosophical, Scientific, and Aesthetic Foundations.* Cambridge, UK: Cambridge University Press, 1986.

Curti, Merle. *The Growth of American Thought.* New York: Harper & Bros., 1943.

"Cushman; Charlotte (1816–1876)." In *GLBTQ: An Encyclopedia of Gay, Lesbian, Bisexual, Transgender and Queer Culture.* https://web.archive.org/web/20070418152943/http://www.glbtq.com/arts/cushman_c.html.

Dallas, Susan, ed., *Diary of George Mifflin Dallas, while United States Minister to Russia 1837 to 1839 and to England 1856 to 1861.* Philadelphia: Lippincott, 1892.

Danly, Susan. *Facing the Past: Nineteenth-Century Portraits from the Collection of the Pennsylvania Academy of the Fine Arts.* New York: The American Federation of the Arts, 1992.

Davis Jr., Donald G." Review of *Quarter of a Millennium: The Library Company of Philadelphia, 1731–1981: A Symposium, an Exhibition, a Man." The Journal of Library History* 17, no. 3 (Summer 1982): 328.

DeFrancis, John. *The Chinese Language: Fact and Fantasy.* Honolulu: University of Hawaii Press, 1984.

D'Elia, Donald J. "Dr. Benjamin Rush and the Negro." *Journal of the History of Ideas* 30, no. 3 (July–September 1969): 413–22.

De Salvo, Donna. *Face Value: American Portraits.* Southampton NY: Parrish Art Museum, 1995.

de Tocqueville, Alexis. "Chapter XVII: Principal Causes Maintaining The Democratic Republic —Part I." In *Democracy in America.* London: Saunders and Otley, 1835; repr. Library of America, 2004.

DeVenney, David P. *Forging America: New Lands and High Culture.* Westport, CT: Praeger, 2003.

Dickens, Charles. *American Notes for General Circulation.* London: Chapman & Hall, 1842.

Diner, Hasia. *A Time for Gathering: The Second Migration, 1820–1880.* Baltimore: The Johns Hopkins University Press, 1992.

"Directors of Library Company to Thomas Penn and Reply, 16 May 1733." *Founders Online.* National Archives, https://founders.archives.gov/documents/Franklin/01-01-02-0095.

Driver, Leota S. *Fanny Kemble.* New York: Negro Universities Press, 1969.

Du Bois, W. E. B. *The Philadelphia Negro: A Social Study.* Philadelphia: University of Pennsylvania Press, 1996 [1899].

Dudden, Faye E. *Women in the American Theatre: Actresses and Audiences, 1790–1870.* New Haven, CT: Yale University Press, 1994.

Dunlap, William. *Diary, 1766–1823.* 3 vols. New York: New York Historical Society, 1930.

———. *A History of the Rise and Progress of the Arts of Design in the United States.* 3 vols. Introduction by James Thomas Flexner. Edited by Rita Weiss. New York: George P. Scott, 1834 [Facsimile reprint NY: Dover, 1969].

Du Ponceau, Peter Stephen, and James L. Whitehead. "The Autobiography of Peter Stephen Du Ponceau." *The Pennsylvania Magazine of History and Biography* 63, no. 2 (April 1939): 189–227.

Durang, Charles. *The Philadelphia Stage from the Year 1749 to the Year 1855.* Philadelphia: Thomas Westcott, 1860.

Ellis, Joseph J. *After the Revolution: Profiles of Early American Culture.* New York: W. W. Norton, 1979.

Evans, Dorinda. *Benjamin West and His American Students.* Washington, DC: Smithsonian Institution Press, 1980.

Fabian, Monroe H. *Mr. Sully, Portrait Painter: The Works of Thomas Sully (1783–1872)* [exhibition cat.] Washington DC: Smithsonian Institution Press, 1983.

———. *Portraits of the American Stage, 1771–1971.* Washington DC: Smithsonian Institution Press, 1971.

Fall, Robert. "Shakespeare in America: A Survey to 1900." *Shakespeare Survey* 18 (1965): 102–18.

Fanelli, Doris Devine, and Karie Diethorn. *History of the Portrait Collection, Independence National Historical Park and Catalog of the Collection.* Philadelphia: American Philosophical Society, 2001.

Feldstein, Stanley. *The Land That I Show You: Three Centuries of Jewish Life in America.* Garden City, NY: Anchor Press, 1978.

Ferguson, Priscilla. *Welfare and the Poor in the Nineteenth-Century City: Philadelphia, 1800–1854.* Madison, NJ: Fairleigh Dickinson University Press, 1985.

Flexner, James Thomas. *Doctors on Horseback: Pioneers of American Medicine.* New York: Viking Press, 1937.

———. *George Washington in the American Revolution, 1775–1783.* Boston: Little, Brown and Company, 1968.

———. *The Light of Distant Skies: American Painting, 1760–1835.* New York: Harcourt, Brace, 1954.

Follini, Tamara. "The Friendship of Fanny Kemble and Henry James." *The Cambridge Quarterly* 19, no. 3 (1990): 230–42.

Fox, W. J. "The Common Interests of Great Britain and America." *The People's Journal* 1. London: Published by Thomas Holmes, 1846.

Franklin, Benjamin. "Compassion and Regard for the Sick." *The Pennsylvania Gazette* (March 18, 1731).

———. *Proposal for Promoting Useful Knowledge among the British Plantations in America*. Philadelphia: Printed by Benjamin Franklin, 1743.

Fried, Stephen. *Rush: Revolution, Madness, and the Visionary Doctor Who Became a Founding Father*. New York: Crown, 2018.

Friedman, Murray, ed. *Jewish life in Philadelphia, 1830–1940*. Philadelphia: Institute for the Study of Human Issues, 1983.

"From Benjamin Franklin to Mary Stevenson, 25 March 1763." *Founders Online*, National Archives. https://founders.archives.gov/documents/Franklin/01-10-02-0123.

Furness, Horace Howard, ed. *Records of a Lifelong Friendship, 1807–1882: Ralph Waldo Emerson and William Henry Furness*. Boston: Houghton Mifflin Company, 1910.

Furness, William H. "Christian duty." In *Three Discourses Delivered in the First Congregational Unitarian Church of Philadelphia May 28th, June 4th and June 11th, 1854, with Reference to the Recent Execution of the Fugitive Slave law in Boston and New York*. Philadelphia: Merrihew & Thompson's Steam Power Press, 1854.

———. *A Discourse Delivered on the Occasion of the Death of John Vaughan*. Philadelphia: J. Crissy, Printer, 1842.

———. *Exercises at the Meeting of the First Congregational Unitarian Society, January 12, 1875: Together with the Discourse Delivered by Rev. W. H. Furness, Sunday, Jan. 10, 1875, on the Occasion of the Fiftieth Anniversary of his Ordination, January 12, 1825*. Philadelphia: Sherman & Co., 1875.

Furstenberg, François. *When the United States Spoke French: Five Refugees Who Shaped a Nation*. New York: The Penguin Press, 2014.

Gaines, James R. *For Liberty and Glory: Washington, Lafayette, and Their Revolutions*. New York: Norton, 2007.

Gale, Robert L. "Thomas Sully." In *American National Biography*, vol. 21, 129–31. New York: Oxford University Press, 1999.

Garlick, Kenneth. *Thomas Lawrence.* London: Routledge & Paul, 1954.

Garraty, John A., and Mark C. Carnes, eds. *American National Biography.* New York: Oxford University Press, 1999.

Garrison, William Lloyd. *Thoughts on African Colonization.* Boston: Garrison and Knaff, 1832.

Garvan, Beatrice B. *Federal Philadelphia, 1785–1825: The Athens of the Western World.* Philadelphia: Philadelphia Museum of Art, 1987.

Gates Jr., Henry Louis, ed. *Lincoln on Race and Slavery.* Princeton, NJ: Princeton University Press, 2009.

Gawalt, Gerard W. "Pierre Étienne Du Ponceau." In *American National Biography,* vol. 7, 112–13. New York: Oxford University Press, 1999.

Geffen, Elizabeth M. "Joseph Sill and His Diary." *The Pennsylvania Magazine of History and Biography* 94, no. 3 (July 1970): 275–330.

———. *Philadelphia Unitarianism, 1796–1861.* Philadelphia: University of Pennsylvania Press, 1961.

———. "Violence in Philadelphia in the 1840's and 1850's." *Pennsylvania History: A Journal of Mid-Atlantic Studies* 36, no. 4 (October 1969): 381–410.

———. "William Henry Furness: Philadelphia Antislavery Preacher." *The Pennsylvania Magazine of History and Biography* 82, no. 3 (July 1958): 259–92.

Geikie, Archibald. *The Founders of Geology.* London: Macmillan, 1905.

Gerdts, William. "The American 'Discourses': A Survey of Lectures and Writings on American Art, 1770–1858." *The American Art Journal* 15, no. 3 (Summer, 1983): 61–79.

———. "Natural Aristocrats in a Democracy: 1810–1870." In Michael Quick, Marvin S. Sadik, and William Gerdts, *American Portraiture in the Grand Manner, 1720–1920,* 27–60. Los Angeles: Los Angeles County Museum of Art, 1981.

Goodman, N. G. *Benjamin Rush, Physician and Citizen.* Philadelphia: University of Pennsylvania Press, 1934.

Goodman, Roy, and Pierre Swiggers. "John Vaughan (1756–1841) and the Linguistic Collection in the Library of the American Philosophical Society." *Proceedings of the American Philosophical Society* 138, no. 2 (June 1994): 251–72.

Gottschalk, Louis Reichenthal. *Lafayette Comes to America.* Chicago: The University of Chicago Press, 1935.

Gougeon, Len. "Militant Abolitionism: Douglass, Emerson, and the Rise of the Anti-Slave." *The New England Quarterly* 85, no. 4 (December 2012): 622–57.

Govan, Thomas Payne. *Nicholas Biddle: Nationalist and Public Banker, 1786–1844.* Chicago: The University of Chicago Press, 1959.

Gray, Austin K. *Benjamin Franklin's Library [Printed, 1936, as "The First American Library," 1731–1931].* New York: The Macmillan Company, 1937.

Gray, Edward G. *New World Babel: Languages and Nations in Early America.* Princeton, NJ: Princeton University Press, 2014.

Griffin, Sean. "Antislavery Utopias." *Journal of the Civil War Era* 8, no. 2 (June 2018): 243–68.

Grimsted, David. *Melodrama Unveiled: American Theater and Culture, 1800–1850.* Chicago: The University of Chicago Press, 1968.

Groseclose, Barbara S. *Nineteenth-Century American Art.* New York: Oxford University Press, 2000.

Gross, Samuel D. *Lives of Eminent American Physicians and Surgeons of the Nineteenth Century.* Philadelphia: Lindsay & Blakiston, 1861.

Hale, Robert Beverly. "American Painting 1754–1954." *The Metropolitan Museum of Art Bulletin* n.s., 12, no. 7 (March 1954): 169–91.

Hall, James. *The Self-Portrait: A Cultural History.* New York: Thames & Hudson, 2015.

Hammond, Bray. *Banks and Politics in America from the Revolution to the Civil War.* Princeton: Princeton University Press, 1991 [1957].

———. *The Second Bank of the United States.* Transactions of the American Philosophical Society, n.s., 43, pt. 1. Philadelphia: American Philosophical Society, 1953.

Harris, Neil. *The Artist in American Society: The Formative Years, 1790–1860*, 2nd ed. University of Chicago Press, 1982.

Hart, Sidney, and David C. Ward. "The Waning of an Enlightenment Ideal: Charles Willson Peale's Philadelphia Museum." *Journal of the Early Republic* 8, no. 4 (Winter 1988): 389–418.

Hatcher, Emily. "The Philadelphia Female Anti-Slavery Society and the Civil War." *The Pennsylvania Magazine of History and Biography* 135, no. 4 (October 2011): 143–66.

Hayes, Walter. *The Captain from Nantucket and the Mutiny on the "Bounty."* Ann Arbor, MI: The William L. Clements Library, 1996.

Heindel, Richard Heathcote, and J. Marshall, "Some Letters of Peter Stephen Du Ponceau." *Pennsylvania History: A Journal of Mid-Atlantic Studies* 3, no. 3 (July 1936): 195–200.

Henderson, Helen W. *The Pennsylvania Academy of the Fine Arts?* Boston: L. C Page & Company, 1911.

Hennessey, William John. *The American Portrait: From the Death of Stuart to the Rise of Sargent.* Worcester MA: Worcester Art Museum, 1973.

Hewitt, Barnard. *Theatre U.S.A., 1665–1957.* New York: McGraw-Hill Book Company, 1959.

Hirschfeld, Fritz. *George Washington and the Jews.* Newark: University of Delaware Press, 2005.

History Making Productions. "Disorder (1820-1854)." *Philadelphia: The Great Experiment.* https://www.youtube.com/watch?v=lTOUquhPKWc&list=PLwEWxvgiPVsXPeZVV0erTz83OyYjD8yjF&index=6.

Hofstadter, Richard, and Walter P. Metzger. *The Development of Academic Freedom in the United States.* New York: Columbia University Press, 1955.

Hone, Philip. *The Diary of Philip Hone.* New York: Dodd, Mead, 1927.

Howe, Daniel Walker. *What Hath God Wrought: The Transformation of America, 1815–1848.* New York: Oxford University Press, 2007.

Jackson, Joseph. "Iconography of Philadelphia." *The Pennsylvania Magazine of History and Biography* 59, no. 1 (1935): 57–73.

James, Henry. "Frances Anne Kemble." In *Essays in London and Elsewhere.* New York: Harper & Brothers, 1893.

James, Marquis. *The Life of Andrew Jackson.* Indianapolis: Bobbs-Merrill Company, 1938.

James, Reese David. *Old Drury of Philadelphia: A History of the Philadelphia Stage, 1800–1835.* Philadelphia: University of Pennsylvania Press, 1932.

Jardine, N., J. A. Secord, and E. C. Spary, eds. *Cultures of Natural History.* New York: Cambridge University Press, 1996.

"To John Adams from Thomas Jefferson, 27 May 1813." *Founders Online,* National Archives. https://founders.archives.gov/documents/Adams/99-02-02-6041.

"John Adams to Thomas Jefferson, 11 June 1813." *Founders Online,* National Archives. https://founders.archives.gov/documents/Jefferson/03-06-02-0171.

Johns, Christopher M. S. "Theater and Theory: Thomas Sully's George Frederick Cooke as Richard III. *Winterthur Portfolio* 18, no. 1 (Spring 1983): 27–38.

Jones, Russell M. "The Flowering of a Legend: Lafayette and the Americans, 1825–1834." *French Historical Studies* 4, no. 4 (Autumn 1966): 384-410.

Jordanova, Ludmilla. "Medical Men, 1780-1820." In *Portraiture: Facing the Subject,* edited by Joanna Woodall, 101–15. Manchester, UK: Manchester University Press, 1997.

Kaplan, Sidney, and Emma Nogrady Kaplan. *The Black Presence in the Era of the American Revolution.* Amherst, MA: University of Massachusetts Press, 1989.

Katkins, Maria. "Almshouses (Poorhouses)." In *The Encyclopedia of Greater Philadelphia.* https://philadelphiaencyclopedia.org/essays/almshouses-poorhouses.

Kayser, Stephen S., and Isidore S. Meyer. "Early American Jewish Portraiture." *Publications of the American Jewish Historical Society* 41, no. 3 (March 1952): 275–94.

Kemble, Frances Anne. *Journal of a Residence on a Georgian Plantation: 1838-1839.* [Place of publication not identified] BiblioBazaar, 2007.

Kennedy, Roger G. *Orders from France: The Americans and the French in a Revolutionary World, 1780–1820.* New York: Knopf, 1989.

King, Cornelia S., and Don James McLaughlin. "Schoolgirl Smashes, David-and-Jonathan Relationships, and Champagne Friendships: Mining the Archive for LGBT History." *Pennsylvania Legacies* 16, no. 1 (Spring 2016): 12–19.

Klamkin, Marian. *The Return of Lafayette, 1824–1825.* New York: Charles Scribners' Sons, 1975.

Kocher, Kurt Lee. "A Duty to America and Africa: A History of the Independent African Colonization Movement in Pennsylvania." *Pennsylvania History: A Journal of Mid-Atlantic Studies* 51, no. 2 (April 1984): 118–153.

Kramer, Lloyd S. "America's Lafayette and Lafayette's America: A European and the American Revolution." *The William and Mary Quarterly* 38, no. 2 (April 1981): 228–41.

Lampert, Sara E. *Starring Women: Celebrity, Patriarchy, and American Theater, 1790–1850.* Urbana: University of Illinois Press, 2020.

Lapsansky, Emma J., and Margaret Hope Bacon, eds. *Back to Africa: Benjamin Coates and the Colonization Movement in America, 1848-1880.* University Park: The Pennsylvania State University Press, 2005.

Lathem, Edward Connery, ed. *Chronological Tables of American Newspapers, 1690–1820.* Barre, MA: The American Antiquarian Society, 1972.

Leach, Joseph. *Bright Particular Star: The Life & Times of Charlotte Cushman.* New Haven, CT: Yale University Press, 1970.

———. "Charlotte Cushman." In *American National Biography,* vol. 5, 921–23. New York: Oxford University Press, 1999.

Lee, Jean Gordon. "Philadelphians and the China Trade." In *Philadelphians, and the China Trade, 1784–1844,* edited by Jean Gordon Lee. Philadelphia: Philadelphia Museum of Art, 1984.

Lemay, J. A. Leo. *The Life of Benjamin Franklin, Volume Two: Printer and Publisher, 1730–1747.* Philadelphia: University of Pennsylvania Press, 2006.

———. *The Life of Benjamin Franklin, Volume Three: Soldier, Scientist, and Politician, 1748–1757.* Philadelphia: University of Pennsylvania Press, 2009.

Levin, Bernard S., and F. R. Kirkland, "Society News and Accessions," *The Pennsylvania Magazine of History and Biography* 64, no. 3 (July 1940): 430–48.

Levick, James J. "Benjamin Hornor Coates, M.D., One of the Founders of the Historical Society of Pennsylvania and for Many Years Its Senior Vice-President." *The Pennsylvania Magazine of History and Biography* 6, no. 1 (1882): 21–33.

Lewin, Judith. "Legends of Rebecca: Ivanhoe, Dynamic Identification, and the Portraits of Rebecca Gratz." *Nashim: A Journal of Jewish Women's Studies & Gender Issues* (Fall 5766/2005): 178–212.

Lewis, Michael. *American Art and Architecture.* London: Thames & Hudson, 2006.

———. "Thomas Sully and the Studious Subjects." *Nineteenth Century* 38, no. 1 (Spring 2018): 30–35.

———. *"Thomas Sully's Philadelphia."* Lecture at the Wagner Free Institute of Science in Philadelphia, October 4, 2003.

Lingelbach, William E. "The Library of the American Philosophical Society." *The William and Mary Quarterly* 3, no. 1 (January 1946): 48–69.

London, Hannah R. *Portraits of Jews by Gilbert Stuart and Other Early American Artists.* New York: William Edwin Rudge, 1927.

———. "Portraits of Rebecca Gratz by Thomas Sully." In *Portrait Painting in America,* edited by Ellen Miles, 162–64. New York: Main Street/Universe Books, 1977.

———. *Shades of My Forefathers.* Springfield, MA: The Pond-Ekberg Company, 1941.

Londré, Felicia Hardison, and Daniel J. Watermeier. *The History of North American Theater: From Pre-Columbian Times to the Present.* New York: Continuum, 1998.

Maclure, William. *Opinions on Various Subjects, Dedicated to the Industrious Producers.* New Harmony, IN: 1837.

Martinez, Katherine, and Page Talbott, eds. *Philadelphia's Cultural Landscape: The Sartain Family Legacy.* Philadelphia: Temple University Press, 2000.

Matson, Cathy. "Putting the *Lydia* to Sea: The Material Economy of Shipping in Colonial Philadelphia." *The William and Mary Quarterly* 74, no. 2 (April 2017): 303–32.

Matthews, Jean V. *Toward a New Society: American Thought and Culture, 1800–1830.* Boston: Twayne Publishers, 1991.

Mayer, Lance, and Gay Myers. *American Painters on Technique: The Colonial Period to 1860.* Los Angeles: J. Paul Getty Trust, 2011.

McElroy, Guy C. *Facing History: The Black Image in American Art, 1710–1940.* San Francisco: Bedford Arts Publishers, 1990.

McFaul, John M. *The Politics of Jacksonian Finance.* Ithaca, NY: Cornell University Press, 1972.

McLanathan, Richard. *Art in America: A Brief History.* New York: Harcourt Brace Jovanovich, 1973.

McManaway, James G. "Shakespeare in the United States." *PMLA* 79, no. 5 (December 1964): 513–18.

McMurtry, Larry. *Sacagawea's Nickname: Essays on the American West.* New York: New York Review Books, 2001.

McNeal, R. A., ed. *Nicholas Biddle in Greece: The Journals and Letters of 1806.* University Park: Pennsylvania State University Press, 1993.

Merrill, Lisa. *When Romeo Was a Woman: Charlotte Cushman and Her Circle of Female Spectators.* Ann Arbor: University of Michigan Press, 1999.

Miles, Ellen, ed. *Portrait Painting in America. The Nineteenth Century*. New York: Universe Books, 1977.

Miller, Floyd J. *The Search for a Black Nationality: Black Emigration and Colonization, 1787–1863*. Urbana: University of Illinois Press, 1975.

Miller, Lynn H. "My Dear General: The Relationship between Lafayette and Washington." *France Revisited* (July 2009): 12–13.

Montgomery, Charles F., and Patricia E. Kane, eds. *American Art: 1740–1950. Towards Independence*. Boston: New York Graphic Society, 1976.

Morton, Thomas G. *The History of the Pennsylvania Hospital, 1751–1895*. New York: Arno Press, 1973 [1895].

Murdoch, James E. *The Stage or Recollections of Actors and Acting From an Experience of Fifty Years*. Philadelphia: J. M. Stoddart & Co., 1880.

Nash, Gary B. *First City: Philadelphia and the Forging of American Memory*. Philadelphia: University of Pennsylvania Press, 2002.

———. *Forging Freedom: The Formation of Philadelphia's Black Community, 1720–1840*. Cambridge, MA: Harvard University Press, 1988.

———. "Slaves and Slaveowners in Colonial Philadelphia." The *William and Mary Quarterly* 30, no. 2 (April 1973): 223–56.

Nash, Gary B., and Jean R. Soderlund. *Freedom by Degrees: Emancipation in Pennsylvania and Its Aftermath*. New York: Oxford University Press, 1991.

Neil, J. Meredith. *Toward a National Taste: America's Quest for Aesthetic Independence*. Honolulu: University Press of Hawaii, 1975.

Newman, Richard S. "The Pennsylvania Abolition Society: Restoring a Group to Glory." *Pennsylvania Legacies* 5, no. 2 (November 2005): 6–10.

Nolan, J. Bennett. *Lafayette in America Day by Day*. Baltimore: Johns Hopkins University Press, 1934.

———. "Lafayette in Pennsylvania." *Pennsylvania History: A Journal of Mid-Atlantic Studies* 1, no. 3 (July 1934): 135–46.

Nolan, James L. Jr. *What They Saw in America: Alexis de Tocqueville, Max Weber, G. K. Chesterton, and Sayyid Qutb*. New York: Cambridge University Press, 2016.

Norris, George W. *The Early History of Medicine in Philadelphia*. Philadelphia: Collins Printing House, 1886.

Nye, Russel Blaine *The Cultural Life of the New Nation, 1776–1830*. New York: Harper & Row, 1963.

Oakes, James. "Ships Going Out." *The New York Review of Books* (September 21, 2023): 60.

Oberholzer, Ellis. *The Literary History of Philadelphia*. Philadelphia: George W. Jacobs & Co., 1906.

Packard, Francis Randolph. *The History of Medicine in the United States*. Philadelphia: J. B. Lippincott Company, 1901.

———. *Some Account of the Pennsylvania Hospital from 1751 to 1938*. Philadelphia: Engle Press, 1938.

Paintings and Drawings by Thomas Sully. New York: Brooklyn Museum, 1921. http://www.brooklynmuseum.org/opencollection/exhibitions/2986/Paintings_and_Drawings_by_Thomas_Sully.

"Paper on the Academy [31 July 1750]." *Founders Online*, National Archives. https://founders.archives.gov/documents/Franklin/01-04-02-0007.

Pelizzari, Maria Antonella. "Thomas Sully." In *America: The New World in Nineteenth Century Painting*, edited by Stephan Koja, 269–70. Munich: Prestel Verlag, 1999.

Philadelphia: Three Centuries of American Art. Philadelphia: Philadelphia Museum of Art, 1976. Exhibition catalog in 2 parts.

Portraits of the American Stage, 1771–1971: An Exhibition in Celebration of the Inaugural Season of The John F. Kennedy Center for the Performing Arts. Washington, DC: The Smithsonian Institution Press, 1971.

Posey, Trisha. "'Alive to the Cry of Distress': Joseph and Jane Sill and Poor Relief in Antebellum Philadelphia." *The Pennsylvania Magazine of History and Biography* 132, no. 3 (July 2008): 215–43.

Poulson, Zachariah Jr., Edward Burd, and Richard Peters. "Some Biographical Letters." *The Pennsylvania Magazine of History and Biography*. 23, no. 2 (1899): 196–209.

Powell, J. H. *Bring Out Your Dead: The Great Plague of Yellow Fever in Philadelphia in 1793*. Philadelphia: University of Pennsylvania Press, 1991 [1949].

Prown, Jules. "Two Manuscript Notebooks of Thomas Sully." *Yale University Library Gazette* 39, no. 2 (1964): 73–79.

Quinn, Arthur Hobson. *A History of American Drama: From the Beginning to the Civil War*. New York: Harper & Bros, 1943 [1923].

———. *The Theatre and the Drama in Old Philadelphia.* Philadelphia: American Philosophical Society, 1953.

Rawle, William. "An Inaugural Discourse Delivered on the 5th of November 1825, before the Historical Society of Pennsylvania." In *Memoirs of the Historical Society of Pennsylvania.* Philadelphia: M'Carty and Davis, 1826.

Rawlings, Peter. *Americans on Shakespeare, 1776–1914.* Aldershot, UK: Ashgate, 1999.

Richards, Leonard L. *"Gentlemen of Property and Standing": Anti-Abolition Mobs in Jacksonian America.* New York: Oxford University Press, 1970.

Richardson, Edgar P. *Painting in America from 1502 to the Present.* New York: Crowell, 1965.

Rosengarten, J. G. "The American Philosophical Society, 1743–1903." *The Pennsylvania Magazine of History and Biography* 27, no. 3 (1903): 329–36.

Rudolph, William Keyse, and Carol Eaton Soltis. *Thomas Sully: Painted Performance.* New Haven, CT: Yale University Press, 2013.

Rush, Benjamin, M.D. *Medical Inquiries and Observations upon the Diseases of the Mind* [facsimile of the 1812 edition, with an introduction by Dr. S. Bernard Wortis]. New York: Hapner Publishing, 1962.

Rutkow, Ira M. *Surgery: An Illustrated History.* St. Louis: Mosby-Yearbook, 1993.

Rutledge, Anna Wells. "Dunlap Notes." *Art in America* 39 (February 1951): 36–43.

Samuel Coates Collection, Clements Library, University of Michigan.

Saum, Lewis O. *The Popular Mood of Pre-Civil War America.* Westport, CT: Greenwood Press, 1980.

Scharf, John Thomas. *History of Philadelphia, 1609–1884,* 3 vols. Philadelphia: L. H. Everts, 1884.

Schmutz, Thomas. "Between Instruction Manuals and Studio Practice: Thomas Sully's Notebooks." *Archives of American Art Journal* 39, nos. 3-4 (1999): 21–31.

Schofield, Robert E. "The Science Education of an Enlightened Entrepreneur: Charles Willson Peale and His Philadelphia

Museum, 1784–1827." *American Studies*. 30, no. 2 (Fall 1989): 21–40.

Schreiber, Lee L. "Bluebloods and Local Societies: A Philadelphia Microcosm." *Pennsylvania History: A Journal of Mid-Atlantic Studies* 48, no. 3 (July 1981): 251–66.

Sellers, Charles Coleman. *Mr. Peale's Museum: Charles Willson Peale and the First Popular Museum of Natural Science and Art*. New York: W. W. Norton, 1980.

Shade, William G. "Nicholas Biddle." In *American National Biography*, vol. 2, 734–35. New York: Oxford University Press, 1999.

Shaw, Gwendolyn DuBois. *Portraits of a People: Picturing African Americans in the Nineteenth Century*. Andover MA: Addison Gallery of American Art, 2006.

Shryock, Richard Harrison. *Medicine in America: Historical Essays*. Baltimore, MD: The Johns Hopkins Press, 1966.

———. *Medicine and Society in America, 1660-1860*. Ithaca: Cornell University Press, 1972.

Sickles, John, Michael J. Winey, and John Mills Bigham. "Southern Soldiers." *Military Images* 21, no. 3 (November–December 1999): 30.

Sill, Joseph. Diaries, Pennsylvania Historical Society, Mss. collection # 600.

———. "The Immigrant." *Godey's Lady's Book* XXV (October and November 1842): 180–88, 217–33.

Simon, Robin. *The Portrait in Britain and America*. Oxford, UK: Phaidon, 1987.

Smith, Billy G., ed. *Life in Early Philadelphia: Documents from the Revolutionary and Early National Periods*. University Park: The Pennsylvania State University Press, 1995.

Smith, Billy G., et. al. "The Precarious Freedom of Blacks in the Mid-Atlantic Region: Excerpts from the *Pennsylvania Gazette*, 1728–1776." *The Pennsylvania Magazine of History and Biography* 113, no. 2 (April 1989): 237–264.

Smith, Murphy D. "Peter Du Ponceau and His Study of Languages: A Historical Account." *Proceedings of the American Philosophical Society* 127, no. 3 (1983): 143–79.

Snyder, Charles McCool. *The Jacksonian Heritage in Pennsylvania Politics, 1833–1848*. Harrisburg, PA: The Pennsylvania Historical and Museum Commission, 1958.

Somkin, Fred. *Unquiet Eagle: Memory and Desire in the Idea of American Freedom.* Ithaca, NY: Cornell University Press, 1967.

Spalding, Paul. *Lafayette: Prisoner of State.* Columbia, SC: University of South Carolina Press, 2010.

Speidel, Judithe Douglas. "The Theater and Early Romanticism in America." PhD diss., Boston University, 1983.

Spero, Patrick, Abigail Shelton, and John Kenney. "The Other Presidency: Thomas Jefferson and the American Philosophical Society." *Proceedings of the American Philosophical Society* 162, no. 4 (December 2018): 321–60.

Staudenraus, P. J. *The African Colonization Movement, 1816–1865.* New York: Columbia University Press, 1961.

Steward Receipt books, 1819–1831. 6 vols. Box 151, Pennsylvania Hospital Archives.

Stroud, Patricia Tyson. "The Founding of the Academy of Natural Sciences of Philadelphia in 1812 and Its Journal in 1817." *Proceedings of the Academy of Natural Sciences of Philadelphia* 147 (1997): 227–36.

Sully, Thomas. *Hints to Young Painters.* New York: Reinhold Publishing Corporation, 1965 [1873].

———. "Journal of Thomas Sully's Activities." Archives of American Art, Smithsonian Institution, Washington, DC, roll no. 18, typescript, 301 pp.

———. "Memoirs of the Professional Life of Thomas Sully, Dedicated to His Brother Artists." November 1851, Henry Francis Du Pont Winterthur Museum, Delaware, Coll. 164.

———. "Memoirs of Thomas Sully." In *The Life and Works of Thomas Sully*, edited by Edward Biddle and Mantle Fielding, 1–79. Philadelphia: Wickersham Press, 1921.

———. "Recollections of an Old Painter." *Hours at Home* no. 10 (Nov. 1869): 69–74.

———. Thomas Sully collection, Pennsylvania Academy of Fine Arts Archives, MS.053, Box 13, Folder 1.

Sully, Thomas, G. Fairman, Geo. Murray, and Benj. Trott, *Letter to the National Register,* 3. Georgetown, District of Columbia: Sept. 1, 1819.

Swan, Claudia. "Looking Behind the Curtain." *Times Literary Supplement* (May 5, 2023): 15.

Swiggers, Pierre. "Americanist Linguistics and the Origin of Linguistic Typology: Peter Stephen Du Ponceau's 'Comparative Science of Language'." *Proceedings of the American Philosophical Society* 142, no. 1 (March 1998): 18–46.

Taylor, Joshua C. *The Fine Arts in America.* Chicago: University of Chicago Press, 1979.

Teague, Frances. *Shakespeare and the American Popular Stage.* New York: Cambridge University Press, 2006.

Thomas, Benjamin Platt. *Theodore Weld, Crusader for Freedom.* New Brunswick, NJ: Rutgers University Press, 1950.

"Thomas Sully (1783–1872)." Worcester Art Gallery. https://www.worcesterart.org/collection/Early_American/Artists/sully/biography/index.html.

Tieck, William A. "In Search of Peter Stephen Du Ponceau." *The Pennsylvania Magazine of History and Biography* 89, no. 1 (January 1965): 52–67, 69–78.

Tinkum, Harry M. "The Revolutionary City, 1765-1783." In *Philadelphia: A 300-Year History,* edited by Russell F. Weigley, 109–54. New York: W. W. Norton, 1982.

Tomek, Beverly C. *Colonization and Its Discontents: Emancipation, Emigration, and Antislavery in Antebellum Pennsylvania.* New York: New York University Press, 2011.

Tomes, Nancy. "The Domesticated Madman: Changing Concepts of Insanity at the Pennsylvania Hospital, 1780–1830." *The Pennsylvania Magazine of History and Biography* 106, no. 2 (April 1982): 268–85.

Torchia, Robert William. *American Paintings of the Nineteenth Century, Part II.* Washington, DC: National Gallery of Art, 1998.

Tuckerman, Henry. T. *Book of the Artists. American Artist Life, Comprising Biographical and Critical Sketches of American Artists: Preceded by an Historical Account of the Rise and Progress of Art in America. With an Appendix Containing an Account of Notable Pictures and Private Collections.* New York: G. P. Putnam & Sons, 1867.

———. "Sully." *The Literary World* no. 27 (August 7, 1847): 14–15.

Turner, Edward Raymond. "First Abolition Society in the United States." *Pennsylvania Magazine of History and Biography* 36, no. 1 (1912): 92–109.

———. "The Abolition of Slavery in Pennsylvania." *The Pennsylvania Magazine of History and Biography* 36, no. 2 (1912): 129–42.

Turner, Jane, ed. *Encyclopedia of American Art Before 1914*. London: Macmillan, 2000.

Turner, William L. *The Charity School, the Academy, and the College Fourth and Arch Streets.* Transactions of the American Philosophical Society, n.s., 43, pt. 1. Philadelphia: American Philosophical Society, 1953.

Unger, Harlow Charles. *Lafayette.* New York: John Wiley & Sons, 2002.

Van Doren, Carl. *Benjamin Franklin.* New York: The Viking Press, 1938.

Verplank, G. C. "Garrick: His Portrait in New York, Its Artist and History." *The Crayon* IV (March 1857): 71.

Vogel, Morris J. *Cultural Connections: Museums and Libraries of Philadelphia and the Delaware Valley*. Philadelphia: Temple University Press, 1991.

Wainwright, Nicholas B. "Nicholas Biddle in Portraiture." In *Portrait Painting in America. The Nineteenth Century*, edited by Ellen Mile, 149–57. New York: Universe Books, 1977.

———, ed. *A Philadelphia Perspective: The Diary of Sidney George Fisher Covering the Years 1834–1871*. Philadelphia: The Historical Society of Pennsylvania, 1967.

Watts, Harvey M. "Thomas Sully—A Revelation of His Art." *Arts & Decoration* 17 (June 1922): 104–5.

Weigley, Russell F., ed. *Philadelphia: A 300-Year History*. New York: W. W. Norton & Company, 1982.

Weisberger, William. "Barnard and Michael Gratz." In *American National Biography*, vol. 9, 430–31. New York: Oxford University Press.

West, Shearer. *Portraiture.* New York: Oxford University Press, 2004.

Wharton, T. I. "A Memoir of William Rawle, LL.D." *Memoirs of the Historical Society of Pennsylvania* IV, pt. I (1840): 5–32.

White, Matthew A. "Science for All: The Wagner Free Institute of Science of Philadelphia." *Pennsylvania Legacies* 15, no. 1 (Spring 2015): 12–17.

Whittier, John Greenleaf. "Justice and Expediency." *Anti-Slavery Reporter* 1, no. 4 (September 1833): 50–64.

Wilentz, Sean. *The Rise of American Democracy: Jefferson to Lincoln.* New York: W. W. Norton, 2005.

Williams, William H. *America's First Hospital: The Pennsylvania Hospital, 1751–1841.* Wayne, PA: Haverford House, 1976.

Wilmeth, Don B., and Christopher Bigsby, eds. *The Cambridge History of American Theatre, Volume One: Beginnings to 1870.* New York: Cambridge University Press, 1988.

Wilson, Garff B. *A History of American Acting.* Bloomington: Indiana University Press, 1966.

Winch, Julie. *Philadelphia's Black Elite: Activism, Accommodation, and the Struggle for Autonomy, 1787-1848.* Philadelphia: Temple University Press, 1988.

———. *A Gentleman of Color: The Life of James Forten.* New York: Oxford University Press, 2002.

Wolf, Edwin, 2nd. *Philadelphia: Portrait of an American City*, rev. ed. Philadelphia: Library Company of Philadelphia, 1990.

Wolf, Edwin, 2nd, and Maxwell Whiteman. *The History of the Jews of Philadelphia from Colonial Times to the Age of Jackson.* Philadelphia: The Jewish Publication Society, 5717/1957.

Wolf, Edwin, 2nd, and Marie Elena Korey, eds. *Quarter of a Millennium: The Library Company of Philadelphia, 1731–1981.* Philadelphia: The Library Company of Philadelphia, 1981.

Wood, George B. *Early History of the University of Pennsylvania, From Its Origins to the Year 1827*, 3rd ed., with supplementary chapters by Frederick D. Stone. Philadelphia: J. B. Lippincott, 1896 [1827].

Wood, Gordon. *The Americanization of Benjamin Franklin.* New York: The Penguin Press, 2004.

Wood, William B. *Personal Recollections of the Stage.* Philadelphia: Henry Carey Baird, 1855.

Woodall, Joanna, ed. *Portraiture: Facing the Subject.* Manchester, UK: Manchester University Press, 1997.

Yoseloff, Sara F. *When Philadelphia Was the Capital of Jewish America.* Philadelphia: Balch Institute Press, 1993.

Index

Page numbers in *italics* refer to illustrations.